# Encyclopedia
## —— of ——
# LIFE SCIENCES

Second Edition

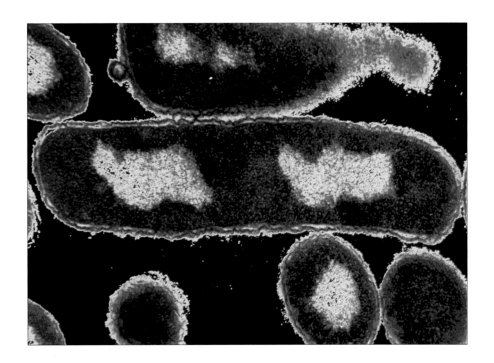

# 11

**Root and tuber crops – Symbiosis**

Marshall Cavendish
New York • London • Toronto • Sydney

Marshall Cavendish
99 White Plains Road
Tarrytown, New York 10591-9001

www.marshallcavendish.com

© 1996, 2004 Marshall Cavendish Corporation

Created by **The Brown Reference Group plc**

**Library of Congress Cataloging-in-Publication Data**

Encyclopedia of life sciences / [edited by] Anne O'Daly.—2nd ed.
    p.    cm.
Summary: An illustrated encyclopedia with articles on
agriculture, anatomy, biochemistry, biology, genetics,
medicine, and molecular biology.
Includes bibliographical references (p.   ).
    ISBN 0-7614-7442-0 (set)
    ISBN 0-7614-7453-6 (vol. 11)
    1. Life sciences—Encyclopedias. 2. Biology—Encyclopedias. [1.
Biology—Encyclopedias. 2. Life sciences—Encyclopedias.] I. O'Daly,
Anne, 1966–
    QH302.5 .E53    2003
    570'.3—dc21

                        2002031157

Printed in Malaysia
Bound in the United States of America

07 06 05 04 03  6 5 4 3 2 1

**Artworks by:**
Darren Awuah, Bill Botten, Jennie Dooge, Dax Fullbrook,
and Mark Walker.

**For The Brown Reference Group:**
Project Editors: Caroline Beattie and Lesley Campbell-Wright
Editors: Richard Beatty, Robert Cave, Simon Hall, Rob Houston,
Jim Martin, and Ben Morgan
Designer: Joan Curtis
Picture Researcher: Rebecca Cox
Managing Editor: Bridget Giles
Design Manager: Lynne Ross
Indexer: Kay Ollerenshaw

**For Marshall Cavendish:**
Project Editor: Joyce Tavolacci
Editorial Director: Paul Bernabeo
Production Manager: Michael Esposito

**Title page:** *Escherichia coli* bacteria ((Biophoto Associates)

# CONTENTS

# USEFUL INFORMATION

Use this table to convert the English system (or the imperial system), the system of units common in the United States (e.g., inches, miles, quarts), to the metric system (e.g., meters, kilometers, liters) or to convert the metric system to the English system. You can convert one measurement into another by multiplying. For example, to convert centimeters into inches, multiply the number of centimeters by 0.3937. To convert inches into centimeters, multiply the number of inches by 2.54.

| To convert | into | multiply by |
|---|---|---|
| **Acres** | Square feet | 43,560 |
| | Square yards | 4840 |
| | Square miles | 0.00156 |
| | Square meters | 4046.856 |
| | Hectares | 0.40468 |
| **Celsius** | Fahrenheit | First multiply by 1.8 then add 32 |
| **Centimeters** | Inches | 0.3937 |
| | Feet | 0.0328 |
| **Cubic cm** | Cubic inches | 0.06102 |
| **Cubic feet** | Cubic inches | 1728 |
| | Cubic yards | 0.037037 |
| | Gallons | 7.48 |
| | Cubic meters | 0.028317 |
| | Liters | 28.32 |
| **Cubic inches** | Fluid ounces | 0.554113 |
| | Cups | 0.069264 |
| | Quarts | 0.017316 |
| | Gallons | 0.004329 |
| | Liters | 0.016387 |
| | Milliliters | 16.387064 |
| **Cubic meters** | Cubic feet | 35.3145 |
| | Cubic yards | 1.30795 |
| **Cubic yards** | Cubic feet | 27 |
| | Cubic meters | 0.76456 |
| **Cups, fluid** | Quarts | 0.25 |
| | Pints | 0.5 |
| | Ounces | 8 |
| | Milliliters | 237 |
| | Tablespoons | 16 |
| | Teaspoons | 48 |
| **Fahrenheit** | Celsius | First subtract 32 then divide by 1.8 |
| **Feet** | Centimeters | 30.48 |
| | Meters | 0.3048 |
| | Kilometers | 0.0003 |
| | Inches | 12 |
| | Yards | 0.3333 |
| | Miles | 0.00019 |
| **Gallons** | Quarts | 4 |
| | Pints | 8 |
| | Cups | 16 |
| | Ounces | 128 |
| | Liters | 3.785 |
| | Milliliters | 3785 |
| | Cubic inches | 231 |
| | Cubic feet | 0.1337 |
| | Cubic yards | 0.00495 |
| | Cubic meters | 0.00379 |
| | British gallons | 0.8327 |
| **Grams** | Ounces | 0.03527 |
| | Pounds | 0.0022 |
| **Hectares** | Square meters | 10,000 |
| | Acres | 2.471 |
| **Horsepower** | Foot-pounds per minute | 33,000 |
| | British thermal units (Btu) per minute | 42.42 |
| | British thermal units (Btu) per hour | 2546 |
| | Kilowatts | 0.7457 |
| | Metric horsepower | 1.014 |
| **Inches** | Feet | 0.08333 |

| To convert | into | multiply by |
|---|---|---|
| **Inches (continued)** | Yards | 0.02778 |
| | Centimeters | 2.54 |
| | Meters | 0.0254 |
| **Kilograms** | Grams | 1000 |
| | Ounces | 35.274 |
| | Pounds | 2.2046 |
| | Short tons | 0.0011 |
| | Long tons | 0.00098 |
| | Metric tons (tonnes) | 0.001 |
| **Kilometers** | Meters | 1000 |
| | Miles | 0.62137 |
| | Yards | 1093.6 |
| | Feet | 3280.8 |
| **Kilowatts** | British thermal units (Btu) per minute | 56.9 |
| | Horsepower | 1.341 |
| | Metric horsepower | 1.397 |
| **Kilowatt-hours** | British thermal units (Btu) | 3413 |
| **Knots** | Statute miles per hour | 1.1508 |
| **Leagues** | Miles | 3 |
| **Liters** | Milliliters | 1000 |
| | Fluid ounces | 33.814 |
| | Quarts | 1.05669 |
| | British gallons | 0.21998 |
| | Cubic inches | 61.02374 |
| | Cubic feet | 0.13531 |
| **Meters** | Inches | 39.37 |
| | Feet | 3.28083 |
| | Yards | 1.09361 |
| | Miles | 0.000621 |
| | Kilometers | 0.001 |
| | Centimeters | 100 |
| | Millimeters | 1000 |
| **Miles** | Inches | 63,360 |
| | Feet | 5280 |
| | Yards | 1760 |
| | Meters | 1609.34 |
| | Kilometers | 1.60934 |
| | Nautical miles | 0.8684 |
| **Miles nautical, U.S. and International** | Statute miles | 1.1508 |
| | Feet | 6076.115 |
| | Meters | 1852 |
| **Miles per minute** | Feet per second | 88 |
| | Knots | 52.104 |
| **Milliliters** | Fluid ounces | 0.0338 |
| | Cubic inches | 0.061 |
| | Liters | 0.001 |
| **Millimeters** | Centimeters | 0.1 |
| | Meters | 0.001 |
| | Inches | 0.03937 |
| **Ounces, avoirdupois** | Pounds | 0.0625 |
| | Grams | 28.34952 |
| | Kilograms | 0.0283495 |
| **Ounces, fluid** | Pints | 0.0625 |
| | Quarts | 0.03125 |
| | Cubic inches | 1.80469 |
| | Cubic feet | 0.00104 |
| | Milliliters | 29.57353 |
| | Liters | 0.02957 |
| **Pints, fluid** | Ounces, fluid | 16 |
| | Quarts, fluid | 0.5 |

| To convert | into | multiply by |
|---|---|---|
| **Pints, fluid (continued)** | Cubic inches | 28.8745 |
| | Cubic feet | 0.01671 |
| | Milliliters | 473.17647 |
| | Liters | 0.473176 |
| **Pounds** | Ounces | 16 |
| | Grams | 453.59237 |
| | Kilograms | 0.45359 |
| | Tons | 0.0005 |
| | Tons, long | 0.000446 |
| | Metric tons (tonnes) | 0.0004536 |
| **Quarts, fluid** | Ounces, fluid | 32 |
| | Pints, fluid | 2 |
| | Gallons | 0.25 |
| | Cubic inches | 57.749 |
| | Cubic feet | 0.033421 |
| | Liters | 0.946358 |
| | Milliliters | 946.358 |
| **Square centimeters** | Square inches | 0.155 |
| **Square feet** | Square inches | 144 |
| | Square meters | 0.093 |
| | Square yards | 0.111 |
| **Square inches** | Square centimeters | 6.452 |
| | Square feet | 0.0069 |
| **Square kilometers** | Hectares | 100 |
| | Square meters | 1,000,000 |
| | Square miles | 0.3861 |
| **Square meters** | Square feet | 10.758 |
| | Square yards | 1.196 |
| **Square miles** | Acres | 640 |
| | Square kilometers | 2.59 |
| **Square yards** | Square feet | 9 |
| | Square inches | 1296 |
| | Square meters | 0.836 |
| **Tablespoons** | Ounces, fluid | 0.5 |
| | Teaspoons | 3 |
| | Milliliters | 14.7868 |
| **Teaspoons** | Ounces, fluid | 0.16667 |
| | Tablespoons | 0.3333 |
| | Milliliters | 4.9289 |
| **Tons, long** | Pounds | 2240 |
| | Kilograms | 1016.047 |
| | Short tons | 1.12 |
| | Metric tons (tonnes) | 1.016 |
| **Tons, short** | Pounds | 2000 |
| | Kilograms | 907.185 |
| | Long tons | 0.89286 |
| | Metric tonnes | 0.907 |
| **Tons, metric (tonnes)** | Pounds | 2204.62 |
| | Kilograms | 1000 |
| | Long tons | 0.984206 |
| | Short tons | 1.10231 |
| **Watts** | British thermal units (Btu) per hour | 3.415 |
| | Horsepower | 0.00134 |
| **Yards** | Inches | 36 |
| | Feet | 3 |
| | Miles | 0.0005681 |
| | Centimeters | 91.44 |
| | Meters | 0.9144 |

# ROOT AND TUBER CROPS

**Root and tuber crops are plants that are cultivated for their edible underground storage organs**

Plants possess a variety of mechanisms that enable them to survive harsh environmental conditions. Many perennial plants, for example, are able to live through cold winters and hot summers by storing food and water in underground storage organs for use by the plant as and when they are required. The storage organs of a number of plant species are edible and are a valuable source of food to many animals, including humans.

The edible portion of the plant may be a root, such as the carrot (*Daucus carota*) and the radish (*Raphanus sativus*). It may be a tuber, an underground stem used for storage, such as the potato (*Solanum tuberosum*; see TUBERS AND RHIZOMES), or a bulb, such as the onion (*Allium cepa*), which is an enlarged bud (see BULBS AND CORMS).

Although all of these storage organs grow underground, they are not all derived from the root system of the plant. However, the term *root crop* in its most general sense may be used to describe any plant whose edible portion lies below the ground. By this definition, tubers and bulbs are regarded as root crops.

## Cultivation of root crops

Root crops are cultivated throughout the world and are used for human consumption as well as for fodder for domestic animals. The early hunter-gatherers collected root crops because they were a readily available source of food when game was scarce. Humans soon learned that obtaining food was much easier in areas where an abundance of edible perennials grew, and the first attempts to cultivate root crops probably began some 8,000 to 10,000 years ago. By the time of the Egyptian pharaohs, tomb paintings show that the people of the Nile valley were already growing black radishes and onions, as well as a number of other vegetables. Native North Americans who lived on the high plains collected the tubers of the Indian potato (*Ipomoea pandurata*) in the spring and ate this apple-sized tuber raw, sundried, or cooked in soups and stews. The hog potato (*Hoffmanseggia glauca*) also has small root tubers that were gathered and eaten. It is also known that carrots were being cultivated in the Mediterranean, China, and northwest Europe by the 13th century.

*Ginseng (Panax spp.) is grown in large fields for its root, which is used in a variety of herbal therapies.*

## Advantages of growing root crops

Grasses, such as rice (*Oryza sativa*) and wheat (*Triticum* spp.), are the staple food of millions of people (see GRAINS). Root crops, however, are easier to grow and maintain. Vegetables such as carrots, beets (*Beta vulgaris*), radishes, and potatoes can be grown in relatively cool climates and are less likely to be affected by adverse weather conditions than grass and grain crops.

For some root crops, such as the potato and sweet potato (*Ipomoea batatas*), the following year's crop can be propagated simply by taking offshoots from the vegetative parts of the plants—such as bulbs and tubers—and replanting them, without the need to sow seeds. Another advantage root crops have over other crops is that they do not need to be harvested immediately and can be stored simply by leaving them in the ground until they are needed, thereby avoiding the risk of spoilage.

---

### CORE FACTS

■ Root crops are cultivated for their underground storage organs, although they are not necessarily true roots.

■ Root crops, although not as important as grain crops, are still a valuable source of carbohydrates.

■ Some roots, such as the mandrake (*Mandragora officinarum*), are credited with medicinal powers.

---

## CONNECTIONS

● Because they contain more water, root and tuber crops have a lower **CARBOHYDRATE** content than **GRAINS** but are valuable providers of **FIBER** and **VITAMINS** in the human diet.

## GINSENG

Asian ginseng (*Panax pseudoginseng*) is a forest herb in the ivy family (Araliaceae) that has been held in high esteem by the Chinese people for centuries. Its thick, fleshy root was prescribed for pain relief and used extensively as a cure for many other ailments. Another Asian species (*Panax ginseng*) is now so rare in the wild that a single well-grown root may be worth thousands of dollars. A North American species also exists (*Panax quinquefolia*), and trade in its root was once more lucrative than furs. Ginseng is considered to be a heart stimulant and a painkiller, and it has also been reported to produce a general feeling of well-being. Some think it even has aphrodisiac properties. Research has now shown that ginseng affects the transport of steroids across cell membranes, but further research is needed to establish how ginseng affects the human body and whether there is any scientific basis for the claims that are made about it.

## A CLOSER LOOK

### Nutritional value of root crops

In the United States, the cereal grasses generally provide over 20 percent of a person's daily energy requirements, while root crops provide less than 10 percent of daily energy needs, partly because they contain only 25 to 30 percent carbohydrates, mostly starch. The bulk of their content is water. Grain crops contain around 70 percent carbohydrate and very little water. However, 1 acre (0.4 ha) of root crop yields two to three times the number of calories that can be obtained from 1 acre of grain because root crops yield a greater mass of edible produce. As well as carbohydrates, root crops usually contain fiber, a small amount of protein, vitamins, and minerals.

### Common root crops

Carrots are edible tap roots (the primary root of a dicotyledonous plant; see ROOTS AND ROOT SYSTEMS). They may be eaten cooked or raw, and a number of varieties exist that differ in shape, color, and size. There are round and long varieties, and the ends may be pointed or blunt. As well as the familiar orange carrot, there are also white, purple, and yellow varieties. Carrots are rich in carotene (provitamin A; see CAROTENES), and a high carotene content is indicated by a bright orange color.

## KALAHARI PEOPLES

The San, or Khoisan, peoples of southern Africa obtain most of their food directly from the land. In the Kalahari Desert, up to 100 species of roots and bulbs are collected and eaten by these people. These plants include *Coccinia rehmanii*, a relative of the cucumber (*Cucumis sativa*), which has edible tubers; various species of *Fockea*, which are related to milkweeds (*Asclepias* spp.) and have tubers whose flavor apparently resembles that of a coconut; and a species of *Eulophia*, an orchid (family Orchidaceae; see ORCHIDS) with a peppery flavored corm that can be eaten raw or roasted. They also collect the bulbs of some species of *Scilla*, a genus in the hyacinth family, which are first roasted, although some species are poisonous. A sedge, *Cyperus congestus*, also has edible sweet tubers. All of these root crops are essential sources of food and water for people who live in arid conditions where other sources are scarce.

The white, or Irish, potato (*Solanum tuberosum*) is a tuber that forms at the end of a rhizome—a horizontal underground stem that bears buds. Potatoes contain large amounts of carbohydrate, vitamin C, and some trace minerals but are low in protein. The potato has been cultivated for at least two thousand years, and there are 150 wild species. It originated in northern South America and Central America and was introduced into Europe in 1537 by Spanish explorers. It is now cultivated in large quantities in Britain, China, France, Germany, Ireland, Poland, and Russia; in the United States over 17.5 million tons (16 million metric tons) are produced annually.

The sweet potato (*Ipomoea batatas*) is a thick, fleshy root. It is grown in parts of the United States, Central America, the Caribbean Islands, China, tropical Asia, the Pacific Islands, the warmer parts of Europe, and in some African countries. Its nearest wild relative is a Mexican plant called *Ipomoea trifida*, from which the modern species is derived. The sweet potato is high in carbohydrates, beta-carotene, and vitamin C and contains a small amount of protein. Over 1 million tons (0.9 million metric tons) are grown annually in the south and southeastern United States.

West Indian yams (*Dioscorea* spp.) are tubers native to Africa and Asia. They are high in starch and contain vitamin C and some protein. Certain species also contain a poisonous substance called dioscorine. The intoxicating yam (*Dioscorea hispida*) has a particularly high content of this substance and must be soaked thoroughly before it can be eaten. West Indian yams also contain a steroid compound called diosgenin, which is extracted and used for the production of drugs, such as cortisone. The southern United States and Central America produce about 275,500 tons (250,000 metric tons) of yams per year.

The cassava (*Manihot esculenta*) has thick, fleshy storage roots that are used as a source of food. It originated in southwestern North America and tropical America but is now an established source of carbohydrates in tropical Asia and Africa. Central America alone produces around 1 million tons (0.9 million metric tons) of cassava per year. In some strains, a cyanide-containing substance is present, so the roots need to be treated before they can be eaten. Cassava is high in carbohydrates and vitamin C but low in other vitamins and protein.

B. TEBBS

**See also:** AGRICULTURE; BULBS AND CORMS; CAROTENES; GRAINS; ORCHIDS; ROOTS AND ROOT SYSTEMS; TUBERS AND RHIZOMES.

**Further reading:**
Hughes, M. S. 1998. *Buried Treasure: Roots and Tubers.* Minneapolis, Minn.: Lerner Publications.
Nayar, N. M. 2003. *Tuber Crops.* Malden, Mass.: Blackwell Science.
Vaughan, J. G., and C. A. Geissler. 1999. *The New Oxford Book of Food Plants.* Oxford and New York: Oxford University Press.

# ROOTS AND ROOT SYSTEMS

The roots of plants have several functions. They provide firm anchorage, they absorb water and nutrients from the soil that are then distributed to other parts of the plant, and they can also act as storage organs. The transport and storage of water and nutrients are also functions that may be carried out by the stem; there are many similarities between the structure of the stem and the roots of a plant. In nonvascular plants, rootlike structures called rhizoids are present (see MOSSES, LIVERWORTS, AND HORNWORTS), but they provide anchorage only and do not perform any other functions and are therefore not considered to be true roots.

> ## CORE FACTS
> - Roots anchor the plant, absorb water and nutrients, and can also act as storage organs.
> - Roots and stems are similar in both structure and function.
> - The growing region of the root, called the apical meristem, is located at the tip and is protected by a layer of cells called the root cap.
> - The volume of root systems underground greatly exceeds that of the plant parts that are visible aboveground.

## Development of roots

In plants the creation of new tissue occurs in several localized areas called meristems, or growing points (see STEMS AND STEM SYSTEMS). The root apical meristem, the main area of growth, is covered by a thin layer of cells called the root cap. This extra layer of cells protects the delicate meristem tissue from damage and is continually sloughed off and replaced by new cells as the root grows into the soil.

As the root meristem produces new cells, the recently formed cells lying behind the meristem begin to elongate and differentiate. The zone of elongation is a short region less than ¼ inch (2 to 5 mm) long situated immediately behind the meristem and root cap. By restricting elongation to this region, the roots avoid buckling, and the fragile root hairs are not dragged through the soil. New cells develop into specialized forms in the zone of differentiation.

Root hairs, which are usually present in large numbers growing from the root, are outgrowths from the epidermal cells (the outermost layer of cells that form the epidermis). Root hairs greatly increase the surface area of the root through which nutrients and water can be absorbed from the soil. The root hairs usually become flattened and intimately entwined around the soil particles.

The concentration of dissolved molecules in root cell sap is higher than that of the surrounding soil. Thus, water is drawn into the root from the soil, through the surface of the epidermis and root hairs,

## Roots provide anchorage, absorb water and nutrients, and may act as storage organs

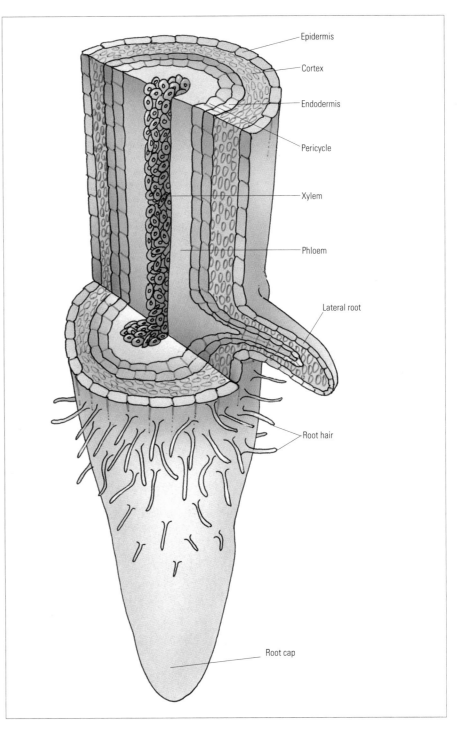

A section of a root, showing the types of cells and cell layers involved in transporting water and nutrients through the plant.

by a process called osmosis. Various elements, called macronutrients, are absorbed at the same time, such as potassium (K), calcium (Ca), magnesium (Mg), sulfur (S), phosphorus (P), nitrogen (N), and silicon (Si). Other elements that are needed by the plant in smaller amounts are also absorbed. These micronutrients include iron (Fe), manganese (Mn), boron (B), chlorine (Cl), molybdenum (Mo), zinc (Zn),

## CONNECTIONS

● **PERENNIAL PLANTS** often have quite extensive root systems, while those of **ANNUAL PLANTS** are likely to be less developed.

*Plant root systems sometimes cover a far greater area than the parts of the plant aboveground. The root systems of trees often stretch many yards.*

## THE BALANCE BETWEEN ROOTS AND SHOOTS

The number of roots and shoots produced by a plant depends on the amount of food the leaves can manufacture and on the amount of water and nutrients the roots can absorb. For example, if the root systems are damaged by fungal attack or breakage during transplantation, they will not be able to supply enough water for all the shoots and leaves, and some of these structures will die. On the other hand, if the shoots are severely pruned, then there will be fewer leaves manufacturing food to support the same sized root system, and thus, many of the roots will die.

copper (Cu), iodine (I), and selenium (Se). In most plants, the root hairs survive for only a few days or weeks. In older roots, the epidermis cell walls become thickened so that eventually water and nutrients are no longer absorbed through them.

The ground meristem cells, which lie beneath the epidermis, develop into the cortex and the endodermis. The latter is a single layer of cells on the innermost edge of the cortex that becomes thickened with age and surrounds the central vascular cylinder. The cortex is made up of parenchyma cells with large spaces between them. These cells are important in the storage of water and nutrients.

### Transport systems

The vascular tissue in angiosperms (flowering plants) consists largely of xylem and phloem, which serve the same function as they do in the stem, namely, the transport of water and nutrients throughout the plant (see ANGIOSPERMS; VASCULAR SYSTEMS). Phloem transports organic and inorganic materials created by photosynthesis in the leaves to other parts of the plant by translocation (see PHOTOSYNTHESIS; TRANSPIRATION AND TRANSLOCATION). The main function of the xylem in roots is to transport water and nutrients from the roots to the leaves and the stem by transpiration.

As water evaporates from the surface of the leaves, more water is drawn up the plant. The concentration of the root cell sap is higher than that of the fluid surrounding it, so water is absorbed from the soil. This pressure helps to force water up the stem. Also, as water is drawn up the stem, the sap within the root cells in turn becomes even more concentrated, and so more water is absorbed; thus, there is a continuous flow of fluid through the plant. There is also a force called root pressure that actively pushes water up the stem from the roots, but very little is known about this mechanism other than that it requires the input of energy.

Between the xylem and the phloem in roots are a few cells that either become vascular cambium, which is important in the formation of secondary growth in woody roots, or sclerenchyma cells. The latter are strengthening cells with hardened walls that may be short (called sclereids) or elongated (called fibers). The thin outer layer of the vascular cylinder is called the pericycle, in which side branches start to develop. The pericycle first starts to bulge, and the outer layers stretch and eventually rupture. This arrangement is in contrast with the stems, where the side branches develop from surface cells near the growing tip. At the center of the vascular cylinder, there is sometimes a core, or pith. This area is also used for storage and is only present in some species, including most monocotyledonous plants (see MONOCOTYLEDONS).

### Types of root systems

A rudimentary root, called the radicle, is already developed in the embryo. When the seed germinates, the radicle extends to become the primary root.

## WHY DO ROOTS GROW DOWNWARD?

The roots of seedlings will always grow downward, even if the seeds are germinated in conditions of all-around light. This response to gravity is called geotropism (see TROPISM AND TAXIS). The mechanism for it is uncertain, but it is thought that free-moving starch grains, called statoliths, are present in some cells at the tip of the root. The grains settle to the bottom of the cells owing to gravity and are thought to stimulate the root to grow downward.

### A CLOSER LOOK

In most dicotyledonous plants (see DICOTYLEDONS), this primary root continues to grow throughout the life of the plant and is called the tap root. It grows fairly straight and downward, and its branches and sub-branches develop at angles of 90 degrees or less. The tap root always remains the dominant root and often becomes thickened to form an important storage organ (see ROOT AND TUBER CROPS). It may be fleshy, as in carrots (*Daucus carota*) and turnips (*Brassica rapa*), or woody, as in oaks (*Quercus* spp.).

Adventitious roots are produced from the base of the stem rather than from the primary root. In most monocotyledonous plants, the primary roots are temporary until the plant becomes established and the adventitious roots become the permanent root system. Numerous adventitious roots usually develop, which then spread and branch outward and downward to form a mass called a fibrous root system. Because it forms an intricate mat in the upper layers of the soil, it is very efficient at extracting the water and nutrients available in this top layer. Tap root systems, on the other hand, are able to penetrate greater depths, sometimes up to 80 feet (25 m), in search of water.

### Storage in roots

Most roots have storage cells located mainly in the cortex, but some may also occur in other root tissues. Food may be stored for only short periods: for example, food produced during the day may be stored for use at night, or it may be stored for months or even years. It may be stored in the form of sugars, but it is usually converted to starch, a complex insoluble carbohydrate (see CARBOHYDRATES) that does not affect the osmotic balance of the cell and can therefore be stored for considerable lengths of time. Food storage in the roots is very important to perennial plants and trees during periods of dormancy (see DORMANCY). In arid regions, the roots are also important for water storage, enabling the plant to survive periods of drought (see DESERT BIOMES).

Some species, such as turnip and parsnip (*Pastinaca sativa*), have specially enlarged tap roots that store food. In some cases, these roots can contribute to vegetative spread. For example, if the tap root of a dandelion (*Taraxacum* spp.) is broken into pieces, each piece may develop into a new plant. Some species, such as dahlias (*Dahlia* spp.) and many terrestrial orchids (family Orchidaceae), produce specialized enlarged structures called root tubers. They are produced from adventitious roots and are used to store the food needed for the following year's growth.

Several modified stem structures are produced underground for overwintering and are often mistaken for parts of the root system. They differ from roots because they have buds from which new plants develop after the dormant period. These structures include stem tubers, such as the potato (*Solanum tuberosum*), bulbs, such as the onion (*Allium cepa*), corms, such as the crocus (*Crocus* spp.), and rhizomes, such as irises (*Iris* spp.; see BULBS AND CORMS; TUBERS AND RHIZOMES).

### Other adaptations of roots

In very dry habitats, root systems generally extend over a wide area and penetrate deeply into the soil to obtain any water that is available. Large amounts

*Boston ivy (*Parthenocissus tricuspidata*) is a climbing plant that attaches itself to the surface over which it grows, using adventitious roots that are produced from the side of the stem.*

## BONSAI TREES

The ancient Chinese and Japanese art of producing miniature trees is called bonsai. The principles used rely on the fact that the number of roots and shoots of a plant, and thus its size, depends on the amount of food the leaves can manufacture and on the amount of water and nutrients the roots can absorb. Seeds of normal tree species are planted in shallow pots, which severely restrict root development, and the roots are also pruned periodically. The growth of the trunks is thus restricted, resulting in trees that would normally be over 60 feet (18 m) tall never growing more than 3 feet (1 m) in height, even after centuries of growth.

## THE SIZE OF ROOT SYSTEMS

Because roots are buried in the ground, their extent is often underestimated, and they often greatly exceed the volume occupied by the stems and leaves above the ground. For example, the roots of a healthy wheat plant (*Triticum* spp.) may extend to about 6 feet (2 m) in depth and about 3 feet (1 m) sideways in every direction. Thus, the roots of plants often compete with each other for water and nutrients long before the foliage aboveground comes into contact. Wheat plants growing on their own are several times larger than those growing in rows only a few inches apart.

In one investigation, scientists counted a total number of 14 million roots on a plant, the combined length of which amounted to 385 miles (620 km). The roots covered a total surface area of 287 square yards (240 m²), and the number of root hairs counted came to 14 billion, produced at a rate of more than 100 million a day. The total surface area of root hairs was calculated to be 478 square yards (400 m²); thus, a total area of 765 square yards (640 m²) of roots and root hairs were in contact with the soil. By comparison, only 80 shoots and 480 leaves were present on the same plant, amounting to a total surface area above ground of only ⅗ square yards (0.5 m²).

### A CLOSER LOOK

of water are needed to compensate for the rapid loss of water through evaporation and transpiration. In wet conditions the rates of transpiration are relatively low; thus, the roots of plants that live in these conditions are less well developed. Aquatic plants can absorb water through the stems and leaves, and most species do not develop root hairs. Some aquatic species do not have roots at all.

A number of other species do not produce root hairs, including firs (*Abies* spp.), redwoods (in the family Cupressaceae), and pines (*Pinus* spp.). These trees have several fungi that are closely associated with their roots (see FUNGI KINGDOM), a relationship called mycorrhizal association. Fungi do not produce chlorophyll and cannot manufacture their own carbohydrates; thus, they obtain their food from the roots of the plant. The plant also benefits from this relationship because the fungi, by breaking down organic matter in the soil, make nutrients more easily available to the plant. This type of association often occurs in plants that grow in very poor soils. These plants are healthier than plants living in similar conditions that do not form a symbiotic mycorrhizal association (see SYMBIOSIS).

In salty habitats, such as salt marshes, the absorption of water through osmosis is more difficult owing to the high concentration of dissolved salts in the surrounding water. To overcome this problem, the plants absorb salt until the concentration in the roots is higher than that of the surroundings.

Adventitious roots usually develop from the base of the stem below the soil surface. However, some species produce aerial roots higher up the stem. These roots often grow obliquely outward from the stems or downward from the branches and provide extra support. Some climbing plants, such as English ivy (*Hedera helix*) and Virginia creeper (*Parthenocissus quinquefolia*), produce roots that cling to the surface over which they are growing (see CLIMBING PLANTS). In humid environments, such as in rain forests, the roots of some epiphytes (plants that grow on other plants but are not parasites) never reach the soil, and they absorb water directly from the air (see EPIPHYTES).

N. STEWART

**See also:** ANGIOSPERMS; BULBS AND CORMS; CARBOHYDRATES; CLIMBING PLANTS; DESERT BIOMES; DICOTYLEDONS; DORMANCY; EPIPHYTES; FUNGI KINGDOM; MONOCOTYLEDONS; MOSSES, LIVERWORTS, AND HORNWORTS; PHOTOSYNTHESIS; ROOT AND TUBER CROPS; STEMS AND STEM SYSTEMS; SYMBIOSIS; TRANSPIRATION AND TRANSLOCATION; TROPISM AND TAXIS; TUBERS AND RHIZOMES; VASCULAR SYSTEMS.

**Further reading:**
Raven, P. H., R. F. Evert, and S. E. Eichhorn. 1999. *Biology of Plants.* 6th ed. New York: W. H. Freeman/Worth Publishers.
Waisel, Y., A. Eshel, and U. Kafkafi, eds. 2002. *Plant Roots: The Hidden Half.* 3rd ed. New York: Marcel Dekker.

# RUMINANTS

**Ruminants are plant-eating, hoofed mammals with specially adapted stomachs and teeth**

A human usually spends between 30 minutes and an hour eating three meals a day. By comparison, a cow feeds on grass for about eight hours a day and then spends the same length of time chewing cud. As grass is neither very nutritious nor easy to digest, cows must eat a huge quantity every day; doing so takes time.

Animals can be classified according to their feeding behavior and the physiology of their digestive systems. For example, cud-chewing animals, such as sheep and cows, are called ruminants, a group of herbivorous (plant-eating) mammals that have evolved a way of digesting their tough, fibrous plant food (see DIGESTIVE SYSTEMS).

## CORE FACTS

- Ruminants have a complex three- or four-chambered stomach. One chamber, the rumen, acts as a fermentation tank, containing a large number of cellulose-digesting microorganisms, which exist in a symbiotic relationship with the ruminant.
- Ruminants must eat large quantities of plant matter because it is difficult to digest and not very nutritious.
- Ruminants are among the most efficient vertebrates at digesting plant fiber.
- Microbial protein is the most important source of protein for ruminants; 10 billion microbes may occur in every milliliter of rumen contents.

## Many-chambered stomach

Ruminants are a suborder (Ruminantia) of the group Artiodactyla, which are ungulates (herbivorous, hoofed mammals; see UNGULATES) whose hooves are formed from their third and fourth toes. Artiodactyla can be divided into three suborders: Suiformes (pigs, peccaries, and hippopotamuses), Tylopoda (primitive ruminants comprising camels and their relatives), and Ruminantia (deer and giraffe families, pronghorn antelope, musk deer, and the bovids—cattle, sheep, bison, goats, and New and Old World antelope. Ruminantia are characterized by a complex three- or four-chambered stomach and specialized teeth. The males also generally have horns or antlers. Like other ungulates, they have a cursorial lifestyle; they are constantly on the move, and their skeletons, muscles, and general physiology are specialized for running to escape from predators.

Although the term *four-chambered stomach* is used, it is more accurate to say that the true stomach (where the digestion of food using enzymes takes place) is preceded by three compartments, the first and largest of which is called the rumen. In the rumen the food is mixed with saliva and fermented by bacteria and protozoans. Unlike more highly evolved animals, these microorganisms can produce cellulase, an enzyme that can digest the tough cellulose cell walls of plants. The rumen is only partly separated from the next chamber, the reticulum, and the two are often referred to together as the reticulorumen.

*As a ruminant, the giraffe (Giraffa camelopardalis), living in the savanna regions of sub-Saharan Africa, feeds mainly on the leaves and shoots of trees and shrubs.*

## CONNECTIONS

● Ruminant **TEETH** have evolved to deal with a diet of tough, fibrous plant material.

● The **BACTERIA** and protozoans living in a ruminant's **STOMACH** can synthesize **AMINO ACIDS** and **VITAMINS**.

● **FERMENTATION** is important in ruminant digestion.

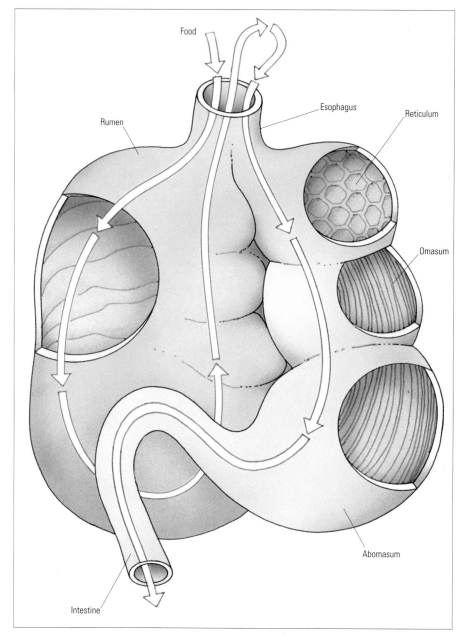

Food

Esophagus

Reticulum

Rumen

Omasum

Abomasum

Intestine

## MICROBES AS A NUTRIENT SOURCE

As many as 10 billion microorganisms may be present in every milliliter of rumen contents. The microbe population is composed of over 60 species of bacteria, as well as protozoans (mainly ciliates) and some fungi. They have all evolved to live only in environments without oxygen and are called obligate anaerobic organisms. In addition to producing waste products that ruminants can use as an energy source, the gut microorganisms have another important function: they are able to synthesize amino acids from inorganic nitrogen (see AMINO ACIDS). Furthermore, they can synthesize the B-complex vitamins and vitamin K (see VITAMINS). Animals require protein that can provide different types of essential amino acids (ones that the body cannot manufacture itself). Meat is a rich source of amino acids, while many plants (especially the green parts) provide little protein and little variation in amino acids. The gut microorganisms manufacture amino acids, vitamins, and other nutrients for themselves, and every day many millions of these organisms pass out of the rumen with the food particles and enter the rest of the gut. The ruminant can then digest them with the plant material and obtain substances it is otherwise unable to obtain in the diet or to synthesize for itself. Thus, ruminants can live on very low-grade forage that other animals would find too poor in essential nutrients to be able to survive on.

*The stomach of most ruminants is composed of four chambers, with food first going into the rumen, then the reticulum, the omasum, and finally, the abomasum.*

Food particles are regurgitated from the rumen, chewed as cud, and then swallowed. Small particles pass from the reticulum into the third chamber, the omasum, where water is pressed out and absorbed. From the omasum, the food travels into the abomasum, or true stomach, where gastric glands secrete enzymes, and from there into the small intestine and the rest of the gut.

### Feeding adaptations

Plant food is difficult to digest and not very nutritious, and so ungulates need to eat a lot of this poor-quality food and spend most of their active time feeding. Ruminants crop vegetation by grasping it between their lower incisors and the hardened gum of the front of the upper jaw (the premaxillary region) and tearing a mouthful away. Their mobile tongue and lips help them to be selective in what they eat; giraffes (*Giraffa camelopardalis*), for example, are able to feed on the leaves of acacia trees without also taking a mouthful of the tree's protective spines.

Ruminants have hypsodont, or high-crowned, cheek teeth composed of enamel, dentine, and cement. They wear down at different rates, so the chewing surface of the teeth is always very rough. These adaptations have evolved to aid in grinding tough, fibrous plant material.

### Microbial activity in the rumen

After vegetation is cropped, chewed briefly, and swallowed, it enters the rumen. The microorganisms in the rumen produce cellulase, an enzyme that breaks down the cellulose molecules, the main structural units of a plant, into their constituent glucose molecules. The microbes obtain their energy by fermenting the glucose. One of the waste products of this process is an organic acid (so-called volatile fatty acid) that is of no use to the microorganisms. However, a ruminant can make use of these waste products. Once the acids have been absorbed through the wall of the rumen, they provide the ruminant with its major source of energy. Therefore, the microorganisms have a mutually beneficial, or symbiotic, relationship with their host (the ruminant; see SYMBIOSIS). Carbon dioxide and methane are also by-products of fermentation and are expelled from the ruminant by belching (see FERMENTATION).

Rumen microorganisms must live in a liquid environment that is not too acidic. The ruminant maintains the right pH (measure of acidity or alkalinity) in the rumen (pH 5.5 to 6.5) by producing large amounts of saliva: 10.5 to 28 pints (6 to 16 l) a day in sheep and goats and 176 to 334 pints (100 to 190 l) a day in cattle. The saliva is a dilute alkaline solution of phosphates and sodium bicarbonate, which buffers the acidic effect of the fatty acids produced by the microorganisms. The ruminant also reduces the level of acidity by quickly absorbing the fatty acids.

## Chewing the cud

When not actively feeding, ruminants spend time regurgitating cuds, or food balls, formed from the tough, fibrous plant material present in the rumen. These cuds are thoroughly chewed (more so than when the food was first ingested) and then swallowed. This process, called rumination, or chewing the cud, gives the group its name. Cattle grazing on pasture ruminate for about eight hours every day, the same amount of time they spend feeding.

The extra mechanical breakdown of food through rumination reduces the food into even smaller particles and releases the digestible cell contents. When the cud is swallowed, small particles pass into the reticulum, while larger particles reenter the rumen for further fermentation.

## Digestion and fermentation

The rumen contents are mixed continuously by rhythmic contractions of the walls. The reticulum acts as a seive, preventing fibrous food from leaving the rumen until it has been reduced to small fragments. Then the semifluid food gradually passes out of the reticulum and into the omasum. Water and electrolytes are absorbed in the omasum, as well as any remaining fatty acids. The residue then passes into the true stomach, the abomasum, where the extremely acidic gastric juices (pH 1.05 to 1.32) begin the process of digestion. The millions of microorganisms that accompanied the food so far are killed by the stomach acids and digested with the food in the abomasum and small intestine. This process has great nutritional benefits for the ruminant (see the box on page 1452).

Ruminants are without doubt among the most efficient vertebrates at digesting fiber. They are foregut fermenters, that is, the site of microbial fermentation (the rumen) is situated in front of the part of the gut (the abomasum and small intestine) where most digestion and absorption take place. Any nutrients released or synthesized by the microorganisms are utilized by the ruminant. Kangeroos, though not ruminants, use a similar strategy. Other animals, such as rabbits and horses, are classified as hind-gut fermenters; microbial fermentation takes place in the cecum or colon, which are located after the stomach and small intestine. These animals are less efficient than ruminants at digesting fiber.

Different animal groups have evolved different ways around the problem of dietary fiber. Rabbits and hares, for example, cope with the fibrous part of their diet by passing it through the gut twice (see RABBITS AND HARES). They produce a fecal pellet formed from the cecal contents, which they swallow whole and so digest for a second time. Dark, dry fecal pellets are then expelled but are not eaten.

## Importance of microbial protein

The advantage of foregut fermentation is that the size of the stomach allows food to slowly ferment there for a long time. Furthermore, microbial protein (and other products synthesized by the

---

### FEEDING BEHAVIOR

Herbivores may be classified according to their feeding behavior. There are three main feeding groups, and ruminants are present in each: concentrate selectors, intermediate feeders, and bulk and roughage eaters. Concentrate selectors, such as deer and giraffes, choose the most nutritious parts of green plants, such as young leaves and shoots, which are low in fiber and high in protein and other nutrients. Intermediate feeders, such as domestic goats (*Capra hircus*), browse on shrubs, while domestic sheep (*Ovis aries*) graze on grass. They are less selective than deer and giraffes but still choose the more nutritious plant material. Larger ruminants are bulk and roughage eaters; they compensate for eating plants low in nutrition by eating a lot of them. Ruminants such as cattle (*Bos* spp.) prefer to feed on fresh grass, while hartebeests (*Alcelaphus buselaphus*) eat dry grasses. Thus, differences in food preference allow many different ungulates to live in grassland areas, such as the Serengeti in East Africa.

### A CLOSER LOOK

microorganisms; see the box on page 1452) can be utilized by foregut fermenters. The main disadvantage is that all food coming into the gut, having already passed through the stomach, is fermented, even the readily digestible parts such as starches and protein, and fermentation may even reduce their nutritional value. Thus, the ruminant strategy is not necessarily the best one for all situations; for example, where an organism has a large amount of easily digestible nutrients in its diet.

E. BRADSHAW

**See also:** AMINO ACIDS; DIGESTIVE SYSTEMS; FEEDING; FERMENTATION; RABBITS AND HARES; SYMBIOSIS; UNGULATES; VITAMINS.

### Further reading:

Givens, D. I., E. Owens, and R. F. E. Axford, eds. 2000. *Forage Evaluation in Ruminant Nutrition*. New York: CABI Publishing.
Owen-Smith, R. N. 2002. *Adaptive Herbivore Ecology*. Cambridge, U.K.: Cambridge University Press.

*The longhorn cow pictured below is chewing cud, mechanically breaking up the plant matter it has eaten into smaller particles to make digestion easier and faster.*

# SALAMANDERS AND NEWTS

**Salamanders and newts (order Caudata) are amphibians with elongated bodies, long tails, and two pairs of legs**

*The tiger salamander (Ambystoma tigrinum) is a mole salamander in the family Ambystomatidae, which lives only in North America. Mole salamanders are so named because they live in burrows for much of their lives.*

## CONNECTIONS

● Salamanders and newts are **AMPHIBIANS** with elongated bodies and **TAILS**.

● Aquatic salamanders and newts live in **RIVERS AND STREAMS, LAKES AND PONDS, WETLANDS**, and **CAVE HABITATS**.

Experts have calculated that if every salamander, bird, and small mammal from a New Hampshire forest were rounded up and piled onto a gigantic balance, the biomass of salamanders would equal that of the mammals and prove more than double that of the birds. Present in substantial numbers, salamanders and newts are secretive amphibians that place little demand on the ecosystem and, unlike frogs, do not advertise their presence by making loud sounds. Their metabolism is among the slowest of any vertebrate.

Characterized in part by their tails, salamanders and newts belong to the order Caudata. There are 10 families, 60 genera, and about 450 known species. They have a streamlined body and four legs, although in some aquatic species the legs are absent or minute. Most are between 2 and 6 inches (5 and 15 cm) long, although the Chinese giant salamander (*Andrias davidianus*) can grow to 6 feet (1.8 m).

### Classification

The most widely distributed family is the Salamandridae, with members living in Europe, Asia, and North America. This family includes newts, brook salamanders, and fire salamanders. Newts are members of the *Triturus*, *Taricha*, and *Notophthalmus* species (among many others), which return to water to breed.

Many salamandrid species are brightly colored, and some produce poisonous secretions. For example, the black and yellow fire salamander produces a neurotoxin (toxin affecting the nervous system), which it squirts from glands on its back to hit aggressors at least 7 feet (2 m) away.

The family Cryptobranchidae includes the world's largest salamanders, the giant salamanders. Hellbenders (*Crytobranchus alleganiensis*) are the largest North American salamanders, measuring 28 inches (71 cm) in length. Giant salamanders live in rivers and streams, and although they lack gills, they can gulp air from the surface and breathe with lungs.

Amphiumas (Amphiumidae) are aquatic salamanders with tiny legs and eel-like bodies. They live in mud burrows in the swamps of the southeastern United States. They have lungs and are the only salamanders also to have internal gills.

Olms, mud puppies, and water dogs (Proteidae) are aquatic salamanders with lungs and external gills. Olms (*Proteus anguinus*) live in subterranean pools and streams in the Balkans and northeastern Italy. Living in a dark environment, they lack skin pigment and are almost blind. Four species of water dogs and one species of mud puppy inhabit aboveground fresh water in the central and eastern United States.

### CORE FACTS

■ Salamanders and newts are amphibians in the order Caudata (also called Urodela), whose members inhabit both terrestrial and aquatic environments.

■ As with most amphibians, salamanders and newts possess a smooth, flexible, and scaleless skin, which is usually moist.

■ The reproductive behavior of salamanders and newts is very diverse: in some species fertilization is external, in others internal; some species lay eggs, and others give birth to live young.

Torrent salamanders (Rhyacotritonidae) live in the United States along the Pacific coast.

Mole salamanders inhabit underground burrows, and most live in North America. Examples include the axolotl (*Ambystoma mexicanum*) and the Pacific giant salamanders (Dicamptodontidae). These salamanders migrate to the head of springs to lay their eggs, which hatch into aquatic larvae. Tiger salamander larvae (*Ambystoma tigrinum*) may be cannibalistic, that is, they feed on larvae of their own species.

Lungless salamanders (Plethodontidae) are the only vertebrates with neither lungs nor gills. They are the largest family of tailed amphibians, with around 300 species distributed from southeastern Alaska to Brazil. A few species are European. They rely on mucous membranes in the mouth and throat for respiratory surfaces and a thoroughly moist skin (see RESPIRATORY SYSTEMS). Some forest-dwelling species are terrestrial; all are confined to moist, shady habitats.

Sirens (Sirenidae) are aquatic salamanders with long, eel-shaped bodies. They live in shallow waters in the central United States and northeastern Mexico. They lack hind limbs, have reduced forelimbs, and breathe through external gills. If the shallow water dries up, sirens bury themselves in the mud. The slimy mucus on their skin hardens to form a protective cocoon. With only their mouth protruding so they can breathe through the mouth lining, they go into a state of dormancy, surviving several months until the next rains come.

## Lifestyle and habitat

Salamanders inhabit moist, temperate regions of Europe, the Mediterranean, Africa, Asia, North America, and tropical Central and South America. They thrive in freshwater lakes, swamps, and streams. Terrestrial species take refuge beneath rocks or logs in moist, shady places and are most active at night and during rainy weather.

Salamanders as a group range from wholly aquatic to terrestrial. Those without gills breathe through lungs, except for lungless salamanders, which absorb oxygen from water or air through the lining of their mouth and throat. Oxygen also diffuses through the moist skin, and skin glands produce mucous secretions that maintain the moisture.

Some species undergo a morphological transformation that coincides with a transition between water and land one or more times during their lives. The axolotl, an aquatic salamander, is one of several types of salamanders that retains larval gills when sexually mature, a phenomenon called paedomorphosis. During drought, the axolotl can lose its gills and become terrestrial.

*The larva of the European fire salamander* (Salamandra salamandra)*, shown below, spends approximately three months in its aquatic habitat before leaving the water as a tiny replica of its parents to begin the terrestrial stage of its life.*

*The palmate newt (*Triturus helveticus*), as with all salamanders and newts, is carnivorous. In addition to small fishes, these newts may also feed on small invertebrates, such as worms, slugs, insects, and crustaceans.*

The red-spotted newt (*Notophthalmus viridescens*) from eastern North America spends its early life as a larva, breathing through gills. It develops legs after three days and loses its gills after three months. It then walks out of water and into a terrestrial life that lasts three to four years. When the newt returns to water to breed, its rough skin becomes smooth, the tail flattens to a shape more useful for swimming, and the eyes change shape to accommodate underwater focusing. Lateral lines develop on the skin, helping the newt detect vibrations and locate prey under water.

All salamanders and newts are carnivorous, taking live prey such as insects, worms, and other small invertebrates. They possess a tongue that can be flicked out some distance to aid in the capture of prey, which is then gripped and chewed with the help of small teeth present on the roof of the mouth and in the jaws. Salamanders may survive extended periods without food, and some species can live for many years, perhaps as many as 15.

## Reproduction

The fertilization of eggs occurs externally in the primitive families Crytobranchidae and Hynobiidae, but in other salamanders the eggs are fertilized internally. With internal fertilization, males produce a gelatinous capsule called the spermatophore, with sperm adhering to the capsule's tip. After the male deposits the spermatophore on the ground, the female picks up the sperm with the lips of her cloaca, leaving the rest of the spermatophore behind.

Salamanders may lay as few as 5 or 6 eggs or as many as 500. Often the eggs are attached to logs or vegetation under water. In some species, one or both parents guard the eggs until they hatch into larvae. The larvae breathe through gills, use their tails when swimming, and unlike tadpoles, are carnivorous. As they grow, terrestrial species develop four legs and lose their gills, finally crawling onto land after metamorphosis (see METAMORPHOSIS).

M. CHU

**See also:** FROGS AND TOADS; METAMORPHOSIS; RESPIRATORY SYSTEMS.

**Further reading:**
Pough, F. H., R. M. Andrews, J. E. Cadle, M. L. Crump, et al. 2001. *Herpetology.* 2nd ed. Englewood Cliffs, N.J.: Prentice Hall.

## AMPHIBIAN ANCESTRY

The earliest known amphibian, *Ichthyostega*, had four short limbs supporting a long body and well-developed tail. In overall body shape, it more closely resembled salamanders than any other modern lineage, although differences in bone structure reflect the approximately 350 million years that separate them.

Amphibian ancestors were lobe-finned fish. These fish had some features that may have predisposed their descendants to life on land. For example, an air bladder connected to the pharynx could fill with air from outside the body—a potential precursor of the lung. Lobe-finned fish gave rise to the first four-limbed vertebrates during the late Devonian period (408 to 360 million years ago), a time of periodic drought. Any creature able to crawl or drag itself across land to seek a larger body of water would have been at a distinct advantage.

Fossils of amphibians that are believed to be the ancestors of modern frogs and salamanders have been discovered in Scotland, dating to 338 million years ago. The earliest fossil evidence for true salamanders is 155 million years old.

EVOLUTION

# SALK, JONAS

**U.S. physician Jonas Salk (1914–1995) developed the original vaccine that led to the control of poliomyelitis**

During his last year at medical school, Salk studied the influenza virus at Woods Hole, Massachusetts. He wanted to find out if the flu virus could be deactivated yet still be used to immunize against illness. His success provided the basis of his work on poliomyelitis (polio, or infantile paralysis), a viral infection of the central nervous system that affects muscle-activating nerves, causing permanent disability and deformity or even death.

In 1942 Salk was awarded a National Research Council Fellowship and went to work with Francis at Ann Arbor in Michigan. He perfected his techniques with vaccines and developed several commercial flu vaccines with Francis.

## The fight against poliomyelitis

In 1947 Salk was appointed head of the virus research laboratory at the University of Pittsburgh, where he worked on poliovirus, which caused poliomyelitis. In the early 20th century, polio epidemics were becoming increasingly regular; in 1952 there were 58,000 cases and 3,000 deaths in the United States. Salk researched the virus for the next eight years. He knew there were three viral types and that Harvard researchers had successfully grown the virus in tissue culture, providing an unlimited supply of poliovirus for study.

In 1949 Salk turned his attention to vaccine production. First, he inactivated the virus by treating it with formalin. Then in 1952, having first tested the vaccine's safety by injecting himself and his family, Salk successfully tested the prototype vaccine. Two years later he began nationwide field trials of his vaccine, during which 1.8 million children were inoculated. In 1955 Salk announced that the vaccine worked. He was hailed as a hero; the more so because he did not patent the vaccine and therefore made no personal profit from its production. The efficacy of his vaccine became clear as the number of new polio cases fell sharply each year. Polio is now virtually unknown in the United States.

Although nominated, Salk was never named Nobel laureate, but he received many other prizes, including a Congressional Gold Medal and a Presidential Citation in 1955 and the Presidential Medal of Freedom in 1977. However, Salk said his greatest reward was the knowledge that he had helped eradicate a terrible disease. He died in 1995 at age 80.

K. DENNIS-BRYAN

**See also:** AIDS; IMMUNE SYSTEMS; IMMUNIZATION; IMMUNOLOGY.

## Further reading:

Barter, J. 2003. *Jonas Salk.* Chicago: Lucent.
McPherson, S. S. 2001. *Jonas Salk: Conquering Polio (Lerner Biographies).* Minneapolis, Minn.: Lerner.

*In 1963 the Salk Institute for Biological Studies was built in La Jolla, San Diego; Salk, above, was its first director.*

## CONNECTIONS

● Research on **VIRUSES**, enabled Salk to produce a vaccine using an inactive form of poliovirus.

Jonas Salk was born to Russian-Jewish immigrant parents on October 28, 1914, and lived in the Bronx, New York. When Salk enrolled at City College, he decided to study medicine to become a medical scientist. After graduating in 1934, he enrolled in the New York University (NYU) School of Medicine, receiving his medical degree in 1939.

At the end of Salk's first year of medical school, he took a year out to study protein chemistry with his professor, R. Keith Cannon. He was awarded a fellowship that allowed him to learn the techniques that would later be useful in his studies on vaccines. During this period, he met bacteriologist Thomas Francis, who became his mentor, research collaborator, and friend. Francis was interested in the production of vaccines, particularly against influenza (flu), and introduced Salk to immunology and viral replication.

During his second year of medical studies, Salk was told it was possible to use chemically treated toxins as immunizing agents against diphtheria and tetanus. In the next lecture, he was informed that one could not be immunized against virus-induced disease in this way but must experience the infection to obtain immunity from it. Salk asked why this was so but no proper explanation was forthcoming.

# SALTS

**Marine birds, such as the glaucous-winged gulls (Larus glaucescens) shown above, remove excess salt from their bodies by secreting a concentrated salt solution from salt glands near their eyes.**

## CONNECTIONS

● **SHARKS** rid their bodies of excess salt with the aid of a gland near the rectum that secretes a concentrated salt solution.

● To remove sodium ions (in a salt solution) from a cell requires **ENERGY**.

## Salts, chemical compounds formed from acids and bases, play important biological roles

$$KCl \Leftrightarrow K^+ + Cl^-$$

Salts cannot continue dissolving in a fixed quantity of water forever. Eventually the solution becomes saturated, and no more salt will dissolve. Different salts have different solubilities, but more salt dissolves as the temperature of the solution is raised.

### Osmosis

The concentration of salts in body fluids remains as constant as possible, whether the organism consumes very salty food, loses water by evaporation, or excretes both water and salts. Animals keep all their internal conditions constant in a process called homeostasis (see HOMEOSTASIS).

The most important mechanism in keeping salt and water levels constant is osmosis, the tendency of water to move through a semipermeable membrane (such as that surrounding a cell), in accord with the relative concentrations of ions and soluble molecules on each side of the membrane. Water tends to move from a site of lower concentration to one of higher concentration. If the salt concentration inside a cell is higher than that in the body fluid outside, water crosses the cell membrane to dilute the cell contents. At the same time, salt moves out of the cell until an equilibrium is reached.

The increasing water raises the osmotic pressure inside the cell, causing it to swell. Plant and bacteria membranes are surrounded by a rigid wall, which restricts the amount of swelling that can occur, but an animal cell with high salt concentration can swell so much that it bursts. Most invertebrates and vertebrates cannot tolerate high salt concentrations in their body fluids; thus, to raise the external osmotic pressure, their body fluids contain organic molecules—such as amino acids and carbohydrates, as well as salt ions—that raise the total concentration of solute molecules close to that of sea water.

For a sugar or amino acid molecule to enter a cell, it must be accompanied by a sodium ion, which raises the salt concentration. Removing sodium ions from a cell requires energy; it is accomplished by an ATP-sodium pump (see ATP PRODUCTION). In all living cells,

All complex animals have an "internal sea" of watery body fluids called the interstitial fluid. This fluid provides the medium through which nutrients, gases, and wastes pass between capillaries (in vertebrates) and cells. The interstitial fluid and the cells of living organisms contain a variety of dissolved salts. They provide ions (charged particles) that are essential to maintain the fluid balance and acid-base balance. In animals these ions maintain nerve and muscle function, blood clotting, bone formation, and other important body functions.

A salt is formed when one or more hydrogen atoms of an acid molecule are replaced by one or more atoms of a base molecule. Typically, the reaction between a hydroxide (an example of a base) and an acid results in the formation of a salt and water:

$$NaOH + HCl \rightarrow NaCl + H_2O$$

If only a part of the hydrogen in the acid is replaced by metal, the product is an acid salt, which has both salt and acidic properties.

Typical salts are those of strong acids, that is, acids that are dissociated largely into hydrogen ions and acid ions. However, weak acids, such as carbonic acid and many organic acids, also form metallic salts. The most common salts are chlorides, sulfates, and nitrates (salts of strong acids) and carbonates, silicates, and phosphates (salts of weak acids).

Salts are solid and usually crystalline at room temperature. Often the crystals also contain water —called the water of crystallization. When salts are dissolved in water, they form positive metallic ions and negative acidic ions.

### CORE FACTS

■ Salts, when not in solution, are solid and usually crystalline at room temperature.

■ The bodies of all complex mammals contain salts.

■ In freshwater organisms, the concentration of salts in the body fluids is greater than in the surrounding water. This situation causes water to move constantly into the bodies of these organisms.

■ Terrestrial animals control the salt balance in their bodies by regulating the amount of water and salt lost in the urine via the kidneys.

energy is stored temporarily in a chemical compound called adenosine triphosphate (ATP; see ENERGY). When one or two phosphates are removed from ATP, chemical energy is released and thus enables sodium ions to be transported out of the cell and into the blood. This pump also controls the concentration of potassium ions; the use of one molecule of ATP results in three sodium ions being pumped out of the cell and two potassium ions being pumped in.

## Freshwater organisms

In freshwater organisms, the concentration of salts and organic molecules in body fluids is greater than in the surroundings. Water tends constantly to move into the body, while salt ions tend to move out. Freshwater fish deal with this problem in four ways: they seldom if ever drink; their bodies are coated with mucus, which slows down water uptake; they excrete large amounts of dilute urine; and they take up salts through their gills (see EXCRETORY SYSTEMS).

Salt-absorbing cells on the gills utilize the ATP-sodium pump in the reverse direction. As the sodium ions are pumped in, either ammonium ions ($NH_4^+$) or hydrogen ions are pumped out. The ammonium ions are the result of the excretion of nitrogen from amino acid metabolism; hydrogen ions are released by the reaction

$$H_2O + CO_2 \rightarrow H^+ + HCO_3^-$$

Thus, the necessary salt is taken up, nitrogen and $CO_2$ are eliminated, and the loss of the hydrogen ions helps keep the body fluids at a constant pH.

## Saltwater organisms

Marine fish must combat the tendency to lose water to their surroundings while also removing excess salts. Thus, they have mechanisms that are effectively the reverse of those used by freshwater fish: they drink sea water, excrete magnesium and sulfate ions in concentrated urine, and excrete NaCl through salt-secreting cells in their gills.

Sharks and their relatives, meanwhile, are very different. The osmotic pressure of their body fluids is higher than that of sea water owing to the presence of urea and trimethylamine oxide (TMO); thus, water uptake is controlled. Urea inhibits enzyme action, while TMO stimulates it. Therefore, the two substances have to be maintained in the correct ratio. To rid themselves of excess NaCl, sharks have a gland near the rectum that secretes a concentrated solution of salt.

## Terrestrial vertebrates

All land animals tend to lose water by evaporation, and so the internal salt concentration rises. With the loss of gills, amphibians lost the ability to get rid of carbon dioxide, nitrogen, and hydrogen ions and to control their salt levels. They have adapted by taking up water through their skin. Another important store of water is the bladder. The drier the habitat, the larger the bladder. When an amphibian begins to dehydrate, it is able to remove water from the bladder and return it to the body fluids.

## BUFFERS

In biological systems, it is essential to maintain a constant pH, and so they must be capable of responding rapidly to pH changes. Chemical substances that are able to adjust to changes in hydrogen concentration (becoming more alkaline as the pH is lowered and more acidic as the pH rises) are called buffers. Salts of weak acids generally make good buffers.

All biological fluids are strongly buffered, with phosphate and carbonate ions playing an important role. In addition, proteins, nucleic acids, and lipids, as well as smaller organic molecules, carry acid and basic groups that can take part in buffering. In medicine, buffer salts are prescribed for those who suffer from stomach hyperacidity.

Acids can have a dramatic effect on the environment. Acids are produced in the atmosphere from gaseous pollutants emitted by automobiles, power plants, and factories. These acids can fall in rain and snow (see ACID RAIN), and when they do, they increase the acidity of lakes and streams and kill fish and other aquatic organisms. Many lakes and streams in the United States contain natural buffers that protect them from acid rain. These waters contain dissolved ions such as $HCO_3^-$ and $Ca_2^+$, which are derived from carbonate-containing bedrock. Other lakes and streams, such as those in high mountain regions, have little buffering capacity and are highly vulnerable to the acids in rain and snow.

Most land vertebrates control the osmotic balance of their bodies by regulating the amounts of water and salts lost in the urine. This regulation is the primary function of the kidneys (see KIDNEYS). Marine and desert birds and reptiles often tend to build up unacceptable levels of salt because of their diet or excessive loss of water by evaporation. They get rid of the excess by means of salt glands near the eye or in the tongue that secrete NaCl in drops similar to tears.

B. INNES

**See also:** ACID RAIN; ATP PRODUCTION; EXCRETORY SYSTEMS; HOMEOSTASIS; KIDNEYS; OCEAN HABITATS.

## Further reading:

Burggren, W. W., K. French, and D. J. Randall. 2001. *Animal Physiology: Mechanisms and Adaptations.* 5th ed. New York: W. H. Freeman.

*The saltbush (Cryptocarpus pyriformis), a salt-tolerant creeping shrub that grows in areas where the soil has a high concentration of salt, often grows in desert habitats, in this case, Death Valley, California.*

# SAPROPHYTES

## Saprophytes are organisms that obtain nutrients from dead and decaying organisms

Bacteria and fungi include many thousands of saprophytic species, including *Escherichia coli* (bacteria present in the human gut and widely used in biological research) and several species of *Clostridium* (see BACTERIA). Fungi vary from single-celled organisms, such as yeasts, to familiar mushrooms and toadstools (for example, the fly agaric mushroom, *Amanita muscari*; see MUSHROOMS AND TOADSTOOLS).

Saprophytes are heterotrophs (they cannot make their own food) and need a source of organic carbon for growth. They digest this food outside their bodies by secreting enzymes to break it down and by absorbing the products of digestion through their cell membrane (extracellular digestion). Digestive products include simple six-carbon sugars (glucose), five-carbon sugars (xylose), and various nitrogen-containing molecules, from amino acids produced by broken-down proteins to pure ammonia.

Saprophytes are present in spore form in large quantities in all but a few extremely hostile environments. The spores germinate as soon as suitable conditions arise and decomposition begins. The time taken for complete decay varies. When leaves fall in deciduous forests, for example, they decay completely in one year. In tropical rain forests, because of the constant moisture and temperature levels, a fallen leaf cannot survive longer than a few weeks. Pine needles from conifers in cool, temperate forests may take up to 10 years to decay. In deciduous forests, each square yard contains about 6½ pounds (3 kg) of leaf litter awaiting decomposition.

### The decay process
On most dead organic matter, there is a definite succession of microorganisms. Dead wood is first invaded by fungi that can utilize simple sugars, such as glucose, fructose, and xylose. These simple compounds are absorbed directly into the net of filamentous fungal hyphae that spreads throughout the wood. Other more complex carbohydrates, such as sucrose and starch, are broken down by the sapro-

*The death cap (Amanita phalloides), shown above, is a member of the fungi kingdom and is a typical saprophytic species.*

## CONNECTIONS

● The dead wood of **TREES** is broken down by saprophytic **FUNGI** and **BACTERIA**.

● Saprophytes secrete strong **ENZYMES** that digest **CARBOHYDRATES** outside the body.

Living organisms continually produce quantities of waste material, and when they die, they produce a further inconvenience, namely a corpse. While they are alive, they deplete the environment of nutrients, locking them into their bodies or excreting an unusable waste. To maintain the continuity of the ecosystem, this material must be recycled into easily accessible nutrients and minerals.

### Earth's decomposers
The organisms performing this vital function of decomposing organic matter are saprophytes (saprobes or saprotrophs), which thrive on general detritus (organic debris from decaying organisms and their waste products), by breaking down complex organic matter and absorbing the nutrients. Without the digestive powers of saprophytic organisms, these essential nutrients would remain locked up in enormous mounds of feces, dead animals, and vegetation. Eventually, life on Earth would grind to a halt.

### CORE FACTS

■ Saprophytes are essential for the world's ecological balance because they decompose organic waste and dead organisms.

■ Without saprophytic decomposition and recycling, organic rubbish would soon pile up on Earth, and life would cease.

■ Saprophytes release and recycle the carbon, nitrogen, and mineral components of organic material; carbon dioxide is released into the atmosphere and minerals are returned to the soil.

■ Harmful effects of saprophytes include food spoilage, denitrification, and destruction of clothes and property.

phyte's enzymes: sucrose is hydrolyzed by sucrase to glucose and fructose; starch is broken down by amylase to form maltose. These products are then absorbed through the saprophyte's cell wall. When these minor carbon sources have been removed, usually by less highly developed fungi, cellulose breakdown takes place. A powerful enzyme called cellulase is needed to break up cellulose, which makes up 60 percent of the dry weight of mature wood, into a readily absorbable form. Cellulase is secreted by the second wave of invaders, usually large fungi such as ascomycetes (yeasts, molds, and truffles) and basidiomycetes (mushrooms, bracket fungi, and puffballs). Cellulase enzymes secreted from the tips of the hyphae work in a distinct three-stage process. First, cellulase attacks the cellulose molecule, breaking it down into long chains. Second, these chains are

## SAPROPHYTES IN EVOLUTION

If the biochemical theory of the evolution of life is accepted, then the first true cells were saprophytic, floating in a soup of amino acids, which they absorbed to produce proteins inside the cell. These cells gradually depleted their surroundings until evolutionary pressure favored cells capable of synthesizing complex polymers from the simple compounds present. In time, these cells evolved into the equivalent of modern-day autotrophic cells (those capable of self-nourishment using inorganic nutrients and photosynthetic or chemosynthetic energy, such as the cells of most plants and some bacteria). Once the cyclical process of building up and breaking down was established, the possibility for the development of cells that lived by ingesting autotrophs existed. These consumer cells started the evolutionary process that eventually led to humans.

### EVOLUTION

*The symbiotic relationship between termites (Reticulitermes lucifugus) and the cellulose-digesting protozoans (Trichonympha) that live within the termites' gut, enables the termites to exist as saprophytes, feeding on dead and decaying wood.*

## BENEFICIAL SAPROPHYTES

Apart from keeping the planet rubbish free, many saprophytes are of enormous benefit to more highly evolved animals that utilize the cellulose-digesting power of microorganisms. For example, cattle possess a four-chambered stomach in which cellulose, present in grass, is acted on and digested by microorganisms of many species. Other ungulates (hoofed mammals), such as sheep, also have this system, and rabbits have an extended gut and an elongated appendix in which such digestion occurs.

Sewage is treated either by using a filtration bed method, in which free bacteria break down finely emulsified sludge, or by using a system where sludge is inoculated with bacteria and kept aerated and stirred. The final products are water, harmless sewage sludge that can be used as a fertilizer or burned, and methane gas. Bacteria can even be used to break down and gradually disperse oil slicks, provided the oil is well aerated, in a process called bioremediation, the use of biological processes to remedy problems, particularly those caused by pollution. On the other hand, the ability of yeast (*Saccharomyces cerevisiae*) to metabolize sucrose in the absence of

oxygen is probably the oldest-known property of a saprophytic organism. The product is alcohol, probably the oldest-known recreational drug. This same reaction is also used in baking, where carbon dioxide production makes bread rise.

Recycling is thought to be a modern concept, but for a long time people have known about leaving garden waste to rot in compost heaps and using heat generated by the saprophytic decomposition of manure to grow heat-loving plants, such as melons. Recycling material by composting is increasingly popular as a method of reducing the enormous quantities of organic waste now produced.

In 1929 the Scottish physician Alexander Fleming discovered penicillin, the antibiotic produced naturally by fungal molds of the genus *Penicillium*. He observed the effects of the fungus on a bacterial culture and found it produced something that inhibited or destroyed bacterial growth. Penicillin production is now a multi-million dollar industry, and many molds are cultivated to produce antibiotics and the drug cyclosporin, which is used to inhibit rejection in foreign-tissue transplants (see ANTIBIOTICS).

### A CLOSER LOOK

## HARMFUL SAPROPHYTES

Saprophytes can be harmful to humans. Many of these organisms are responsible for food spoilage, for example. Food spoilage can vary from the growth of fungi, bacteria, and yeasts on carbohydrate-rich substances, such as jam or bread, which causes little real harm except in aesthetic appeal, to the lethal effects of botulism in canned food. Botulism is caused by *Clostridium botulinum*, a bacterium that can produce a neurotoxic substance so deadly that a 5-gallon (23 l) drum would be sufficient to wipe out the world's population. Fungi also synthesize unpleasant by-products; some *Aspergillus* species grow on peanuts and produce aflatoxin, which can cause liver cancer.

Saprophytic bacteria and fungi can also harm the environment by removing nitrogen in gaseous form from ecosystems (a process called denitrification). This process occurs under anaerobic conditions (where no oxygen is present).

Eutrophication, especially of lakes, in which excessive growth of algae and other organisms occurs because of an accumulation of nutrients, for example, from fertilizer runoff, gives saprophytes an excellent opportunity to proliferate. As saprophytes decompose and decay these nutrients, oxygen levels in the water fall, and the lake habitat dies. Recovery from eutrophication is slow or completely irreversible.

Some saprophytes can break down the structure of artificial (human-made) materials. This decay is not so bad when it is only the cellulose in cotton cloth that becomes mildewed and rotten; however, it is much more serious if the cellulose is present in wood, and the culprit is *Serpula lacrymans*, the dry rot fungus. This fungus is one of the most serious agents of timber decay in buildings, attacking both softwoods and hardwoods.

## A CLOSER LOOK

*Many bacteria, such as Escherichia coli (shown below), live as saprophytes, some of which can have harmful or toxic effects, while others can be beneficial to people.*

cut into cellobiose, consisting of a few polymerized glucose units. Third, these units are hydrolyzed further to glucose, which is absorbed by the fungal mycelium and fed into the metabolic cycle.

This sudden increase of six-carbon sugars is soon noticed, and there is competition for available sugar from a secondary crop of sugar fungi and bacteria. These organisms grow in close association with cellulose digesters, live as opportunists (growing only under certain conditions), and can usually secrete

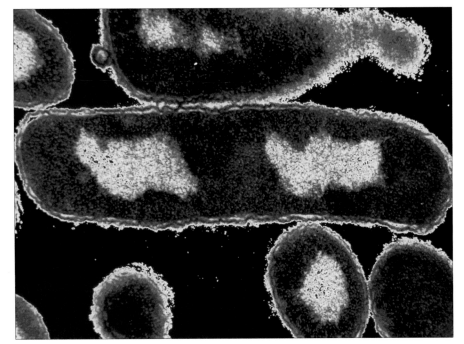

enzymes to hydrolyze cellobiose to glucose. Other interested parties also rapidly become aware of the food source. Of these parties, termites have an advantage. They are unable to digest cellulose and so have formed a partnership with something that can. In their expanded rear gut lives a single-celled protozoan named *Trichonympha*, capable of digesting wood particles (cellulose) to easily absorbed simple sugars (carbohydrates), which are used by the insect. This association is called a mutual or symbiotic relationship (see SYMBIOSIS).

### A new ecosystem

Once other organisms move in, the wood becomes as busy as a construction (or more accurately, a demolition) site. Fungi and bacteria attack various parts of the wood and digest structural elements, such as lignin, a polymer of alcohols containing a phenyl group, which is resistant to attack from the average decay organism. Only a few fungi, such as some basidiomycetes and ascomycetes, have the required enzymes to digest lignin.

Eventually the dead wood becomes an ecosystem. Whole life cycles take place in it, as organisms move in, grow, and die, providing even more microhabitats for different saprophytes. Gradually the dead tree becomes transformed by microbial action, aided and abetted by larger organisms. Simple sugars and starches, celluloses, and other structural elements are recycled many times before the tree has decayed. Saprophytic species present in the dead wood increase dramatically, both in quantity and diversity. Eventually the number of species falls, as the last of the tree decays. The final components are returned to the ecosystem, and the recycling process is complete.

Other saprophytes decompose animal parts or dead animals. The presence of animals leads to the production of dung, detritus (such as shed skins), and corpses. All of these materials have their own decomposers; some saprophytes handle the chitin in shed insect skins, while others decompose the nitrogenous waste in droppings. Yet others recycle dead bodies.

While some saprophytic action allows in other decomposers to exploit the products, some fungi positively discourage "freeloaders." They secrete toxic substances (antibiotics) to inhibit the growth of other microorganisms, reduce competition, and leave the field free for themselves. Some of these antibioitcs are of use to humans (see the box on page 1461).

B. TEBBS

**See also:** ANTIBIOTICS AND ANTIMICROBIALS; BACTERIA; FUNGI KINGDOM; MOLDS AND MILDEWS; MUSHROOMS AND TOADSTOOLS; SYMBIOSIS.

### Further reading:

Carlile, M. J., and S. C. Watkinson. 1994. *The Fungi.* Boston: Academic Press.
Facklam, H., and M. Facklam. 1994. *Bacteria.* New York: Twenty-first Century Books.
Money, M. P. 2002. *Mr. Bloomfield's Orchard: The Mysterious World of Mushrooms, Molds, and Mycologists.* Oxford: Oxford University Press.

# SAVANNA BIOMES

**Savanna biomes are areas of grassland, with varying degrees of tree cover, that exist within the tropics**

*The Masai Mara in Kenya, shown above, is an example of a savanna with open grasslands and a small number of trees.*

## CONNECTIONS

● Savanna biomes support a range of living organisms, including a wide variety of **UNGULATES** and **CARNIVORES**.

● **GRASSES** dominate the vegetation of savanna biomes.

● The **SOIL ECOLOGY** of savanna biomes is unique, with limited **NUTRIENTS** available to plants.

Savannas are tropical grasslands with trees that are present in a belt across the equator from the tropic of Cancer (15 °N) to the tropic of Capricorn (15 °S). Most savannas exist in Africa, Australia, and South America. Savannas may include a range of habitats. The driest have only grasses; this extreme is one of open-plains grasslands with hardly any trees, typified by the Serengeti Plains of Tanzania and Kenya. With more rainfall, sufficient water is available to support the growth of scattered trees. With more rain still, savannas become tropical woodlands where the canopy cover (the area of ground covered by trees) may exceed 30 percent. These woodlands are present in the south of Africa as well as in parts of Australia and South America. Like temperate grasslands, the savanna is dominated by plants in the family Gramineae (see GRASSLAND BIOMES).

The climate present in the savanna is distinctive. Temperatures are commonly well over 103 °F (40 °C) in the daytime, dropping to between 50 to 60 °F (10 to 15 °C) at night. The seasons are dictated by the pattern of rainfall rather than by temperature. There is never very much rain; an average rainfall of about 20 inches (50 cm) per year (range 12 to 60 inches, or 30 to 150 cm, per annum) occurs either in one long or two shorter rainy seasons. The relative scarcity of rain is compounded by the fact that in many savanna ecosystems, rainfall is unpredictable,

and thus, they are prone to relatively frequent and long droughts and rare but spectacular floods.

In addition to determining the seasons, the amount of rain falling on the savanna also determines the relative contribution of grasses and woody vegetation to the biome. At the lower end of the rainfall scale (12 to 24 inches, or 30 to 60 cm), grasses

### CORE FACTS

■ Savannas are tropical grasslands, often including trees, usually present in parts of Africa, Australia, and South America.

■ Savanna regions vary from areas of mainly grassland to those of tropical woodland.

■ Temperatures in the savannas are often extremely high during the day but fall drastically at night.

■ The relative contribution of grass and woodland to the savanna is determined by the amount of rainfall and type of soil present.

■ The savanna is host to a huge variety of animals. In Africa, these animals include ungulates (hoofed animals) and the carnivores that eat them. The Australian savanna is dominated by an introduced ungulate, the domestic sheep, as well as by a variety of pouched animals, such as kangaroos and wallabies. In South America, birds and rodents are abundant.

# SAVANNAS AND TOURISM

As human populations expand rapidly in many parts of Africa, conservation of the great savanna ecosystems becomes more and more difficult. The demands for wheat, corn, and grazing land make it very hard for many African governments to justify setting aside large areas of their countries exclusively for wildlife.

One solution that protects wildlife and provides a critical source of income to people of developing nations is wildlife tourism. In Kenya, the African country with the most developed tourist industry, the money that tourists bring to the country earns more for the Kenyan government than the export of their two major cash crops, coffee and tea. It has been estimated that each acre (0.5 ha) of national park earns at least 20 times as much per year for Kenya than if these areas were used simply for grazing. The viewing of elephants alone contributes many millions of U.S. dollars per year.

In addition to viewing animals from a minibus or four-wheel drive car, a small but significant number of people go to Africa to hunt the exotic wildlife of the savanna. The amount of money earned for a country, or a local community, can be staggering. In Zimbabwe, a hunter licensed to shoot a single elephant can earn the country tens of thousands of U.S. dollars.

In the past decade, South Africa has begun to allow very limited hunting of the white rhinoceros (*Ceratotherium simum*), the population of which is now growing. With payment for a single rhinoceros rising well above $100,000, shooting a few can support a huge conservation project, wildlife helping pay its way. Despite these economic benefits, many countries see a total ban on hunting as the only way to preserve the numbers of rhinoceroses.

## SCIENCE AND SOCIETY

dominate; as the rainfall increases, woody vegetation begins to replace grasses. However, rainfall is not the only ecological factor that determines the balance between grasslands and woodlands. Some soils, for example, old lake bottoms rich in calcium carbonate, are almost always dominated by grasses, and rich, loamy soils that hold moisture may be more likely to be covered by shrubs and trees. The balance between grasslands and forests is further complicated by fire and grazing. Both factors tend to keep shrubs

*The activities of the dung beetle (*Geotrupes*) ensure the recycling of nutrients in the grassland ecosystem.*

and trees from becoming established. Areas of grassland regulated by fires include the floodplains of great rivers, such as the Zambesi in Africa or the Orinoco in Venezuela. In contrast, when fires are infrequent, trees have a chance to establish themselves, and the occasional burn tends to clear out grasses and small shrubs.

The tropical grasslands of savannas usually have poor soils, as opposed to the rich soils of the temperate grasslands. Most of the nutrients are held in the grasses themselves. With the grasses drawing out nutrients, how are these nutrients returned to the soil? The animals that live in these areas and eat the grasses are the first stage in the nutrient-recycling process. Animals convert the nutrients in grass to dung. In the rainy seasons, the dung of the grazing animals breaks down and returns many minerals and elements to the soil. However, for much of the year, these grasslands are arid, and dung cannot decompose. During these dry periods, a family of insects called dung beetles is critical to the recycling of nutrients in grassland ecosystems. The beetles lay their eggs in balls of dung and then bury the balls; the dung is thus returned to the soil. In a study of one large national park in Africa, scientists found that over 500 species of beetles are involved in recycling dung. Many of the beetles are specific to the species of ungulate whose dung they recycle.

Dung beetles help to promote seed banks. Seeds, eaten by grazing animals with the grass, pass undigested into their dung; dung beetles then transfer them to the soil. Here the seeds of many annual plants, including grasses, are stored and protected against drought and fire. For example, in one study, 31,300 seeds of a common grass species, *Poa annua*, were found when 1½ square yards (1 m²) of soil was excavated. The longevity of these seeds is astounding. While the seeds of most species will last for only around 5 to 10 years, in certain conditions the *P. annua* seeds can survive in soils for hundreds if not thousands of years.

## Wildlife of the savannas

The grasslands and woodlands of the tropical savanna are perhaps best known for their animals, and those of Africa are perhaps the most spectacular. There is a huge variety of birds, including the flightless ostrich (*Struthio camelus*), with pipits, larks, and guinea fowl being the most common. However, Africa is best known for its huge variety of ungulates (hooved animals; see UNGULATES) and the carnivores that eat them. In many parts of the African savanna live up to 15 species of ungulates and seven or more large carnivore species (including lions, hyenas, jackals, and wild dogs; see CARNIVORES).

The ungulates can be classified by what they eat, with grazers (grass-eating animals) being dominant in the open plains and browsers (animals that eat trees and shrubs) being more common in the woodlands. In the Serengeti and in the Ngorongoro Crater, areas of few trees and extensive grasslands in Tanzania, several million grazing ungulates—

wildebeests (*Connochaetes taurinus*), Thomson's gazelles (*Gazella thomsoni*), and plains zebras (*Equus burchelli*)—acting as lawnmowers, maintain the grasslands. In other more heavily wooded areas, such as the national parks at Tsavo in Kenya, Hwange in Zimbabwe, or Kruger in South Africa, the most common ungulates are browsers, medium-sized species, such as impala (*Aepyceros melampus*) and greater kudu (*Tragelaphus strepsiceros*). In terms of sheer mass, however, both grasslands and woodlands are dominated by Africa's ultimate browser, the African elephant (*Loxodonta africana*; see ELEPHANTS AND MAMMOTHS).

Australia is now dominated by an introduced ungulate—the domestic sheep. Living side-by-side with the sheep, however, is a wide variety of marsupial mammals, including dasyurids, wallabies, and kangaroos (see MARSUPIALS). Large-footed, or macropod, kangaroos (such as the red or gray kangaroo, *Macropus rufus* and *M. giganteus*, respectively), while not at all closely related to Africa's ungulates, fill the same ecological role, grazing down the dominant grasses of the outback. Only a few species of large (110 pounds, or 50 kg) kangaroos exist now, but before the arrival of humans in Australia, approximately 40,000 years ago, these savannas were full of 15 genera and perhaps 40 species of large kangaroos. Scientists believe that a combination of a climate that was becoming drier, overhunting by humans, and the introduction of the dingo, or Australian wild dog (*Canis dingo*), contributed to the extinction of most of these animals.

In South America, the birds of the savanna—including pipits, tinamous, and buntings—are abundant. However, in both the temperate dry savannas (the pampas of Argentina and Chile) and the tropical wet savannas of Venezuela and Brazil, there are very few species of grazing animals. Wet tropical savannas mostly support large numbers of two species of large rodents, capybaras (*Hydrochoeris hydrochoeris*) and coypus, or nutrias, (*Myocastor coypus*)—rather than ungulates or macropod marsupials. The reason for a lack of large herbivores is historical; it appears that a large group of herbivores living in South America, the Notoungulates, became extinct, and no new group of animals came forward to replace them.

J. GINSBERG

**See also:** BIOMES AND HABITATS; CARNIVORES; DESERTIFICATION; ELEPHANTS AND MAMMOTHS; GRASSES; GRASSLAND BIOMES; MARSUPIALS; UNGULATES.

**Further reading:**
Furley, R. A., J. Proctor, and J. A. Ratter, eds. 1992. *Nature and Dynamics of Forest-Savanna Boundaries*. New York: Chapman and Hall.
Longman, C. 2001. *African Grasslands*. New York: Peter Bedrick Books.
Ricciuti, E. R. 1996. *Grassland (Biomes of the World)*. New York: Benchmark Books.

## THE NGORONGORO CRATER

The Ngorongoro Crater in northwest Tanzania is a vast collapsed volcano, or caldera, approximately 7½ miles (12 km) wide and one of the world's wildlife wonders. Surrounding the crater is a vast expanse of woodland and forest on the eastern side of the Serengeti Plains. The sides of the volcano, up to 1,640 feet (500 m) tall, are covered in dense forest. However, the floor of the crater is a sea of grasslands extending nearly 88½ square miles (230 km2), an isolated patch of grasslands comprising a practically self-contained ecosystem.

While a few species of common ungulates do not inhabit the crater (for example, warthogs and giraffes), many of the common Serengeti ungulates and all of the predators, with the exception of African wild dogs, are present. Yet while the Serengeti is known for the spectacular migration of many of its animals, the wildebeests, zebras, and Thomson's gazelles living in the crater do not migrate; they live there all year round. The animals of the Ngorongoro are remarkably tame, perhaps a reflection of their long isolation.

Although isolated from other open plains, the crater is not isolated from humans. People have been part of the Ngorongoro ecosystem since time immemorial, and the fossils of one of humans' oldest ancestors were found in the nearby Olduvai Gorge. Perhaps it is therefore fitting that the Ngorongoro Conservation area, separated from the Serengeti National Park in 1956, is one of the oldest experiments aimed at integrating humans and wildlife. The Masai, a tribe known for their nomadic ways and cattle herding, use the crater during the dry season, grazing their cows, goats, and sheep among the wildebeests and gazelles. To preserve this precious resource, the Masai ensure that their animals do not overgraze the land.

### A CLOSER LOOK

*The gray kangaroo* (Macropus giganteus*) is a marsupial; pouched mammals are the dominant group of naturally occurring mammals in the Australian savanna regions.*

# SCHIZOPHRENIA

**Schizophrenia is a mental disorder that affects a person's ability to perceive reality or react to it in a rational way**

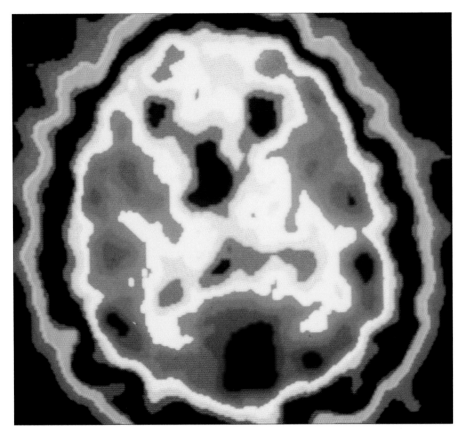

*A brain scan of a person suffering from schizophrenia. Brain-scanning and imaging techniques are now providing more information about the anatomy and physiology of the brain and finding some differences between the brains of people with schizophrenia and those without. This research may enable the illness to be recognized and treated more efficiently and effectively.*

## CONNECTIONS

● **GENETICS** plays a part in the development of schizophrenia.

● Structural abnormalities in the **BRAIN** have been linked to schizophrenia.

Between 1 and 2 percent of the world's population develop an episode of schizophrenia at some time or another. The illness is a major psychiatric disorder, which gives rise to many symptoms that affect an individual's personality and behavior. These symptoms include hallucinations, delusions, emotional disturbances, thought disorders, and movement disorders. The presence of these symptoms is sometimes called psychosis (see PSYCHOSIS). Hallucinations are most frequently voices that comment on the sufferer's behavior or thoughts, although other sounds are also commonly heard. Hallucinations can also include visions, tastes, smells, and skin sensations.

Delusions experienced by people with schizophrenia and those with other mental illnesses (see MENTAL DISORDERS) are strongly held false beliefs. A person may believe he or she is being followed, persecuted, or watched. The illness may also be dominated by delusions of grandeur. Those who suffer from schizophrenia whose symptoms are characterized primarily by persecutory or grandiose delusions or hallucinations are said to have a paranoid type of schizophrenia.

Most people with schizophrenia suffer from a variety of thought disorders, which disturb concentration and clear thinking. Sufferers often say their thoughts are blocked, inserted into, or withdrawn from their minds by some outside force. Disordered thinking can create muddled and disjointed speech. In some cases, speech disintegrates into odd phrases and detached syllables. People who suffer from this type of disorganized thought are classified as having disorganized schizophrenia (or a hebephrenic form).

Profound emotional disturbance is also typical of schizophrenia, although it can take many forms. Sufferers may giggle or laugh in completely inappropriate situations. Some people with schizophrenia experience flattened emotions, showing little variation from day to day; others experience periods of agitation or violent rage. Another more rare type is catatonia, a movement disorder. Such a patient can alternate between sitting motionless for many hours or behaving in an excited and often agitated manner.

## Treatment

Treatment for schizophrenia tends to focus on managing the symptoms rather than curing the sufferer. In most cases schizophrenia is chronic (long-term), and treatment may last a lifetime. Sometimes permanent adaptations to the sufferer's environment are needed; for example, placing him or her in a long-term care facility, such as a hospital or group home.

In most cases, treatment typically includes the use of medication, traditionally the antipsychotics. One of the first of these drugs to emerge was chlorpromazine (Thorazine), which became widely used as a treatment from the 1950s. Antipsychotics work by reducing the main symptoms of schizophrenia (hallucinations, delusions, and thought disorders). It has also become obvious that other types of therapies can work in conjunction with medications to treat schizophrenia—for example, social-skills training, education about medication (to increase compliance) and the disorder, and family therapy. Hospitalization can also form an important part of treating schizophrenia because hospital staff can observe the patient's behavior and symptoms and provide suitable therapy. The best types of hospital activities, or treatments, are those that carry over into the person's life and teach him or her the skills to manage the disorder in the community.

Genetic factors have been shown to play an important part in the development of schizophrenia. Some research has indicated that first-degree relatives of people with schizophrenia have a more than 10 percent chance of illness. If someone has two parents with the illness, he or she has an approximately one in two chance of developing schizophrenia. However, nongenetic factors must also be considered, such as the influence of a person's upbringing, stress, social status, and brain damage.

M. RIESKE

**See also:** EMOTIONS; MENTAL DISORDERS; PSYCHOSIS.

## Further reading:

Miller, Rachel, and Susan E. Mason, eds. 2002. *Diagnosis: Schizophrenia.* New York: Columbia University Press.

# SCIENTIFIC METHOD

**Scientific method is the rigorous process that scientists use to follow a line of scientific inquiry**

*Experimentation is an important part of scientific method. Experiments test hypotheses put forward to explain observations.*

Scientists, whatever their discipline, seek answers to their questions. All scientific inquiry follows a similar course: an observation is made, a hypothesis is advanced to explain the observation, a study is designed to test the hypothesis, an interpretation is made of the results, and a conclusion is reached concerning the validity of the original hypothesis. The rigorous progression of this process is called the scientific method.

## Observations and hypotheses

The scientific method relies on two kinds of logical reasoning, deductive logic and inductive logic. The laws of deductive logic were first defined by Greek philosopher Aristotle (384–322 BCE; see ARISTOTLE). The basic form of logical argument is called the syllogism, which has the following form:

> All animals with feathered wings are birds.
> This ostrich has feathered wings.
> Therefore, this ostrich is a bird.

One should notice that the first statement is a generalization. It may be that, somewhere in the world, so far undiscovered, there is an animal with feathered wings that is not a bird. However, on the basis of many observations, one feels justified in using this statement as a definition of a bird. It enables people to classify the animal kingdom into birds and "not-birds." The correct form of the syllogism must always be

> A is B.
> C is A.
> Therefore, C is B.

This line of thought is called deductive reasoning; it is the basis on which a scientist plans a study and

reaches conclusions from the results. However, one should remember that the statement "A is B" is a generalization and must be generally agreed to be true. For example, a scientist observes that a piece of copper is a good conductor of electricity. He or she can find that all the samples of copper investigated and all the samples investigated by other scientists are good conductors. It is therefore justifiable to assume that the statement "copper is a good conductor" is valid in all cases. However, if somebody discovers a piece of copper that is not a good conductor, then everybody will want to discover why. When somebody has discovered why, people's understanding of the world will have been increased.

The making of considered generalizations is called inductive reasoning. Using inductive reasoning, one argues that from the particular ("this is what one observes, and no observations contradict it") must follow the general ("therefore, one will assume, until proved wrong, that it is always true"). Philosophers have frequently questioned the validity of inductive reasoning, although everyone does it. Scientists tend to be more cautious in their use of induction than people are in daily life.

These generalizations are only the foundations on which scientific investigation is built. Scientists ask themselves "Why is copper a good conductor?" or "Why do birds have feathered wings?" Their studies must be based on observations. Scientists cannot evaluate the results without a clear idea of what they are looking for. They must first put forward a hypothesis, that is, a possible explanation.

To a large degree, a hypothesis is intuitive. It must be (at least to the scientist advancing it) sensible, drawing on all of the observations and hypotheses made by other scientists. However, it will be tested again and again to see if it resists falsification. If the hypothesis holds true, then it may be general enough to be called a theory. Austrian-born philosopher Karl Popper (1902–1994) noted that one can only disprove but never prove hypotheses. Most modern science follows Popper's line of thought.

## CONNECTIONS

● The significance of any experimental result increases with the size of the sample and the percentage of the **POPULATION** it represents.

● Many scientists have claimed that the **PSYCHOLOGY** of the researcher is likely to affect the results— the so-called experimenter effect.

---

### CORE FACTS

■ Scientific method relies on both deductive and inductive logic.

■ The scientist proposes a hypothesis (a possible explanation) and then conducts a study to test the hypothesis.

■ If the hypothesis remains true through a number of studies, the hypothesis could contribute to a theory.

■ If a study is repeated exactly, the results of an experiment should remain the same.

■ Statistics are often used to interpret the results of a study.

## Research to test the hypothesis

The next stage is the planning of a study that tests whether the hypothesis is true. The study should be designed to disprove the hypothesis. If the hypothesis resists disproof, there is justification to conduct further studies to test the hypothesis. If the hypothesis holds true across a number of studies, the scientist can combine the hypothesis with others to contribute to a theory. Theories, unlike hypotheses, are major parts of scientific knowledge. Examples are the theory of gravity and the theory of natural selection.

A requirement of a scientific study is that someone should be able to repeat it. If a study is repeated exactly, the results should be the same. To ensure this repeatability, researchers can devise a controlled experiment based on a comparison of an experimental group with a control group. The control group is identical except for one factor, and the effects of that factor are tested. During an experiment, the scientist measures variables in both the control group and the experimental group. Any differences observed are a result of differences in the factor tested.

This experimental approach has been a stumbling block to objective investigation of psychic events (see PARAPSYCHOLOGY; PSYCHOLOGY) and psychological responses because many practitioners have claimed that the mental attitude of the researcher can affect the results—the so-called experimenter effect. To overcome this problem, scientists have devised double-blind experiments. In some double-blind experiments on drug performance, for example, neither the scientists nor the subjects know any details about the drugs under test.

In general, the possibility of repeating identical experiments is greatly reduced when living organisms are involved. Tests of a certain drug, for example, may suggest that it has a harmful effect on those who take it. Few medical researchers would want to repeat such an experiment. In addition, outside the laboratory, it is impossible to guarantee that, for example, the weather, temperature, and a host of other variables, will remain the same.

## Results and conclusions

Methods to design successful studies with living organisms and to analyze the results were developed during the 1920s by English statistician and geneticist Ronald Aylmer Fisher (1890–1962). He developed statistical methods of assessing the probability that experimental results arose by chance and of calculating the significance of the results. Fisher applied his techniques to modernizing Darwin's theory of evolution by natural selection. He combined it with the developing science of genetics and published *The Genetical Theory of Natural Selection* in 1930.

Scientists owe a great debt to Fisher's work on the design of experiments. By investigating the effects of fertilizers on crops, he worked out how statistics could be used to show how the effects of several different treatments and the interactions between them could be measured at the same time. Each experiment is divided into subexperiments, differing from one another by variation of one or more factors. A relatively simple mathematical formula shows whether the outcome of the experiments is likely to be due to chance or to the variables being tested.

The significance of any result increases with the size of the experiment (the number of samples tested) and the percentage they represent of the so-called population (the total number of possible samples). If, for example, there is a 50 percent probability a certain result will be occur by chance, a single experiment is valueless. Results become significant only as the size of the sample increases.

Fisher and his colleagues began their work in agriculture, but their methods have been applied to nearly all branches of physical and biological science. They have been used to investigate the effects of acid rain on forests and fish, and they even monitor the long-term effects of radioactivity.

B. INNES

*Ronald Aylmer Fisher (1890–1962) contributed greatly to the development of methods of experimental design. He also devised statistical methods of assessing the probability and significance of experimental results.*

**See also:** ANALYTICAL TECHNIQUES; ARISTOTLE; BIOLOGY, HISTORY AND PHILOSOPHY OF; PARAPSYCHOLOGY; PSYCHOLOGY.

## Further reading:
Carey, S. S. 1994. *A Beginner's Guide to Scientific Method.* Belmont, Calif.: Wadsworth Publishing.
Cohen, M. R., and N. Ernest. 2002. *An Introduction to Logic and Scientific Method.* Safety Harbor, Fla.: Simon Publications.

# SCORPIONS

**The imperial scorpion (Pandinus imperator), pictured above, displays the characteristic structure of true scorpions, with prominent clawlike pincers and a long curled tail.**

Scorpions are menacing in their appearance, with their large clawlike pincers and a long, narrow tail, bearing a poison gland opening into a stinger. They belong to the class Arachnida. All arachnids have a body consisting of two sections, the cephalothorax and the abdomen. The cephalothorax consists of the thorax and head, which bears the eyes and mouthparts but no antennae. The four pairs of legs are also attached to the cephalothorax.

Scorpions are distinguished from other arachnids by having an elongated body with a long, segmented tail that ends in a stinging organ. A scorpion often carries its tail curled up over its back.

At the front of its body, the scorpion has a pair of pincerlike appendages called pedipalps, which it uses in defense, for grasping prey, and for courtship. Also present on the underside of the scorpion are organs called pectines. Their function is unknown, although they may be cleaning organs for the legs; organs of respiration or hearing; organs with a sexual function; or organs for detecting ground vibrations.

## Evolution

The ancestral arachnids, scorpion-like animals, were probably the first arthropods to leave the water and adapt to terrestrial habitats. When moving from the sea to land, these arachnids had to change their methods of locomotion and respiration.

The earliest fossil arachnid, a scorpion, dating around 400 million years ago, existed during the Paleozoic era (570 to 245 million years ago).

Modern-day scorpions have changed little from the primitive scorpions that existed at that time.

## Diversity

True scorpions are grouped into the order Scorpiones and subdivided into eight families. The more than 1,200 species of scorpions occupy most land masses, except Greenland, Antarctica, New Zealand, and many small islands. They live in a range of habitats, including deserts, grasslands, and rain forests. While scorpions generally prefer warm climates, they live as far north as southern Germany, and the scorpion *Euscorpius flavicaudis* has even been found in England.

Similar arachnids include small (less than 5 mm) pseudoscorpions (order Pseudoscorpiones) that resemble tiny tailless scorpions; tiny 2 mm long microwhip scorpions (order Palpigradi), which have a long flagellum (whiplike appendage); wind scorpions (order Solifugae, or Solpugida), which have no tail but enormous jaws; and whip scorpions, or vinegaroons (order Uropygi), which also have a flagellum.

## CONNECTIONS

● Scorpions have a mainly **NOCTURNAL LIFE**, feeding at night on **INSECTS** and **SPIDERS**.

● Although successful predators, scorpions can be prey to other **ARACHNIDS, BIRDS, LIZARDS,** and **SNAKES.**

## CORE FACTS

■ Scorpions are terrestrial arthropods in the class Arachnida, which also includes mites, ticks, and spiders.
■ Scorpions use their stinging tail for defense and to paralyze prey.
■ Scorpions generally prefer warm environments and are almost all nocturnal.

## CLASSIFICATION

The order Scorpionida is divided into eight families:

**Buthidae:** The oldest family with about 600 species, including the most dangerous scorpions; worldwide distribution in the tropics and temperate zones.
**Bothriuridae:** South American scorpions except for one genus in Australia; approximately 80 species.
**Chactidae:** Mostly in South America but a few species in Mexico, Australia, and the Mediterranean; approximately 75 species.
**Chaerilidae:** 15 species confined to the Malay peninsula.
**Diplocentridae:** Native to the Middle East, Mexico, and the Antilles; approximately 50 species.
**Luridae:** 20 species in the arid regions of the Americas and the Aegean region of Europe.
**Scorpionidae:** Worldwide distribution except North America, mostly in the Eastern Hemisphere; about 175 species, including the largest scorpions.
**Vejovidae:** About 125 species divided among western North and South America and the Middle East, spreading to eastern Asia.

Scorpions vary greatly in size. The smallest is a Caribbean species (*Microtityus fundorai*), which measures less than ½ inch (1.3 cm). The longest is a South African species (*Hadogenes troglodytis*), which can grow to more than 8 inches (20 cm). The heaviest scorpion, *Pandinus imperator*, is 7 inches (18 cm) long and weighs more than 2 ounces (57 g).

Scorpion coloring also varies. Some are light brown or tan, while others are brown or black. Almost all scorpions are nocturnal and probably hunt cockroaches and crickets, many of which are also nocturnal. Scorpions often find shelter in rock crevices or under stones during daylight hours. That they also shelter in human belongings, such as shoes, clothing, and sleeping bags, poses a threat to people living in areas favored by poisonous scorpions.

### Feeding
Scorpions emerge mostly at night to hunt for food. Vibrations or possibly air currents made by poten-

*After birth, young scorpions climb onto the back of their mother. In this way they are transported for up to 50 days until they are sufficiently developed to live independently.*

tial prey enable the scorpion to detect the whereabouts of its next victim. When the prey is close enough, the scorpion grasps it with its pincerlike pedipalps and, if necessary, bends its tail over its head to sting the prey and paralyze it. A feeding scorpion may take several hours to devour its meal.

Scorpions possess only a small mouth opening, and the prey is picked to pieces by the movements of the jaws, or chelicerae. The crushed soft tissues and juices of the meal are then pumped into the mouth by the action of the pharynx. Once the scorpion has eaten, it may not need to feed again for some time. Most scorpions do not drink very much because they have efficient body mechanisms for retaining water (see HOMEOSTASIS).

### Reproduction
Some species of scorpions undertake an elaborate mating ritual, in which the male holds the female by her pedipalps and leads her back and forth across the ground. The sperm is deposited on the ground in the form of a spermatophore (packet of sperm). The male maneuvers the female into a position where the sperm can be taken into her genital opening. Both the male and female can mate more than once. The sperm in the female can fertilize a number of generations of offspring.

The fertilized eggs are retained in the female's body for up to a year. The young, which number from one to a hundred, will be born live over several hours or even days. In many species, the birth occurs during the hours of darkness, sometimes in two batches separated by a 24-hour period. The young scorpions then emerge and mount the female's back. After a period that varies from 1 to 50 days, the young molt (see MOLTING) and leave the mother.

### Dangerous scorpions
Most scorpions are relatively harmless and inject a mild toxin from their stinger that causes slight swelling and pain in humans (see DEFENSE MECHANISMS). However, some types of scorpions are much more venomous. These scorpions can inject venom, called a neurotoxin, that affects the nervous system. *Centruroides exilicauda*, for example, is a highly venomous species that lives in Arizona, New Mexico, and Mexico. Scorpions do not normally attack humans but often will sting if inadvertently disturbed. Antivenins are now available against most scorpion stings and can prevent death if they are administered quickly enough.

L. BLASER

**See also:** ARTHROPODS; DEFENSE MECHANISMS; HOMEOSTASIS; MOLTING.

### Further reading:
Harvey, Bev. 2002. *Arthropods (The Animal Kingdom)*. Philadelphia: Chelsea House Publishing.
Hawkins, D. R. 1996. *Goodbye Scorpion; Farewell, Black Widow Spider*. Sedona, Ar.: Veritas Publishing.

# SEABIRDS

Many different species fit into the category of seabird, and their lifestyles vary a great deal. Some seabirds, such as albatrosses and penguins, remain constantly in their marine environment and return to land only to breed. Others, such as most gulls, base themselves on land but feed out at sea, and some, such as loons and grebes, spend only part of the year at sea and the rest of the time in freshwater habitats. Although 70 percent of Earth is covered by sea, of the 8,900 species of birds, only a fraction (260 to 300 species) are seabirds—perhaps because the sea provides a smaller diversity of niches for birds than a terrestrial environment does. Conditions at sea differ mainly in terms of water and air temperatures; type, direction, and strength of the wind; water depth and salinity; and food availability.

## What is a seabird?

Ornithologists disagree as to exactly which birds are seabirds. While there is no dispute over some families (phalaropes, jaegers, gulls, terns, penguins, albatrosses, shearwaters, petrels, storm petrels, diving petrels or tubenoses, tropic birds, gannets, boobies, skimmers, and auks), a number of others (loons, grebes, pelicans, frigate birds, and sheathbills) are considered by some to be borderline seabirds.

True seabirds are pelagic (they inhabit open sea) and usually come ashore only to breed. These families of ocean-going birds, highly evolved for marine environments, are found in the orders Sphenisciformes (penguins, which have lost the ability to fly) and Procellariiformes (albatrosses, fulmars, shearwaters, petrels, storm petrels, diving petrels, and prions, which spend most of their life traveling the air currents far out at sea).

The order Charadriiformes contains the phalarope, jaeger, gull, tern, skimmer, and auk (alcid) families, all of which are adapted to marine environments, especially the auks. However, not all members of the gull family depend on the sea for all or even part of their livelihood. Some gull species spend their entire life inland, and sometimes different individuals of the same species (for example, the herring gull, *Larus*

*Tufted puffins (**Fratercula cirrhata**), as with most seabirds, spend much of their lives at sea, coming ashore only to breed.*

*argentatus*) may be either pelagic or terrestrial. The sheathbills, which breed in the Antarctic or live year-round on remote sub-Antarctic islands, are terrestrial seaside scavengers. They do not fly very much (unless migrating) and are not semiaquatic, as the auks (puffins and murres) are; thus, they have the most tenuous claim to the title of seabird. Other families in this order are not classed as seabirds, even though they live by the sea. For example, shorebirds and waders (such as plovers and sandpipers) are adapted for feeding on invertebrates along the shoreline or in shallow waters and so have different characteristics from their seabird cousins (see WATERBIRDS AND WADERS).

In the order Pelecaniformes, the gannet, booby, and tropic bird families easily qualify as seabirds, but some ornithologists argue that the pelican, cormorant, and frigate bird families do not because,

## CORE FACTS

- True seabirds include penguins, albatrosses, frigate birds, boobies, shearwaters, petrels, and storm petrels, which inhabit open seas and come ashore only to breed.
- Seabirds have many adaptations for marine life, including large, paired, nasal salt glands that help to regulate the fluid and ion balance in their bodies.
- All seabirds breed on land and so must be able to survive in both marine and terrestrial environments.
- Penguins and auks "fly" under water to hunt their prey, often reaching depths of 800 feet (265 m).

## CONNECTIONS

- Seabirds include penguins, **FLIGHTLESS BIRDS** that use their wings for **SWIMMING** under water.

although they feed out at sea, they have to spend at least part of their day resting ashore, and frigate birds do not even have waterproof feathers.

The loons or divers (Gaviiformes), grebes (Podicipediformes), and sea ducks (Anseriformes) are all highly adapted for life at sea. Loons and grebes are so specialized for swimming and diving that adult loons cannot walk on land and grebes do so only with great difficulty.

Ornithologists sometimes doubt whether loons and grebes are seabirds because they spend only the nonbreeding season at sea and the rest of their time on fresh water. Sea ducks are also considered borderline seabirds because they are not truly ocean going. They feed by diving for bottom-dwelling invertebrates and so, unlike loons and grebes, could never survive in deeper water.

## Adaptations to marine life

Seabirds show many distinctive adaptations for life in a marine habitat. They have large, paired nasal salt glands, usually located in a shallow depression in the bone of the top of the head, just above the eye. The glands secrete a salt-rich fluid whenever the seabird ingests sea water or salty foods and thus helps the bird to maintain the correct fluid and ion balance. A few seabirds drink fresh water but others, such as petrels and shearwaters, never do.

All seabirds must return to land to breed and so have to deal at some point with two very different environments, marine and terrestrial. Some species have adapted to make the best use of both habitats; others have become adapted mainly for their aquatic environment. For example, auks, grebes, loons, and cormorants are rather clumsy on land because their feet are set far back on the body for propulsion or steering when swimming. Compromises have also been made in wing structure because adaptations for flight are very different to those needed for activity in water.

Almost all seabirds rely to some extent on their ability to swim to get food. In addition, they have had to evolve ways of staying warm when immersed in water. The body feathers form a dense insulating layer by trapping a layer of air against the skin, and waterproofing oil from the preen gland above the tail base is spread over them by the bill during preening. Some birds also have a layer of fat below the skin, which is particularly important for penguins when swimming down to great depths because water pressure squeezes insulating air from the feathers and thus removes the first line of defense against the cold. Seabirds also have a heat exchanger called the rete mirabile in the legs and feet to prevent loss of body heat to the water. In this adaptation of the circulatory system, blood vessels going into and out of the legs are very closely associated, so that chilled blood coming from the feet is warmed by blood going into them. Most seabirds have webbed feet for surface paddling (albatrosses and gulls), underwater propulsion (cormorants), or for use as rudders (penguins and auks). Webbed feet are also useful in flight—for steering, braking, providing lift when flying at slow speeds, and for running over water to help with takeoff.

## Feeding techniques

Seabirds feed on other animals. They are mostly active hunters, although many will scavenge dead material; frigate birds, jaegers, and gulls also steal prey from other birds, an activity called kleptoparasitism. Most seabirds feed on fish, many eat invertebrates (from squid to jellyfish), and some specialize on tiny zooplankton. The diversity of seabirds' prey and fishing techniques are reflected in the different shapes and sizes of their bills.

Among the most spectacular feeding strategies is that of the plunge divers: tropic birds, gannets, boobies, and some pelicans. Plunge divers have long, pointed bills and mainly eat fish small enough to swallow whole. They catch prey by dropping into the water, sometimes from great heights. They usually fold their wings directly backward at the last

*Common terns (Sterna hirundo) feed primarily on fish (sometimes squid and crustaceans), which they catch by plunging into the water and seizing with their beaks.*

moment, though gannets might fold their wings 30 feet (10 m) above the water so that they drop like a stone, plunging to depths of 30 feet (10 m).

Brown pelicans (*Pelecanus occidentalis*) have very specialized bills, the lower mandible having an elastic pouch that expands as it hits the water and surrounds the targeted fish while the upper mandible snaps shut to prevent their escape.

Auks, penguins, loons, and grebes dive down from the surface and literally fly under water in pursuit of their prey, using their wings for propulsion. Auks and penguins can reach great depths; emperor penguins (*Aptenodytes forsteri*) have been recorded at nearly 800 feet (265 m). One problem facing this group is how to reduce body buoyancy; they cannot build up momentum for a dive in the same way as the plunge-divers. Unlike those of other birds, the bodies of these divers tend to be heavier than water; these birds are also able to deliberately compress the air from beneath their feathers. However, cormorants have adopted a completely different strategy; they swim under water using their feet rather than their wings. In addition, the wing feathers are wettable, so trapped air is removed (see SWIMMING). Seabirds that feed solely on fish, including cormorants, tend to have longer, narrower bills than others, such as auks and penguins, that also (or only) feed on plankton and crustaceans.

Albatrosses and shearwaters are versatile feeders; they may feed while surface swimming (particularly if scavenging for food), but they can also plunge dive or pluck food from the surface when flying. Their large hooked bills are adapted for gripping and tearing up large prey, such as squid. However, the true generalists are the gulls: efficient hunters of open water or shoreline but also scavengers and opportunists adapted to a wide range of natural and artificial habitats, some of them far removed from the sea.

Among the specialist feeders are prions (such as the blue petrel, *Halobaena caerulea*), shearwaters, and skimmers (*Rynchops* spp.). Prions filter plankton from sea water using tiny flat plates (lamellae) on the bill. Skimmers, also called scissor bills, have a longer lower than upper mandible and hunt by flying just above the sea surface, skimming the bill through the water and snapping up fish.

## Seabird morphology

Pelagic species, such as albatrosses and petrels, have long, thin wings and small, light bodies in relation to wing size. This arrangement allows them to glide easily, covering long distances using the minimum amount of energy. Frigate birds are also excellent ocean gliders; despite a 6-foot (2 m) wingspan, they weigh only 2 to 3⅓ pounds (1 to 1.5 kg). However, auks and other species that swim under water are fairly poor fliers. Their stout, heavy bodies and short wings are excellent adaptations for underwater activity but poorly suited for flight. Despite the rapid, whirring action of their stiffly outstretched wings, they can fly only in a straight line, taking short occasional glides. Some seabirds have lost the ability to fly altogether, such as penguins and the Galápagos cormorant (*Compsohalieus harrisi*), which has lost the specialized breastbone to which a bird's flight muscles are usually attached.

## Breeding and nesting

Seabirds that cannot move rapidly on land and find takeoff difficult are vulnerable to terrestrial predators such as weasels, dogs, and rats. Therefore, many seabirds breed on high cliffs (where updrafts aid landings and takeoffs), offshore islands, isolated headlands, or sandbars.

## RIDING THE WIND

The flight of albatrosses is called dynamic soaring. These seabirds take advantage of the fact that the wind speed near the ocean surface is decreased by friction across the surface of the water. An albatross flying about 50 feet (17 m) above the water and facing into the wind receives little uplift, so it does not make much progress forward (see FLIGHT). Consequently, it glides downward, with the wind. The nearer the albatross gets to the ocean the slower the wind becomes and the faster the bird moves relative to the air. It will usually glide into a wave trough (where the wind is at its slowest) and turn into the wind once more at the front of the wave. As it shoots above the crest of the wave, the increasing wind speed lifts it rapidly upward. As the albatross gains height, it gradually loses speed and thus forward momentum, at which point it turns again to glide downward with the wind and repeats the cycle.

*The albatross's large wingspan is adapted more for gliding than flapping.*

### A CLOSER LOOK

*Although some seabirds build nests in which to lay their eggs, others, such as the little tern (*Sterna albifrons*), shown above, lay their eggs directly on the surface of the ground.*

About 95 percent of seabirds are colonial breeders; they breed in groups that range from a few pairs to literally millions, sometimes because nesting space is limited (such as in cliff-nesting species) but often to reduce predation. Synchronized egg laying also helps decrease egg and chick loss because predators quickly become glutted (see PREDATION). Nesting densities can be very high, each pair having only enough room for itself and its chick. The alternative way of avoiding predation is to nest well away from other birds, as do mainland ground-nesting gulls. Grebes build floating nests on water using weeds, reeds, and other vegetation.

Some cliff-nesting species, such as gannets (*Morus* and *Sula* spp.) and kittiwakes (*Rissa* spp.), build nests; others do not. For example, the common murre, or guillemot (*Uria aalge*), has pear-shaped eggs that roll in a circular direction to prevent them from falling off the nesting ledge. Similarly, ground-nesting birds may either build a nest or simply lay their eggs on the ground. Many auks, tubenoses, and penguins lay their eggs in crevices, natural holes, or burrows. Boobies, cormorants, frigate birds, and some terns and gulls are tree nesters. Seabirds' webbed feet are often used for incubation; emperor penguins use their feet to insulate the egg from the cold ground, while cormorants, gannets, and boobies, which lack a brood patch (bare abdominal skin that radiates heat), place their feet on the egg to keep it warm.

Once adulthood is reached, the lifespan of many seabirds is high; albatrosses and fulmars live for 30 to 40 years or more, for example. Many seabirds pair with the same mate for years or for life, although divorces are common among penguins and among pairs with poor breeding success. Territorial and pair displays are often elaborate, especially among ground-nesting colonial birds, such as gannets, boobies, and cormorants. Young seabirds may be extremely precocial and leave the nest soon after hatching (for example, grebes), or they may be altricial (needing parental care), staying in the nest until more or less fully grown (as do albatrosses).

## Migration and navigation

Seabirds often have amazing migratory movements and navigational abilities. For example, several species of shearwaters nest on islands off the coasts of Australia and New Zealand and yet spend their nonbreeding season many thousands of miles away in the Bering Sea (between Alaska and Siberia) or farther south along the Pacific coast of North America.

Wilson's storm petrel, which is no larger than a starling, and south polar skuas breed on sub-Antarctic islands and then migrate to spend their nonbreeding season in the North Atlantic or North Pacific. The Arctic tern migrates some 24,000 miles (38,500 km) per year between its breeding grounds in the Arctic and winter grounds in the Antarctic.

In one study, a Manx shearwater was removed from its nesting burrow in Britain, taken to the New England coast, and released. Within a week, the bird was back in its own burrow.

E. BRADSHAW

**See also:** BIRDS; FLIGHT; OCEAN HABITATS; PREDATION; SHORE HABITATS; WATERBIRDS AND WADERS.

**Further reading:**
Enticott, Jim, and David Tippling. 1997. *The Complete Reference: Seabirds of the World.* Mechanicsburg, Pa., and U.K.: Stackpole Books and New Holland Publishers.
Harrison, Peter. 1997. *Seabirds of the World: A Photographic Guide.* Princeton, N.J.: Princeton University Press.

## SEABIRDS AND ENVIRONMENTAL PROBLEMS

While some seabirds have benefited from their association with humans, most have not. The success stories include increased populations of many gull species because they have been able to colonize new artificial habitats and exploit new food resources, such as household waste. However, sometimes gulls reach pest proportions, and attempts are made to reduce numbers by damaging the eggs (for example, by puncturing them) of nesting pairs, who continue to defend their territory but do not rear any young. Cormorants have started to breed inland, causing problems by fishing in fish farms and areas stocked for anglers. However, other seabirds suffer greatly from human-related activities. Many thousands, particularly diving birds, are killed each year by oil pollution and toxic wastes dumped at sea, as well as by less obvious, easily corrected forms of pollution, such as discarded plastic and other human wastes, which, if eaten, may choke the birds. Millions of diving birds, including auks and albatrosses, drown annually in fishing nets, a major conservation problem in many countries. Such accidental killings may be responsible for the steady decrease in common guillemot (murre) breeding populations since the 1960s, for example. Overfishing itself is a problem of increasing seriousness, adding to the effect of natural seasonal food shortages and creating an overall shortage.

### AT RISK

# SEEDS AND SEED DISPERSAL

**Seeds, which contain the embryo plant, are spread in a variety of different ways**

*Seed-bearing plants, such as the wild strawberry, have existed for 360 million years.*

## CONNECTIONS

● Plants that rely on **BIRDS** to scatter their seeds often produce small, brightly colored fruits.

● Formation of a seed follows **FERTILIZATION**.

● The food store in the seed breaks down at **GERMINATION**.

A seed contains the embryo plant from which a new plant develops. Although the seeds from different plant species vary in shape and size, they have certain factors in common. Food is stored in most seeds to provide the growing seedling with nourishment until it is able to obtain its own. Surrounding the embryo and food store there is usually a hard, highly resistant covering called the seed coat, which protects the delicate embryo tissue until conditions are suitable for germination. Many plants have developed elaborate seed-dispersal mechanisms that help locate the seed to new, favorable sites. These dispersal mechanisms allow plants to inhabit new areas.

## Evolution of seed plants

The development of seeds was an important step in the evolution of land plants that enabled them to grow in a much wider variety of environments than they had previously. In more primitive plants there are two alternating phases in the life cycle: a sexual gametophyte phase and an asexual sporophyte phase (see FERNS AND FERN ALLIES). These two phases occur as separate plants, which may be similar in size; in the more advanced lower plants, however, the gametophytes are very much smaller. In the gametophyte phase, the presence of a film of water is essential for the male gamete (the sperm) to reach and fertilize

the egg cell. Dispersal occurs by single-celled spores produced by the sporophyte. In seed plants these two phases are still present, but the gametophyte phase is so much reduced that it occurs within the tissue of the sporophyte (in the ovary). This arrangement eliminates the need for water and allows the plant to spend its whole life in much drier conditions and makes it possible for the early stages of growth of the new plant embryo to occur protected within the tissue of the parent plant. Thus, the embryo is fairly advanced by the time it leaves its parent and has a better chance of survival.

The first seeds evolved in the Devonian period about 360 million years ago. They originated in a group of fernlike plants called seed ferns (Pteridospermales). These now extinct plants belonged to the division Gymnospermae, so called because members of the division have naked seeds (seeds that do not have coverings and are exposed to the elements; see GYMNOSPERMS). The next important development was the enclosure and protection of the developing ovule and seeds in an ovary. These plants, called angiosperms, evolved in the Cretaceous period about 100 million years ago (see ANGIOSPERMS). They now number over 250,000 species and are the dominant plants in most of the world.

## Formation of the seed

When a pollen grain (containing the male gamete) of one flower lands on the stigma (female organ) of another flower, the process of fertilization is initiated. A tube grows through the tough outer coat of the pollen grain, which then penetrates the tissue of the stigma until it reaches an ovary. The male gamete then travels down the pollen tube and fertilizes the egg cell within an ovule. In angiosperms, two male gametes are present in the pollen; one fertilizes the egg cell to form the embryo, while the other fuses with the primary endosperm nucleus to form the endosperm nucleus. This nucleus divides to form the endosperm itself. The endosperm is a structure that frequently stores food materials for the embryo plant, which are broken down and used during germination (see GERMINATION).

The two male gametes are surrounded by a tissue called the nucellus, which in turn is surrounded by the integuments. Integuments are one or two protective layers of the ovule that eventually give rise to

---

### CORE FACTS

■ A seed contains an embryo plant and stored food.
■ The seed coat protects the embryo from damage.
■ Seeds are dispersed in a number of different ways, including by wind, water, animals, and other mechanisms.

---

the seed coat, or testa. As the newly formed embryo develops, it absorbs food from the nucellus or, sometimes, from the endosperm. The embryo then grows at a steady rate until it reaches maturity.

When the seed is mature, it contains the embryo plant and stored food and is surrounded by the testa. The embryo has two main parts, the radicle, or embryonic root, which develops into the primary root, and the shoot. The shoot eventually develops into the plant above the ground. Between the embryonic root and shoot is a part of the embryo called the hypocotyl. A minute shoot tip called the epicotyl is at the end of the hypocotyl. Next, one or two cotyledons, or seed leaves, are present in the seed, depending on which major angiosperm division the plant belongs to. Most species produce two or more cotyledons and are called dicotyledons (see DICOTYLEDONS). Grasses (family Graminae, or Poaceae; see GRASSES), lilies (family Liliaceae, especially Lilium spp.), orchids (family Orchidaceae; ORCHIDS), rushes (family Juncaceae), and various other families belong to the division Monocotyledoneae; they have only one seed leaf (see MONOCOTYLEDONS). The tip of the radicle is positioned at the micropyle, a small pore that is usually present close to the scar left by the seed stalk (the hilium).

The food supply in the seed may be stored in several places. In many species, it is provided by the endosperm, but often the endosperm is absorbed in the formation of the seed, and the food is stored in the embryo itself, predominantly in the cotyledons. In a few plants, part of the nucellus remains as a store of food, called the perisperm. The food is often stored in the form of starch, but some species store it as fats and oils, proteins, or sugars or a combination of several of these. Annual plants die when the seeds

are produced, the seeds being the main storage organ of the plant (see ANNUAL PLANTS). Many of the staple cereal crops throughout the world are annual species.

In some species, the seeds do not have a food store, and thus, establishment of the seedling is more difficult. For example, orchid seeds rely on developing a symbiotic link with fungal hyphae to provide them with food for germination (see SYMBIOSIS). The advantage of not storing food is that the seeds are very light and easily dispersed over long distances by the wind.

The seed coat protects the embryo until conditions are suitable for growth. In less developed seeds, the seed coat consists of an inner woody layer and an outer fleshy layer. However, in many seeds the two layers are fused together and are hard and dry. In some species, the seed coat becomes covered with mucilage, hairs, or fibers that aid the dispersal of the seed. The role of protecting and dispersing the seed is often accomplished by the fruit in flowering plants.

Gymnosperms, such as conifers (*Coniferae* or *Pinopsida*), differ from other plants in that the ovules and seeds are borne and carried naked on the scales of cones. After pollination, it often takes a year or so for fertilization to take place, and it may take another year for the seed to form. There is no endosperm, but the seed is fed by the female gametophyte in which the embryo is lodged.

### Transport of seeds and fruits
In the simplest cases, the seed capsule opens, and the seeds simply fall off the parent plant. However, it is often an advantage for the seeds to be dispersed some distance from the parent plant so that the seedlings do not have to compete with it for water, nutrients, and growing space. There are numerous

*The seed contains the embryo plant and a food store. The embryo consists of a radicle and a shoot apex, and food is usually stored in the endosperm. Seed leaves (cotyledons) and a protective seed coat are also present.*

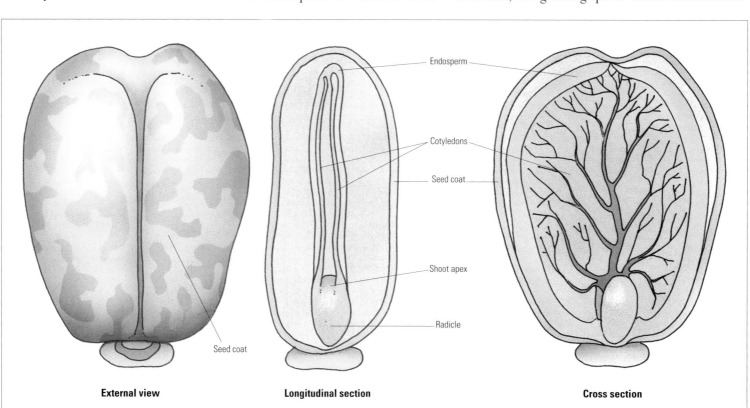

| External view | Longitudinal section | Cross section |

Endosperm

Cotyledons

Seed coat

Shoot apex

Radicle

Seed coat

adaptations of seeds and fruit capsules that encourage dispersal. Some species, such as orchids, have very light seeds that can be easily blown away by the wind. Other species have various types of hairs that act as parachutes. These species include, for example, dandelion (*Taraxacum* spp.), cotton (*Gossypium* spp.), and willow herb (*Epilobuim* spp.). Some seeds have wings or other appendages that act as gliders, such as sycamore (*Acer pseudoplatanus*) and ash (*Fraxiuns* spp.). In some dry areas, the whole plant may come loose and be blown for several miles by the wind, distributing the seed as it goes. This strategy is used by plants such as Russian thistle (*Salsola kali*) and tumbleweed (*Carex* spp.).

Many seeds float and can be washed to new sites by rivers and streams. Some species aid this process by producing air bladders (for example, sedges in the family Cyperaceae, especially *Carex* spp.); spongy coats (for example, white water lily, *Nymphaea alba*); or light, fibrous coats (for example, coconut, *Cocos nucifera*). A number of species rely on raindrops falling on the stems to catapult the seed out of the capsules, and some capsules open only when the weather is wet, for example, members of the family Aizoaceae.

Many species rely on their seeds being eaten by birds and other animals for dispersal. The seed is enclosed in a succulent fruit that encourages the animal to eat it. The plant embryo is protected from the action of digestive juices by the tough seed coat. The seed is then passed out in the feces; it is deposited with a convenient supply of fertilizer to help it grow into a new plant. Alternatively, some species have toxins in their seeds that encourage the animal to regurgitate them. Birds are particularly common transporters of seeds, and plants that rely on birds for dispersal typically have fruits that are small, thin-skinned, and brightly colored. They also have no smell and remain attached to the plant (for example, most berries). Those that tend to be transported by mammals are often large and dull in color and have a pleasant aroma. They may also have hard shells, usually falling to the ground when ripe (for example, many nuts), where they are eaten by animals. Most nut-producing trees rely on rodents, such as squirrels, to hoard the nuts, some of which are forgotten and develop into new plants.

Many species, including some aquatic and marsh plants and mistletoe (*Phoradendron*) produce various barbs, hooks, or sticky hairs that become attached to the coats of passing animals. Seeds become attached when an animal bends back a stem as it brushes past; when the stem is released, seeds are catapulted out of the capsules and scattered, and some become lodged in the animal's fur. These seeds later fall or are brushed off the animals. The seeds of a number of wetland species are small and easily transported on the feet of wildfowl; some have sticky coats that aid dispersal.

Some species have developed their own means of seed dispersal. Balsams (*Impatiens* spp.) produce capsules that explode when they are mature. Many

legumes, such as broom (*Cytisus* spp.) and geraniums, have capsules in which tension builds as they begin to dry out. The capsules eventually crack, catapulting the seeds. The storksbill (*Erodium* spp.) has a coil mechanism for drilling its seeds into the ground.

### Fruit capsules

The simplest method of dispersal occurs when the ovary opens when the seeds are mature so that seeds can disperse on their own. In many cases, plants have found it an advantage to shed the ovary with the

*The seeds of the dandelion (*Taraxacum spp.*) are very light and easily dispersed by the wind.*

*Seeds can survive for a long time. One-thousand-year-old seeds of the Oriental lotus flower* (Nelumbo nucifera)*, shown above, have been germinated successfully.*

seeds inside or in some cases with other flower parts, whole flowers, or even the whole plant. For example, the ovary forms the hard outer shell of many nuts and the fleshy parts of many soft fruits, such as strawberries and raspberries. These structures are given the general term *fruit capsules*. Their advantage is that they often give better protection to the seed and allow many more elaborate mechanisms and appendages that enable the seed to travel farther. In some cases the fruit capsules also provide food for the germinating seed.

## Dormancy

When a seed is fully mature, it goes into a period of dormancy that results from a considerable reduction in the water content of the seed (see DORMANCY). While normal stems and leaves contain around 80 percent water, seeds usually contain only around 15 percent. This dehydration greatly reduces metabolic activity and makes the seed very resistant to unfavorable conditions. Different seeds can survive for different lengths of time. Some may survive for only a few days or weeks, but others can live for many years. For example, 1,000-year-old seeds of the Oriental lotus flower (*Nelumbo nucifera*) have been made to germinate successfully.

Some seeds require a definite period of dormancy. This prerequisite is often the case where

there are periods of unfavorable weather, such as drought or cold winters. In these cases, germination may be controlled by factors that prevent the seedling from developing even though suitable conditions may occur during the period of dormancy. For example, seeds may have to go through a period of freezing conditions before they are able to germinate. This procedure ensures the seeds do not germinate on warm days that might occur in the fall. Some species contain chemical inhibitors in their seed coats that need to be washed out before germination. Others may need to be abraded (rubbed), perhaps by mechanical movement. Some seeds are sensitive to daylength, assurance that they will germinate at the most favorable time of year.

## Germination of the seed

When suitable conditions for germination occur, the seed starts to absorb water and begins to swell. The seed coat (and fruit capsule if this is present) bursts, and the food reserves become available for use. The first stage of development of the seedling begins when the radicle bursts through the seed coat and begins to extend downward. Soon afterward, the shoot begins to uncurl and extend. Often, the cotyledons are the last structures to emerge from the seed coat.

If an endosperm or perisperm is present, it is absorbed by the stem as it pushes toward the surface. In monocotyledons, such as grasses, the cotyledon usually remains underground in the seed and breaks down the endosperm. In many dicotyledonous plants, the cotyledons find their way above the soil surface, where they turn green and start to photosynthesize and produce their own food.

In a few plants, the seed starts developing while still attached to the parent plant. This process is called vivipary. It occurs in a number of species that grow in cold climates; a notable example is provided by some species of mangroves that inhabit the harsh environment of salt marshes. The seedling radicle and hypocotyl of these plants may grow up to 3 feet (1 m) in length while still attached to the parent plant. When the seedlings finally come away from the parent, they stick into the mud or are washed away by the tide. They stand a better chance of survival because they are already well developed by the time they leave the parent plant.

N. STEWART

**See also:** ANGIOSPERMS; ANNUAL PLANTS; DICOTYLEDONS; DORMANCY; FERNS AND FERN ALLIES; FRUITS AND FRUIT PLANTS; GRAINS; GRASSES; GYMNOSPERMS; MONOCOTYLEDONS; ORCHIDS; SYMBIOSIS.

## Further reading:

Baskin, C. C., and J. M. Baskin. 2001. *Seeds: Ecology, Biogeography, and Evolution of Dormancy and Germination.* London: Academic Press.
Kigel, J., and G. Galili, eds. 1995. *Seed Development and Germination.* New York: Marcel Dekker.

# SELECTIVE BREEDING

**Selective breeding is the process of controlling which animals or plants in a population are allowed to reproduce**

Thousands of years ago, when people began to keep animals and plants for food, they also started to affect how these organisms would inter-breed to produce the next generation. These early farmers were not deliberately planning to alter their animals and plants; much of this first selective breeding was probably a side-effect of domestication (see DOMESTICATION). For example, individual wheat plants that do not let their seeds (grains) fall to the ground to sprout are at a disadvantage in the wild. However, this feature makes gathering in their seeds at harvesttime much easier. Early farmers would have obtained their grain more easily from such plants and therefore had more of it available to plant next year's crop. In this and similar ways, domesti-cated wheat soon became different from wild wheat.

Similarly, smaller, less aggressive cattle and sheep were easier to control, and castration of excess males reduced competition and fighting for females. Once tamed, animals were no longer subject to natural selection, and because the captive populations were small and gentically isolated, regional breeds started to develop (see NATURAL SELECTION).

Even in ancient times, more deliberate breeding was carried out. For example, a 5,000-year-old inscription found in present-day Iran appears to record selective breeding carried out with donkeys. The ancient Egyptians also developed several breeds of dogs. The first domestic breed for which detailed pedigrees (records of parentage) were kept was the Arabian horse, the ancestor of modern thoroughbred racehorses. However, it was not until the 1700s that people began breeding farm animals with the delib-erate intention of improving them. The most famous innovator of this period was Englishman Robert Bakewell (1725–1795), whose great success in breeding longhorn cattle and Leicester sheep inspired many other plant and animal breeders. Bakewell kept his breeding methods largely secret to protect his profits; he also hired out his prize bulls and rams rather than selling them outright.

These pioneer breeders achieved their success long before the science of genetics was understood. The founder of genetics, Austrian botanist and monk Gregor Mendel (1822–1884), owed much to earlier experiments carried out by plant breeders, while English naturalist Charles Darwin's (1809–1882)

*About 10,000 years ago, wheat and barley were two of the first plants cultivated. Now more than half of the world's wheat comes from selective breeding methods.*

theory of evolution by natural selection was inspired partly by the way that animals and plants were selected for breeding purposes (see DARWIN, CHARLES; MENDEL, GREGOR).

The laws of genetics, however, make it much easier to understand and discuss what occurs during selective breeding. All modern breeding takes account of the fact that plants and animals have two copies of every gene in their bodies but pass only one of these copies to their offspring in their sperm or eggs. To take a simple case, Mendel's pea plants had either purple or white flowers, controlled by a single gene that occurs in one of two alleles (versions), P and p. An individual pea plant can have one of three genetic makeups for this gene: PP, Pp, or pp. Plants that are PP or Pp both have purple flowers, while those that are pp have white ones. (In this case, the

## CORE FACTS

- Hybridization between existing plant varieties or animal breeds is an important tool of selective breeding.
- Inbreeding (breeding between close relatives) can help selective breeding but also carries genetic dangers.
- Modern techniques, such as artificial insemination and embryo transfer, have speeded up the breeding process.

## CONNECTIONS

● In prehistoric times, an early result of the **DOMESTICATION** of animals and plants was selective breeding.

● Traditional selective breeding has now been supplemented by the techniques of **GENETIC ENGINEERING**.

allele P—the purple allele—is termed dominant and the allele p is recessive.) Where both alleles are the same in an individual plant (PP or pp), the plant is described as homozygous; where they are different (Pp), it is heterozygous. By isolating homozygous plants and animals, it is possible to breed "true," even if the characteristic is recessive. However, many characteristics of interest to farmers, such as the milk yield of cows, are influenced by many genes and also by the environment: this fact makes their genetics much more difficult to interpret.

### Animal breeding

Over the centuries, people have bred animals for food, wool, pulling carts, racing, and fighting, as well as for show or ornament. Sometimes the goals of breeding change; during the 20th century, for example, there was a move away from high-fat to leaner meat in farm animals, and new breeds had to be developed to meet this changed demand.

When the goal of a breeding program has been decided on, the next step is selection—choosing which animals to breed from. This step is not as simple as it sounds. The most obvious strategy, probably thousands of years old, is to select the best-looking animals (or at least to avoid any obviously

defective ones). However, an individual animal may be superior because it has had a better upbringing rather than because of its genes, and it may also be carrying "bad" recessive alleles. So it is a good idea to look also at the animal's pedigree (ancestral line), its siblings (brothers and sisters), and its half-siblings.

The best method is progeny testing, where the earlier offspring of an animal are checked for quality before deciding whether to carry on breeding from the animal. This technique is done, for example, with bulls used to breed dairy cattle, because individual cattle are expensive to rear and it is important to get the best result. Often, statistical techniques are needed to show that one bull's progeny are better than another's.

Another problem with selection is how to measure a particular trait if it is not obvious from the outside. In the past (and to some extent in the present), judging animals was more of an art than a science. One example of using more objective methods is the measuring of milk yields in cows, which began systematically in Denmark in 1895. Other traits, such as the thickness of fat on a pig's back, can now also be measured directly using ultrasound or other imaging techniques.

The pattern of breeding also has to be decided on. Inbreeding (see the box on page 1482) can result in quick progress, especially in the early stages of a breeding program, but it can also bring disadvantages. (Conversely, where there is a danger of unwanted inbreeding in a small herd, computer programs can help plan the best breeding program to avoid this situation.) Sometimes a new breed is created by crossing two existing breeds; for example, Indian brahman cattle were crossed with local breeds in the United States, the result being the production of new strains of heat- and drought-tolerant cattle.

It is also common to crossbreed sheep; lower-yielding pure breeds are crossed regularly to produce sheep that grow and fatten faster. Sometimes a wild or a low-yielding form of an animal is revealed to have a useful trait such as disease resistance: in this case, it is often bred with a cultivated animal using a method called backcrossing, in which the breeder tries to ensure that only the useful gene and not others end up in the domesticated animal.

Animal breeding can also be carried out on a more short-term basis, as is particularly true of hybridization—breeding between different strains or breeds or sometimes between different species. A well-known example is the mule, the hardy but infertile animal created by crossing a donkey with a horse. A mule can work harder in harsh conditions than either of its parents and thrives on poorer-quality food. (This phenomenon of hybrids doing better than their parents is called heterosis, or hybrid vigor.)

### Plant breeding

Plant breeding has much in common with animal breeding, but there are important differences. To begin with, plants are usually kept in far greater numbers than animals, so there is a much greater

*The picture below shows an olive shoot being grafted onto an old trunk. This practice enables the grafted shoot to grow and develop into a new plant with all the desirable qualities of the original donor, while taking advantage of an existing root system.*

chance that a useful mutation will appear naturally and be noticed by a plant breeder; many ornamental varieties of flowers have arisen in this way. Natural hybrids or mutations that result in extra sets of chromosomes (polyploidy) are also far more common in plants and often result in larger, more vigorous varieties. In addition, once a new variety is identified, it is often propagated by cuttings rather than having to grow it from seed. Some plants, such as wheat, rice, and beans, are naturally self-pollinating and so can be interbred only by artificial means.

In the 20th century, plant breeders had great success in producing new varieties to meet commercial demands. Staple cereals such as corn (maize) and rice now produce several times the yield of grain that they once did, while varieties have been bred to provide many specific traits, such as resistance to pests and fungal attack or tolerance of heat and drought. For mechanical harvesting of crops such as tomatoes, newer varieties that ripen at the same time are an advantage. Trees have also been bred to grow much faster than before. However, high-yielding crops often depend heavily on artificial fertilizers (see FERTILIZERS).

Hybridization has been particularly important in plant breeding. The European exploration of the world from the 16th century onward provided many opportunities for botanists to bring together and hybridize plants from different continents. For example, the main types of strawberries now grown originate from a Chilean species that was crossed with a North American one.

In plants, such as maize, hybridization between purebred lines is used to create high-yielding crop plants. These hybrids do not themselves breed true (they are heterozygous: see above); thus, new hybrid seed has to be created from pure strains every year.

## New directions

Throughout the 20th century and into the 21st, many technical advances—some of them controversial—have had an impact on how animal and plant breeding is carried out. There have also been organizational changes, with many specialized breeding institutes set up by governments and private corporations.

In animals one important innovation has been artificial insemination, in which sperm taken from an award-winning bull, for example, is frozen and used to inseminate (fertilize) cows worldwide. This technique has helped to increase the milk yields of cattle in the United States, although in the longer term it may increase the risk of inbreeding. A more recent practice applied to female animals (especially cows) is embryo transfer, in which developing embryos are taken from the womb of cows judged to be superior and implanted into other cows, which act as surrogate mothers. Thus, the best cows can have far more calves than they otherwise would.

Plants, too, have benefited from innovative technologies. One technique practised from the early 20th century involved treating plants and seeds with chemicals or radiation to try to increase the natural mutation rate (see MUTATION) and produce new varieties. This technique produced a few commercial

*A longhorn bull. In the 18th century, pioneering cattle breeders selectively bred longhorn cattle to produce animals with specific favorable characteristics.*

# INBREEDING

*The Hawaiian nene goose (Branta sandvicensis), threatened by extinction in the 1940s, was reestablished successfully after careful captive breeding.*

The simplest definition of inbreeding is "breeding between close relatives." The word can be used in subtly different ways, however; geneticists define inbreeding as any pattern of breeding in which the mating individuals are more closely related than the average in that population. (The opposite practice is called outbreeding.) For example, if zoos are trying to preserve an endangered species by captive breeding, the scientists in charge of zoo breeding programs swap animals with each other so that the least-related animals mate (outbreeding). However, after a few generations, the animals may still remain related to each other simply because the total zoo population is so small. A third definition of inbreeding is used by animal breeders; they often restrict the term to mating between very close relatives such as father and daughter, calling mating of more distant relatives linebreeding.

One drawback of inbreeding within a genetically varied population, such as humans, is that every individual carries a few single copies of recessive alleles that would be damaging if the individual had them in a double dose. When human near-relatives mate, any offspring would be more likely to inherit matching doses of one of these defective alleles (one from each parent) and thus go on to develop a genetic disease. In addition, noninbred individuals are believed to benefit positively from so-called heterozygous advantage (that is, being heterozygous for many genes). In the long run, too, the species as a whole should be better able to resist new diseases or other challenges if there is more genetic variety in the population.

Inbreeding is not all bad, however. If it is carried out for a long enough period of time, strains that are homozygous for damaging alleles are usually eliminated, and so the only alleles that are left should be genetically healthy. Many wild plants, for example, are naturally self-pollinating and so are completely inbred. Inbred laboratory mice have been kept for many generations, while in China inbred pigs have recently been developed; their genetic similarity may help with the program to use pig organs for transplanting into humans.

From the time of animal breeder Robert Bakewell onward, inbreeding has also been a useful tool to fix new advantageous alleles in a breed so that it subsequently breeds true (is homozygous) for the new characteristic.

## A CLOSER LOOK

successes, including new short-stemmed cereal varieties. More recent advances in propagating plants from tiny pieces of tissue have speeded up the rate at which new strains can be developed and launched in the marketplace.

The spread of a few high-yielding breeds or strains is threatening the storehouse of genetic diversity contained in many older breeds of plants and animals. While traditional breeds may be less productive, they often contain useful inherited traits, such as frost or pest resistance. Wild relatives of domesticated species also represent a storehouse of useful genes for the future, but they, too, are often under threat, especially because of habitat destruction. In response to this situation, governments and other organizations are setting up gene banks (stores of genetic material, such as seeds) in an effort to safeguard this rich genetic heritage for the future.

Traditional selective breeding now has competition in genetic engineering (see GENETIC ENGINEERING). Genetic engineering techniques can add a desired gene directly into an animal or plant breed without the need for an elaborate breeding program. In practice, however, it will probably be a long time before genetic engineering replaces traditional breeding. Quite apart from people's worries about eating genetically modified food, present-day genetic engineering has its limitations. Currently it works best when adding a single gene to an organism—one for herbicide resistance, for example, or to make an animal produce a human protein for use in medicine.

Traditional breeding, by contrast, is often concerned with mixing whole sets of interacting genes from different varieties, a feat that would be more difficult for genetic engineering to imitate. In addition, cloning, the production of genetically identical individuals, allows rare breeding lines to be maintained and has implications for breeding endangered species (see CLONING).

Apart from genetic engineering itself, modern genetic knowledge may bring other benefits. Genetic screening is already being used so that pedigree dogs, for example, can be tested for hidden disease-causing alleles before they are used for breeding. Now that the complete genetic maps (genomes) of some animals are becoming known, humans may also soon be able to solve some longstanding mysteries of how, when, and in what order human domestic breeds originated.

R. BEATTY

**See also:** AGRICULTURE; ANIMAL DISEASES; CLONING; DARWIN, CHARLES; DOGS; ENDANGERED SPECIES; FERTILIZERS; GENETICALLY MODIFIED FOODS; GENETIC DISEASES; GENETICS; MENDEL, GREGOR; MUTATION; NATURAL SELECTION; PLANT DISEASES; REPRODUCTIVE SYSTEMS.

**Further reading:**
Clutton-Brock, J. 1999. *A Natural History of Domesticated Animals*. Cambridge, U.K.: Cambridge University Press.
Price, E. O. 2002. *Animal Domestiction and Behavior*. New York: CABI Publishing.
Smith, B. D. 1999. *Emergence of Agriculture*. New York: W. H. Freeman.
Zohary, D., and M. Hopf. 2001. *Domestication of Plants in the Old World*. Oxford: Oxford University Press.

# SEXUAL SELECTION

**Sexual selection is a type of natural selection that directly affects mating success**

*A male peacock displays his colorful tail plumage. With an elaborate display and enthusiastic courtship behavior, the male is more attractive to female peacocks and thus is more likely to mate.*

The biological term *sexual selection* was first used by the English naturalist Charles Darwin (1809–1882), who—with fellow naturalist Alfred R. Wallace (1823–1913)—published the *Theory of Evolution by Natural Selection* in 1858 (see DARWIN, CHARLES). In essence, the theory of natural selection asserts that individuals in a population that have inherited characteristics that better fit them to the environment are more likely to survive, reproduce, and leave behind offspring (see NATURAL SELECTION). Over generations, the inherited characteristics of survivors and successful reproducers will accumulate in the population, giving rise to evolutionary change (see EVOLUTION).

Darwin noted that in many sexually reproducing animal species, there appeared to be another type of selection at work, other than natural selection (see REPRODUCTION; SPECIES). He called this second type sexual selection, because it acted specifically on one or the other sex. Sexual selection could give rise to marked differences between males and females. For example, male stag beetles are larger than females and have prominent mandibles (grabbing mouthparts) that they use to joust with other males for possession of female mates. The name stag beetle comes from the comparison of the beetle's mandibles with the antlers of male deer (stags), which use their antlers in fighting contests over access to mate with the females in a herd.

In other cases of sexual selection, it is not so much males competing violently for the possession of females, as females choosing males. For example, in peacocks and peahens—birds that originate from the forests of Asia—adult males have extraordinarily large and elaborate tail feathers. This tail plumage, coupled with a vibrant courtship display, appears to form the basis for the female's choice of mate. The tail and courtship display improve the

## CORE FACTS

- In sexual selection, males usually compete with other males for female mates. Competition between males can give rise to adaptations, such as advanced weaponry that favor success in male–male conflicts over possession of mating partners.
- Because females usually choose males, in many animal species, males have more ornate coloring and engage in elaborate courtship behavior to attract females.
- Sexual selection can be a key factor in the evolution of new species, as was the case with some species of *Haplochromis* fish of Lake Victoria in Africa.
- Sexual selection in humans is partially culturally determined. Sexual preferences within human societies are complex and are determined by many factors. Social norms for sexual preference often vary greatly between cultures and between social levels and generations within the same culture.

## CONNECTIONS

- According to **CHARLES DARWIN**, famous for his theory of **EVOLUTION** by **NATURAL SELECTION**, sexual selection was a process separate from natural selection. Most modern evolutionists regard sexual selection as a form of natural selection.

- **COMPETITION** between males is a common factor in sexual selection, but so, too, is female choice. The two processes operating at the same time can lead to **COEVOLUTION** of males and females.

## SEA HORSES AND PIPEFISH

In sea horses and pipefish, males look after the eggs before they hatch by taking their female partner's eggs and incubating them in a pouch on their belly. The young hatch out and emerge through an opening in the male's pouch. In this case, because the male invests energy in reproduction, males are in demand. In some species of pipefish, the females are more brightly colored than the males and presumably compete with one another to be chosen by a male.

## EVOLUTION

*Male southern elephant seals fight for the right to claim and mate with a harem of females. Bull elephant seals are much larger than females; in this form of sexual selection, the larger the male, the more successful he is likely to be in terms of mating and passing on his genes.*

male peacock's chances of mating and bearing off-spring. On the other hand, these characteristics make the male more conspicuous and less able to fly well, and thus, he is more likely to be eaten by a tiger or other predators. Sexually attractive peacocks have reduced chances of survival compared with drab pea-cocks. In evolutionary terms, flamboyant peacocks will be successful provided that their attractiveness to females more than compensates for their tendency to be preyed on, so that they leave more offspring than drab males do (see PREDATION).

Sexual selection, whether by male competition or female choice, accounts for many of the striking differences between males and females of the same species and the large and elaborate structures present in the males of some species, such as the peacock's colorful tail plumage, a stag's large antlers, and a bull (male) elephant seal's giant size. Such differences between the sexes are examples of sexual dimorphism (see COMPETITION; DIMORPHISM AND POLYMORPHISM).

Sexual selection has become a major field of interest among modern evolutionary biologists. Many evolutionary biologists now regard sexual selection as a form of natural selection and not, as Darwin did, as distinct from natural selection itself.

### Competition or choice

Sexual selection takes two major forms—intra-sexual selection and intersexual selection. They are not mutually exclusive; both can operate in the same individuals at the same time. The first form of sexual selection involves competition between indi-viduals of the same sex (intrasexual selection) for mates of the opposite sex. Males usually compete because females tend to invest more energy in the production of young. Females produce eggs and invest energy in caring for the eggs before they hatch or the live young before they are born, and they often care for the young in the first few days, weeks, or months after hatching or birth. On the other hand, in most sexually reproducing species, males produce sperm by the million—at much less cost in energy terms than it takes to produce eggs. In many species, males have little involvement in parental care, although there are many exceptions, particularly among birds and mammals. As a general rule, in most animal species, males compete for the attentions of females (but see the box above left).

Competition between males can involve fighting for possession of or access to females. In such cases, successful males tend to be those with great fight-ing prowess. In this way, males of some species are selected for larger size and more powerful weaponry, as in the case of elephant seals. Adult male elephant seals are several times the size of females and have large canine teeth with which they stab rival males and thick skin over the neck region for protection. The male's elongated, elephant-like snout acts as a resonating tube, enabling him to roar a threat to ward off other males. Often an impres-sive display is enough to discourage a rival male, fights and injury thus being avoided; in ungulates in particular (for example, hippopotamuses, elephants, and rhinoceroses), serious fights usually occur only when the males are approximately the same size. Among elephant seals, the largest males, the best fighters, and the most successful at roaring gain the largest harems of females.

However, traits other than fighting ability can be selected for in males of many species. For example, in frogs and toads that have an extended mating sea-son, persistence seems to pay off. Males that croak their mating call night after night for several weeks are the ones that tend to have greatest mating success (see SOCIOBIOLOGY).

In some species, the ability of males to manipulate or deceive male competitors can be a successful approach. This strategy is called the "sneaky male" strategy (see the box below).

The second form of sexual selection is mate choice, in which an individual chooses a mate of the opposite sex among those on offer. This type of selection is called intersexual selection because it involves selection between the sexes. In many species, for reasons of energy investment, the female does the choosing and males compete for her attention (see box on page 1486).

## Runaway success

In the 1920s and 1930s British population geneticist Ronald Aylmer Fisher (1890–1962) developed a theory about how mate choice could lead to rapid evolutionary change. According to Fisher, if some males, perhaps with special ornamentation or coloration, are especially attractive to some females, the genes for these male features and the genes for females to be attracted to such features will both be passed on together to offspring. In a matter of a few generations, the two traits will become linked together by nonrandom mating. The genes, effectively linked together, will come to spread like wildfire through the population in what Fisher called a runaway process. In this way, males and females coevolve (see COEVOLUTION).

Fisher's theory is a workable explanation, whether or not there is some other reason why females select certain types of males. Other researchers have since looked for deeper explanations behind female choice.

## Good genes

The so-called good-gene hypothesis, also called the handicap hypothesis, proposes that females prefer males that display honest, costly signals that they are vigorous and healthy. The "good gene" stresses the male's fitness, as demonstrated by his ability to gather resources and keep himself in fine condition. For example, males of some species of hanging flies attract females by offering them dead insects. A female hanging fly will mate with a male if he provides her with a food item. The bigger the morsel, the longer she mates with him and the more eggs he fertilizes. A female benefits because the food gives her energy for producing eggs. Male flies fight for ownership of dead insects, and thus, a male with a large insect is likely to be a good fighter and in fine health.

The use of the word *handicap* emphasizes the costliness of displaying the honest signal. The signal requires energy to maintain and could be costly in survival terms, as in spectacularly tailed peacocks being more likely to be killed by predators than less well endowed males.

## Coming to their senses

In the 1980s some researchers sought a physiological (body function) explanation as to why females chose certain colors or types of ornamentation in males. Some workers thought that perhaps certain shape or color preferences were already wired into the nervous system of the species. Distinguishing certain stimuli, such as color, shape, or movement, might be useful in contexts other than breeding, such as in foraging for food. According to the so-called sensory bias hypothesis, an existing preference becomes taken up by sexual selection.

One researcher, A. F. Basalo, tested this idea with species of tropical freshwater platyfish belonging to the genus *Xiphophorus*. In recently evolved species belonging to this group, males have an elongated sword at the tail. In one still-living but apparently ancestral species, males lack a sword. Basalo tested whether females of this species would prefer their normal swordless males or a male with an artificial sword attached. The females preferred the sworded males. Such results suggest that female

## THE ROCK-PAPER-SCISSORS GAME WITH LIZARDS

In the Coast Range of California, males of the side-blotched lizard (below) exist in three throat-color forms—orange, blue, and yellow. Behavioral differences are associated with the three color forms. Orange-throated males tend to mate with as many females as they can. Blue-throated males tend to concentrate on a single mate and prevent other males from approaching her. Yellow-throated males tend to hang around the territories of orange-throated males and sneak matings with females while the orange-throated male is occupied elsewhere. All three behavioral strategies are successful in their own way, rather like the different choices in a game of rock-paper-scissors: rock beats scissors, scissors beats paper, and paper beats rock. In these lizards, the multiple-partner strategy of the orange throat beats the single-partner strategy of the blue throat. The blue throat's strategy, however, beats the sneaky strategy of the yellow throat. The yellow throat's strategy, in turn, beats that of the orange throat. All three forms of males coexist in the local population, and no one form appears to gain the upper hand to the exclusion of the others.

**A CLOSER LOOK**

SCIENCE AND SOCIETY

# SEXUAL SELECTION IN HUMANS

The application of sexual selection theory to humans is controversial. Male competition and female choice play their part but so, too, do female competition and male choice. Patterns of sexual selection and reproductive success vary from one culture to another. For example, in some traditional Islamic cultures, wealthy men have many wives and sire many children. In some Westernized countries, there is now a tendency for couples with moderate-to-high incomes to have relatively few children compared with couples who are less well off economically. In many Westernized countries, cultural norms about selecting a sexual partner have changed within a generation, and in many cases, choice of sexual partner appears more fluid than ever before.

This stag's large set of antlers enables it to fight and compete with other male deer for the right to mate with females in a herd. The larger the antlers, the older and more successful the stag is likely to be.

# LONG TAILS BETTER THAN SHORT

Some of the best evidence for sexual selection comes from studies on African long-tailed widow birds. One researcher shortened the tail of some males by cutting tail feathers and lengthened the tail of other male widow birds by sticking on additional feathers. Some birds were left with a normal tail length. All three types of males demonstrated equal prowess in fighting with other males, but the females definitely preferred the males with a longer tail. Those birds with a long tail successfully mated with, on average, two females in a season, those with a normal-length tail, one female, and among those with a shortened tail, only one male in two was successful in gaining a mate.

A CLOSER LOOK

platyfish have an ancestral bias for swordedness. This evidence offers support for sensory bias.

## Sexual selection and new species

In some circumstances, sexual selection can be an important factor in the formation of new species. Lake Victoria in Africa dried out during the peak of the last Ice Age some 15,000 to 18,000 years ago. Since then the depression has flooded, and in that time more than 500 species of fish belonging to the genus *Haplochromis* have evolved in the lake. Sexual selection is probably a key factor in the rapid evolution of at least some species. In some cases, closely related species living in the same locality appear very similar, but a striking difference between them lies in male coloration. In one species males are red, in another blue, and in a third yellow. Females are drab by comparison, and laboratory experiments show that the females choose the males. Under light conditions similar to those present in the lake, a female of a red-male species will choose a red male over a blue male of a related species. If only a blue male is provided, he may well be rejected. If the lighting conditions are changed so that color differences are masked, the female preference disappears, and she is as likely to mate with a blue male as a red one. A key factor in the female's choice of mate appears to be color and not some other feature, such as shape or behavior.

New species arise when members of an existing population split into two or more populations that do not interbreed. Over time, the two populations can become sufficiently different that they are incapable of interbreeding even if encouraged to do so. Some species of *Haplochromis* in Lake Victoria demonstrate that sexual selection can be a factor in causing the split. The males of some species display several different colors, showing perhaps the so-called ancestral condition before some species evolved into two or more species, with male color difference playing a leading role.

T. DAY

**See also:** DIMORPHISM AND POLYMORPHISM; HUMAN EVOLUTION; PREDATION; REPRODUCTION; SOCIOBIOLOGY; SPECIES.

## Further reading:
Basolo, A. L. 1990. Female preference predates the evolution of the sword in the swordtail fish. *Science* 250: 808–810.
Buss, D. M. 1994. The strategies of human mating. *American Scientist* 82: 238–248.
Darwin, C. 1871. *The Descent of Man, and Selection in Relation to Sex.* London: Murray.
Fisher, R. A. 1958. *The Genetical Theory of Natural Selection.* 2nd ed. New York: Dover.
Fryer, G., and T. D. Iles. 1980. *The Cichlid Fishes of the Great Lakes of Africa.* Edinburgh: Oliver and Boyd.
Stearns, S. C., and R. F. Hoekstra. 2000. *Evolution: An Introduction.* New York: Oxford University Press.

# SHARKS

Sharks, belonging to the class Chondrichthyes, are a group of often large, mainly marine, cartilaginous fish

harks are fish, but unlike most fish, they have a skeleton made of cartilage, several gill slits, and skin covered with toothlike scales. Although sharks occasionally kill humans, only a few of the 350 species of sharks are dangerous. Many shark attacks on humans are provoked or are thought to be a case of mistaken identity (from below, surfers can look remarkably like turtles or seals). In the United States, there are fewer than 12 shark attacks each year, only 1 or 2 of which are fatal. A person is 50 times more likely to be struck by lightning than to be attacked by a shark. The two largest sharks, the whale shark (*Rhincidon typus*, 59 feet, or 18 m long) and the basking shark (*Cetorhinus maximus*, 32 feet, or 10 m long) are both plankton feeders and do not attack any large vertebrates, much less

humans. Research shows that far from being mindless killing machines, sharks are relatively sophisticated and intelligent animals.

## Survey of the sharks

Sharks probably evolved 350 to 400 million years ago from the placoderms, a group of primitive jawed fish. They have remained basically unchanged for 60 to 100 million years, a testimony to the success of their body shape and their ability to adapt to a variety of ecological niches.

Sharks are members of the class Chondrichthyes, the cartilaginous fish. Embryos of bony fish (class Ostichthyes) have a cartilaginous skeleton, but it is replaced by a bony skeleton in the adult; the Chondrichthyes have cartilaginous skeletons even as adults. Thus, scientists once thought sharks represented the primitive earlier stages of fish evolution, but this theory is now known to be untrue.

Within the Chondrichthyes, sharks, dogfish, rays, and skates form the subclass Elasmobranchii. There are 8 orders of living sharks, containing a total of 30 families and about 350 species. The biggest order, the ground sharks (Carcharhiniformes), includes about 197 species in 8 families.

*The great white shark (Cargarodon carcharias), a pelagic shark, is often regarded as potentially the most dangerous fish in the ocean.*

## CORE FACTS

- Sharks are fish of the class Chondrichthyes.
- Sharks inhabit all the seas of the world, in both warm and cold waters.
- The shark's body is perfectly adapted for slow continuous swimming.

## CONNECTIONS

- Sharks are unusual among **FISH** in that their **SKELETAL SYSTEMS** are made of **CARTILAGE**.

- Shark **SPECIES** that feed on **PLANKTON** are not generally dangerous or aggressive.

The cat sharks are the largest family with 92 species. These mainly small, deep-water slope sharks feed on invertebrates and fish.

## Distribution

Sharks live in all the major seas of the world. One species, the bull shark (*Carcharhinus leucas*), also enters freshwater rivers. The distribution of most sharks depends on both water temperature and depth. Tropical species are subdivided into benthic (bottom-dwelling) species and the more active pelagic (ocean-going) species.

Benthic sharks are generally small (less than 6⅔ feet, or 2 m, long) and rarely move more than a few miles from where they were born. Tropical and temperate benthic sharks live in fairly shallow warm waters. Cold-water species live in water that has a temperature of 50 °F (10 °C) or less, including water beneath ice floes and in the cold depths of temperate and tropical regions. Pelagic sharks may travel very large distances in one day. They also undertake seasonal migrations, following the changes in water temperature. Their active, migratory lifestyle makes them more widely spread than benthic sharks.

## Body form

The shape of a shark's body and the type of locomotion it uses are determined by its way of life. Most sharks, such as the blue shark (*Prionace glauca*) and the whale shark, are adapted for slow, continuous swimming (see SWIMMING). They have a long snout and large pectoral fins to give lift to their forward motion (guarding against sinking) and control direc-

*The rare whale shark (Rhincodon typus), the largest fish on Earth, lives in most tropical waters.*

tion, and they move by swinging their body and tail from side to side. They also have a slim, streamlined shape: the upper lobe of the tail is bigger than the lower one, and the forward part of the body and the part near the tail are flattened. This body shape reduces water resistance and thus helps to conserve energy. About 11 percent of the body muscle is red muscle, present in a thin layer beneath the skin. It is well supplied with blood and is used for sustained, slow swimming. The inner white muscle is used for sprinting, but because it is poorly supplied with blood, most sharks cannot sprint for long.

In contrast, mackerel sharks (family Lamnidae) and thresher sharks (*Alopias vulpinus*) are adapted for relatively fast cruising, with rapid bursts of acceleration to pursue prey. These sharks have spindle-shaped bodies, with the maximum width well forward on the body. The tail provides most of the propulsion; it is adapted to produce maximum thrust forward with minimum drag.

Mackerel and thresher sharks are often called warm-bodied fish. They have an internal countercurrent system: oxygenated blood coming from the gills (which is cold) passes via a complicated capillary network system alongside the deoxygenated blood returning to the gills, which has been warmed by heat generated in the muscles and gut. This heat-exchange mechanism helps to maintain a relatively high temperature in the red muscle, and therefore these sharks are able to swim at high speeds regardless of changes in water temperature.

Benthic species have little use for moving quickly and so do not need to be streamlined. Many species

have a large head, tapered body, and a thin, weak tail. They have a sinuous, eel-like form of locomotion, undulating the rear of their body and tail.

All sharks have a skeletal cartilage made of flexible, translucent, elastic tissue full of cell spaces (see SKELETAL SYSTEMS). It is formed from proteins enclosing a network of very fine connective collagen fibers. Sharks maintain the osmotic balance of their body fluids by reabsorbing nitrogenous waste into the blood and secreting excess salt from a rectal gland (see EXCRETORY SYSTEMS; SALTS).

Sharks do not have a swim bladder. Their large, oily liver (up to 20 percent of their body weight) helps them control buoyancy. They slowly sink if they stop swimming, but they are better able to cope with the pressure changes associated with depth than are bony fish. Some pelagic sharks must keep swimming to maintain the water flow over their gills for breathing; benthic species actively pump water over their gills, and thus, they can breathe when motionless.

## Feeding

Most sharks are selective feeders. Whaler sharks (*Carcharhinus* spp.) and some of the dogfish sharks (family Squalidae) feed mainly on fish and squid. Other sharks specialize in feeding on echinoderms, crustaceans, or octopuses. The plankton feeders (basking, whale, and megamouth sharks, *Megachasma pelagios*) use modified gill rakers to filter plankton from sea water.

Omnivorous species, such as the tiger shark (*Galeocerdo cuvier*) and sharks that eat marine mammals, such as the great white shark, are generally the most dangerous to humans. Their teeth are not attached directly to the jaw but are embedded in a membrane (the tooth bed) in rows. Behind the front row of teeth lie six or more rows of replacement teeth, which gradually work their way forward as they are required. Most sharks have pointed teeth for seizing prey or sharp-edged teeth for slicing. The powerful jaws are only loosely attached to the skull and can be extended as the mouth opens.

Sharks cannot chew their food, so large chunks are swallowed whole and may remain in the stomach for some time being digested. Because sharks are cold-blooded (they obtain their body heat from the environment), they require less food than a mammal of the same size, which must generate its own body heat (see HOMEOSTASIS).

The sense of smell in sharks is more acute than the sense of sight. The nostrils and eyes of the hammerhead shark (family Sphyrnidae) are located far apart at the ends of the hammer. This arrangement, coupled with the shark's habit of swinging its head from side to side as it swims, is thought to enable the shark to sample smells.

Shark eyes are adapted to detect brief, flickering movements of prey in poor light conditions. In some species, including hammerheads, a membrane protects the eyeball during attack. The great white shark, however, simply rolls its eye backward. Sharks also have other sensory systems, including

*A swell shark (*Cephaloscyllium ventriosum*) hatches from an egg case called a mermaid's purse.*

hairlike cells along the lateral line (present along the side of the shark and branching over its head), which detect the direction and the extent of local water movement; hair cells in the inner ear, which detect low-frequency sounds; and a sensitive electroreceptor system based on gel-filled canals connected to pores in the skin, which allows sharks to detect weak electrical voltages and enables them to locate prey and use Earth's magnetic field for orientation.

## Reproduction and life cycle

Courtship in sharks may be elaborate and last for up to two hours. Fertilization is internal; the male's

---

## SHARK EVOLUTION

Although the scales and teeth of sharks are readily fossilized, the cartilage skeleton rapidly disintegrates unless it is quickly buried by sediments. Thus, the shark fossil record is rather fragmentary. Remains of one of the most ancient and primitive sharks, *Cladoselache*, has been found in rock in Ohio, Kentucky, and Tennessee, dating back nearly 400 million years. *Cladoselache* was about 3 feet (90 cm) long, with a tail fin similar to that of active modern species, suggesting it was fast and agile. Around 350 million years ago, an intense period of shark development produced the ancestors of the modern rabbit fish and rat fish (chimaeroids). In evolutionary terms, little happened to sharks from 300 to 150 million years ago. Most fossil sharks of this time belong to two groups: the freshwater xenacanths and the hypodonts. The hypodonts appeared about 320 million years ago and occupied fresh and salt water throughout the dinosaur era. Modern sharks appeared much later. Fossil mako and mackerel shark teeth dating from 100 million years ago have been recorded. The oldest white shark teeth date from 65 to 60 million years ago. One of the most famous fossils from this period is that of *Carcharadon megalodon*, a great white shark that existed 25 to 10 million years ago. Its teeth were more than 7 inches (18 cm) long and its body length was 39 feet (12 m) or more.

### EVOLUTION

## SHARK HUNTING

Sharks have long been used by humans to supply a variety of needs. The body may be made into fertilizer or eaten and the teeth made into ornaments or weapons; the liver provides oils, vitamin A, and squalene (a hydrocarbon used by the high technology and cosmetics industries); the skin is used for sandpaper and leather; and the cornea of the eye is used as a substitute for human corneas in transplant operations. The main uses of sharks now are recreational fishing and food.

Despite evidence that some species are being overfished, there is virtually no monitoring of global shark fisheries. The barbarous and wasteful practice of finning (cutting fins off live sharks before throwing the sharks back in the water), to supply the fin-soup trade, was banned in U.S. waters in 1993 and in Canadian waters in 1994; however, the practice continues elsewhere. Overall, at least 100 million sharks are deliberately killed each year and millions more are killed accidentally as bycatch in other fishing operations. It seems that sharks need protecting from humans far more than humans need protecting from sharks.

## AT RISK

pelvic fin guides the sperm into the female's vent. Oviparous sharks lay eggs, each encased in a leathery so-called mermaid's purse. In other species, the young are born fully developed. The female keeps the eggs inside her body, where the young feed off their yolk sacs, a process called ovoviviparity. The piked dogfish (*Squalus acanthias*) retains its young in this way for 22 months. The lemon shark (*Negaprion brevirostris*) and some others are viviparous and nourish their young using a type of placenta (see GESTATION).

*The silky shark (*Carcharias falciformis*) is abundant in tropical waters in many parts of the world. This oceanic shark is active and quick moving and can grow to a maximum of 10 feet (3 m).*

### Behavior

Large sharks, such as the great white, are mainly solitary, but many other species spend at least part of their life in groups. Scalloped hammerheads (*Sphyma lewini*) form huge daytime schools off the Californian and Mexican coasts. Social hierarchies exist between species as well as within species; bigger species or individuals are usually dominant. Little is known about shark behavior, including why such groups form; they may help sharks to find food, or to avoid predation (see ANIMAL BEHAVIOR).

Experiments with captive sharks indicate they have a substantial learning capacity. This evidence is supported by the ratio of their brain size to their body weight, which is comparable to that of some birds and mammals. Sharks can be taught to distinguish targets of different shapes and to recognize sound cues. Some sharks have even been taught to take fish from the hand. This ability suggests that the reasoning powers and general awareness of sharks have been greatly underestimated in the past.

Although it is difficult to kill a shark outright because of the organization of its nervous system, the shark's relatively soft skeleton and susceptibility to shock lead to it being easily damaged during capture and transport. Great whites cannot survive in captivity, but scientists are learning how to keep some other species, such as blue sharks.

Sharks sometimes live in association with other fish. This association may be mutually beneficial, for example, in the shark's relationship with remoras, or suckerfish, the smaller fish feed on the parasitic copepods attached to the shark's skin. Other shark parasites are flatworms, roundworms, marine leeches, and tapeworms.

E. BRADSHAW

**See also:** ANIMAL BEHAVIOR; EXCRETORY SYSTEMS; GESTATION; HOMEOSTASIS; JAWS; OCEAN HABITATS; SALTS; SWIMMING; TEETH.

### Further reading:
Allen, T. B. 1999. *The Shark Almanac.* Guildford, Conn.: Lyons Press.
Hamlett, W. C., ed. 1999. *Sharks, Skates, and Rays: The Biology of Elasmobranch Fishes.* Baltimore: Johns Hopkins University Press.

# SHORE HABITATS

**Shore habitats, of differing but specific physical characteristics, are the areas along the coast created by the sea**

*A sandy beach. Shorelines, molded by the activities of the sea, particularly by the action of waves, are diverse environments undergoing continual change.*

For more than three billion years the sea and shore have been locked in endless combat, with land being created in some areas and destroyed in others. The sea is responsible for many of the coastal features present all over the world, from gently sloping beaches to the rocky sculptures formed by the constant pounding of waves against the shore. Over the same length of time, fluctuations in sea level caused by tides have led to Earth's shores being submerged in sea water and reexposed some two trillion times. Coastal areas are therefore constantly undergoing change, sometimes violent change, and would appear to be fairly inhospitable places to live. However, a number of organisms have developed various mechanisms that enable them to survive these conditions, and an amazing diversity of life-forms thrives in coastal areas throughout the world.

## Estuaries

Creatures that live in coastal areas have to adapt to the numerous changes that occur in their habitat. Perhaps the coastal region that is most challenging to survival is an estuary. An estuary is formed at the point where fresh water in a river flowing toward the sea meets the sea water surging inland. The clash of these very dissimilar masses of water produces turbulence, showers of sediment, temperature variations, and even more critical to living things, great swings in the salinity (salt levels; see SALTS) of the water. In the United States, the largest

### CORE FACTS

■ Rocky shores can be divided into four regions: splash zone, high intertidal zone, middle intertidal zone, and low intertidal zone. Each zone has particular physical characteristics.

■ An estuary is formed at the point where fresh water in a river meets the sea. Organisms that live in estuaries are specially adapted to survive changes in salinity and temperature.

■ Large coastal animals, such as seabirds and turtles, often inhabit rocky coastal areas, the sea providing their major source of food.

■ The creatures living on sandy beaches are mainly burrowing animals, such as worms.

## CONNECTIONS

● The **ANIMAL KINGDOM** is well represented in shore habitats by many **INVERTEBRATES, FISH, SEABIRDS,** and **MAMMALS.**

● Shore habitats are increasingly threatened by **POLLUTION** and other human activities.

# SEA TURTLES

The navigational feats accomplished by sea turtles far outweigh even those of the world's greatest human navigators. These marine reptiles can find their way across thousands of miles of open sea to precise locations, with no knowledge of astronomy and without the aid of landmarks, compasses, or other navigational instruments.

There are two families and seven species of sea turtles, the largest of which is the leatherback (*Dermochelys coriacea*), which can reach a length of 8 feet (2.4 m), a weight of 1,300 pounds (590 kg), and a flipper span of 9 feet (2.7 m). Other species include the endangered green turtle (*Chelonia mydas*), the loggerhead (*Caretta caretta*), and the hawksbill (*Eretmochelys imbricata*).

The navigational abilities of sea turtles are clearly apparent in a population of green turtles that feeds in the warm waters off the east coast of Brazil. These animals travel long distances to lay their eggs. The females find their way to the sandy beaches of Ascension Island, a 34-square-mile (88 km2) dot of land in the middle of the South Atlantic Ocean, some 1,370 miles (2,200 km) to the west. What is perhaps even more amazing is that the female turtles return to the same beaches where they were born years earlier.

When the female turtle reaches a point on the beach above the highest tide, she digs a 16-inch (40 cm) deep hole with her hind flippers. She then deposits about 100 leathery shelled eggs into the hole and sweeps sand over them. Afterward she drags herself back to the surf and swims into the sea. Before journeying back to Brazil, she returns to different spots on the beach three more times during the breeding season to deposit clutches of eggs.

Two to three months later, her eggs hatch, and the hatchlings emerge from the sand. Within a very short period of time, perhaps seconds, the hatchlings identify the direction in which the sea lies and scurry toward the water. Ascension Island harbors only one predator of the hatchlings, the frigate bird, which will intercept only a small number of the little turtles. Those that make it to the sea must avoid further water-dwelling predators before eventually finding their way to the feeding grounds off the coast of Brazil.

*The female green turtle leaves the water to lay her eggs on the beach and then returns to the sea, leaving the eggs to hatch some two to three months later.*

estuary is Chesapeake Bay, which stretches 200 miles (322 km) between Maryland and Virginia, covers 1.5 million acres (607,000 ha), and sports 4,000 miles (6,437 km) of ragged shoreline.

In Chesapeake Bay, as in other estuaries, sediment carried by the river from the land is deposited on the riverbed and on the shore when the flow of water slows as it nears the sea. So much sediment is deposited that, in time (some 10,000 years or more), the estuary will fill up and be transformed into land. This sediment consists of inorganic material, such as pieces of rock, phosphorus, and nitrogen compounds, as well as organic substances derived from the remains of dead plants and animals. Thus, creatures that inhabit an estuary have access to a rich source of nutrients.

The salinity of the water and its distribution are crucial factors that determine where in the estuary a particular species of living organism is able to live. Most species, being unable to adapt to salinity changes, are restricted to certain areas of an estuary, depending on their salt-tolerance levels. However, some animals, such as blue crabs (*Callinectes sapidus*), mullet (*Mugil* spp.), and sturgeon (*Acipenser* spp.), are able to adapt to waters of widely different salt concentrations and can live anywhere in the estuary.

Tides and storms frequently—and, in the case of tides, regularly—change the salinity of estuarine waters. The salinity falls as the tide goes out or during a rainstorm. The salinity rises when the tide comes in or during periods of drought. Most organisms that live in estuaries have developed various ways to overcome and survive these changes. For example, protozoans that function best in relatively salty water cope with deluges of fresh water by selectively pumping it out of their body through a small pore. The shells of crustaceans, such as lobsters and crabs, are impervious to water and salts and thus can maintain an appropriate internal salt concentration regardless of changes occurring in their environment.

## Adaptations to estuary life

Among the most prolific animals of the estuary are tiny shrimplike crustaceans called copepods. Around 60,000 of these animals are present in every gallon of Chesapeake Bay water. Copepods share their ever-changing environment with sponges and fish, such as striped bass (*Roccus saxatilis*), herring (*Clupea harengus*), and shad (*Alosa sapidissima*). Just as salmon (*Salmo salar*) are adapted to life in both fresh water and salt water, so too are herring and shad.

The salmon is able to adjust to extreme changes in salinity because of the action of certain tissues or organs in the body of the fish. Salt glands present in the gills are able to concentrate and rid the animal of excess salt (see SALTS). Its highly efficient kidneys can maintain a safe internal concentration of salts. In addition, a salmon's skin is virtually waterproof and saltproof.

The plants of estuaries and tidal marshlands provide the food for many animals, and like the animals of the area, these plants must also be able to survive the changes associated with this habitat. One of the most impressive plant inhabitants of tidal marshlands is cord grass (*Spartina* spp.), which can grow 9 feet (2.7 m) tall. As with most land plants, cord grass cannot tolerate high levels of salt in its tissues, and yet the roots of these plants are constantly submerged in very salty water. These plants possess a number of adaptations that protect them from the salt. For example, the membrane surrounding the roots is selectively permeable and allows water but not salts to be absorbed. Although this membrane is not entirely efficient at excluding salts, any that are absorbed are then excreted from the plant by structures present in the leaves.

## Seacoast

The open sea lies downstream from the estuary and beyond the salt marshes and mangrove wetlands (see the box on page 1494). Wetland water is always salty, but tidal pools can become even saltier as the water evaporates at low tide. Also, a sudden deluge of rain can greatly dilute the salt in the pool; thus, animals that find themselves trapped in a pool must be able to adapt to these changing conditions or they die.

Whether they live in a pool, cling to rocks, or bury themselves in the sand, animals living along the coast are exposed to a number of other hazards, including the force of the waves, which may crush the animal or sweep it away. The ebb and flow of the tide causes the animal to be alternately covered and uncovered with water, the result being its exposure to heat and the drying effects of the air at regular intervals during the day.

## Rocky shores

Rocky coasts can be divided into a number of regions, each with a particular set of physical characteristics. The uppermost region, often called the splash zone, lies beyond the highest tide but is splashed by waves, ocean spray, and rain. This zone is home to black marine lichens, blue-green algae, limpets, and periwinkles. Usually algae would be vulnerable to drying out in exposed conditions, but these primitive organisms possess a slimy covering that protects them from the effects of the Sun and air. This slime makes the rocky splash zone a particularly slippery place along which to walk. The periwinkle, a type of snail, can survive a month without water because it has a structure called the operculum, which it uses to seal off its shell. When the periwinkle is in danger of drying out, the operculum slams shut and traps the remaining water inside the shell.

Down from the splash zone lies the high intertidal zone, in which creatures are covered with seawater for only 10 percent of the time. In this zone, where ocean waves routinely smash into sand and rock, live acorn barnacles, rockweed, and shore crabs. Acorn barnacles possess a hard plate cover-

ing that protects their delicate organs from the onslaught of the waves. The plates also protect acorn barnacles against foraging predators. These primitive crustaceans produce a powerful cementing agent to attach themselves to rocks and so avoid being swept away. Just as periwinkles have structures that seal in moisture during extended periods of dryness, so, too, do barnacles.

Black-shelled mussels (*Mytilus* spp.) abound at the upper level of the next ocean zone, the middle intertidal zone. The creatures in this zone lie below and above the water for equal amounts of time and so are less vulnerable to drying out or being swept away. Goose barnacles, red algae, and sea cabbage are also typical inhabitants of this zone. These organisms spend much of their time covered with sea water, and all are primarily sea creatures that depend on the sea for food and shelter. They are generally more loosely anchored to the seafloor than, say, acorn barnacles because creatures living in the middle intertidal zone do not have to withstand the force of crashing waves.

Farther out to sea lies the low intertidal zone, which is exposed to the air for only 10 percent of the time at most. This region is inhabited by color-

*The high and middle intertidal zones of rocky coasts are often characterized by the presence of rock pools at low tide. These rock pools enable many organisms that could not survive out of the water to remain in these zones during the periods between high tides. Rock pools are extreme environments, however, especially the smaller pools because the temperature and salinity ranges can be considerable.*

ful sea anemones, purple sea urchins, pink coraline algae, kelp, sponges, multihued sea stars, visiting fish, and an abundance of other creatures. Of all the intertidal zones, this one is richest in life-forms.

### Sandy beaches

Although sandy beaches can also be divided into the various intertidal zones, the absence of rocks limits the diversity of animal and plant life, which is restricted largely to burrowing animals such as soft-shelled clams, cockles, ghost shrimp, annelid worms, and various species of crabs.

These creatures are adapted to a life beneath the sand, where moisture tends to persist even at low tide. Few animals live in the dry sand above the high-water mark. The adaptations of sand-burrowing animals vary from one species to another. Mollusks, such as clams and cockles, possess siphons that protrude from the sand so that they can obtain food when the sea water sweeps over them. The siphons indiscriminately take in tiny particles of food as well as larger undesirable bits of sand. When this mixture reaches the animal's gills, they reject the sand particles, which are then expelled through the siphon.

### Large coastal animals

Birds, marine mammals, and reptiles, such as sea turtles, inhabit both rocky and sandy coastal areas and are an important part of the food webs in this habitat, many of them situated high up on the food pyramids (see FOOD WEBS). Although these animals are tied to the land in many ways, primarily for nesting and breeding, for example, the sea is their major source of food.

Birds, such as cormorants and pelicans, visit coastal waters in search of small and medium-sized fish (see SEABIRDS; WATERBIRDS AND WADERS). The mouth pouch of the pelican is perfectly adapted for carrying the fish they catch. Some marine birds, such as sanderlings (*Calidris alba*), patrol beaches where the backwash of water leaves small sea creatures momentarily stranded. Using their sharp pointed beaks, sanderlings pick up their prey before it has the chance to burrow into the sand. Marine mammals, such as seals, sea lions, walruses, and sea otters feed on the abundance of food in the coastal waters.

C. PROUJAN

**See also:** CRUSTACEANS; FISH; FOOD WEBS; OCEAN HABITATS; SALTS; SEABIRDS; TORTOISES AND TURTLES; WATERBIRDS AND WADERS; WETLANDS.

### Further reading:

Bertness, M. D. 1999. *The Ecology of Atlantic Shorelines.* Sunderland, Mass.: Sinauer Associates.
Haslett, S. K. 2001. *Coastal Systems.* New York: Routledge.

## THE MANGROVES OF THE TROPICS

The coastal areas and estuaries of the tropics support populations of living organisms different from those of temperate regions. One of the most distinctive of the tropical and subtropical coastal habitats is the mangrove wetland, which is present in many places around the world, usually between 25 °N and 25 °S latitude. The only mangrove wetland in the United States is situated on the Atlantic and Gulf coasts of southern Florida. In Florida, mangrove wetlands extend from 27 °N to 29 °N latitude.

Appearing to stand on stilts, which are their roots (see the picture at right), mangrove trees are the dominant plants of these wetlands and are well adapted to their environment. However, they expend an enormous amount of energy in maintaining constant salt levels. Like cord grass, mangroves are able to survive in this environment by preventing salt from entering their roots and by excreting excess salt from their leaves. They reproduce by forming fully developed seedlings rather than by producing undeveloped seeds. The seedlings have a greater chance of surviving in the shallow, oxygen-poor water than seeds, which would be unable to germinate under these conditions. The seedlings either put out roots in the sediment underneath the water or float along until they find a place to root.

Most other plants cannot afford to expend so much energy on maintaining salt levels, and thus few plants share the wetlands with mangroves, although a diverse population of animals does. In Florida, these animals include 220 species of fish, such as tarpon (*Tarpon atlanticus*), spotted sea trout (*Cynoscion regalis*), and jack (*Caranx* spp.); 181 species of birds, including the wood stork (*Mycteria americana*), brown pelican (*Pele-canus occidentalis*), and white ibis (*Eudocimus albus*); 24 species of reptiles, such as alligators, turtles, and snakes; and 18 species of mammals, such as wildcats, and rats.

The tangle of mangrove roots also serves another function. The roots trap sediment, which slowly builds up to become dry land. Over the past 50 years, mangrove trees have been planted on about 1,500 acres (607 ha) of land along the edges of Florida's Biscayne and Florida Bays to recover useable land from the ocean.

### A CLOSER LOOK

# SKELETAL SYSTEMS

**Skeletal systems are the structural forms providing a supporting framework for different animals**

Every animal needs to support its body tissues. Without a skeleton, an animal would be just a formless mass of cells. A skeleton is a structural framework that performs three important functions: it provides support to keep an animal from collapsing under its own weight, it helps to protect an animal's soft tissues from damage, and it provides a framework for the action of the muscles. Without a skeleton to push against, muscles would be unable to produce movement.

The common image of a skeleton is the hard and bony structure inside human bodies, but skeletons are not always internal and neither are they always hard. Many simpler animals have a skeleton that is composed mostly of fluid, called a hydrostatic skeleton. Other animals have tough, external shells called exoskeletons. Internal skeletons, such as that of humans, are called endoskeletons.

Each animal's skeleton is adapted to suit its unique characteristics and its environment. Some marine animals have soft, flexible endoskeletons made of a fibrous tissue called cartilage (see CARTILAGE). Most land animals, including amphibians, reptiles, birds, and mammals, have a similar type of endoskeleton called a vertebrate skeleton. Vertebrate skeletons are characterized by a backbone constructed from a chain of bones called vertebrae.

## Hydrostatic skeletons

The hydrostatic skeleton is one of the simplest types of skeleton. It consists of one or more water-filled cavities that support the body by exerting pressure. Body fluids are dominated by water, which, unlike air, is not compressible. When water is squeezed it does not take up less space. Hydrostatic skeletons take advantage of the incompressibility of water. When muscles squeeze the fluid-filled body cavities, the fluid inside is forced to flow. This flow can change the animal's shape and help it move.

Tiny aquatic animals called hydras have hydrostatic skeletons and are able to elongate their bodies and extend their tentacles using hydrostatic flow.

*Jellyfish, such as the compass jellyfish (Chrysaora hysoscella) above, possess hydrostatic skeletons, where the shape of the animal's body is maintained and manipulated by water pressure.*

Inside a hydra's body is a fluid-filled space called the gastrovascular cavity, which functions as the creature's stomach and also as its means of locomotion. The cavity stretches throughout the hydra's body and into the tentacles that the hydra uses to catch prey. When a hydra closes its mouth and contracts muscles in its body walls, the fluid in the gastrovascular cavity is forced from the main part of the body into the tentacles. Like a water balloon that has been squeezed, the hydra's body elongates and the tentacles extend. In this extended position, the hydra is more likely to catch microscopic prey in its tentacles.

Jellyfish, which are closely related to hydras, also have a hydrostatic skeleton (see JELLYFISH, SEA ANEMONES, AND HYDRAS). The domelike shape

## CORE FACTS

- The skeleton performs three major functions: it provides structural support for the body, an attachment point for muscles important in locomotion, and protection for internal organs.
- There are three types of skeletons: hydrostatic skeletons, comprising fluid-filled cavities; exoskeletons, in which the structure is formed from a hardened exterior; and endoskeletons, where the skeleton is within the body.
- All arthropods (including insects, spiders, lobsters, and crabs) have exoskeletons.

## CONNECTIONS

- **SHARKS** have a skeletal system that is composed entirely of **CARTILAGE**.

- The **BRAIN** is protected from damage by the skull **BONE**, cerebrospinal fluid, and layers of tissue.

- The **EVOLUTION** of bones in **BIRDS** has included reduction in bone weight, which enables **FLIGHT**.

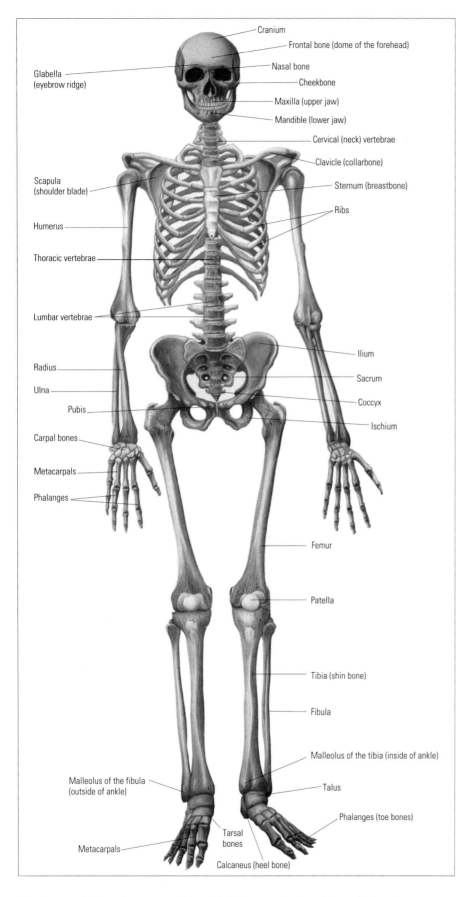

Cranium
Frontal bone (dome of the forehead)
Nasal bone
Glabella (eyebrow ridge)
Cheekbone
Maxilla (upper jaw)
Mandible (lower jaw)
Cervical (neck) vertebrae
Clavicle (collarbone)
Scapula (shoulder blade)
Sternum (breastbone)
Ribs
Humerus
Thoracic vertebrae
Lumbar vertebrae
Ilium
Radius
Sacrum
Ulna
Coccyx
Pubis
Ischium
Carpal bones
Metacarpals
Phalanges
Femur
Patella
Tibia (shin bone)
Fibula
Malleolus of the tibia (inside of ankle)
Malleolus of the fibula (outside of ankle)
Talus
Phalanges (toe bones)
Tarsal bones
Metacarpals
Calcaneus (heel bone)

*The human skeleton is well adapted to the bipedal (standing and walking on two legs) lifestyle into which humans have evolved.*

of the jellyfish is maintained largely by the support provided by the water inside. A jellyfish moves by contracting muscles in the dome. These contractions force water out of the central cavity, called the coelenteron, and propel the jellyfish forward.

Not all animals with a hydrostatic skeleton live in water. The earthworm, for example, is a common land dweller with a hydrostatic skeleton (see ANNELIDS). Earthworms have a fluid-filled body cavity called a coelom, and their movements represent a complex orchestration of hydrostatic flow within this coelom. An earthworm is capable of such precise movement because its coelom is divided into many separate compartments, two in each segment of the earthworm's body. There are two types of muscles in each segment: circular muscles that encircle the body and longitudinal muscles that run through the length of the body. Contracting the circular muscles in a segment causes the segment to elongate; contracting the longitudinal muscles causes the segment to shorten and thicken. By coordinating these contractions, an earthworm can crawl and burrow with remarkable speed and force.

The pressure of the fluid inside the hydrostatic skeleton helps cushion and protect the earthworm's internal organs and keep the body relatively firm. If a worm dries out, it loses this protection as well as the ability to move because, without the pressure of fluid in the coelom to work against, the worm's muscles are useless. When worms are stranded and die on the sidewalk, it is because their hydrostatic skeletons have lost too much water to be able to function properly.

## Exoskeletons

Exoskeletons evolved from hydrostatic skeletons. An exoskeleton is the hardened exterior of an animal. Like a suit of armor, an exoskeleton supports and protects the soft body within. Lobsters, crayfish, crabs, spiders, insects, and all other members of the arthropod phylum have exoskeletons (see ARTHROPODS).

An arthropod's exoskeleton is a coating of dead tissue called a cuticle, which is made up of a mixture of protein and a tough substance called chitin. The entire body is covered by the cuticle; the cuticle even forms the lenses of the eye. In insects the cuticle also extends inside the body and forms the tracheal tubes that insects use to breathe. The cuticle is often waterproof and so helps the arthropod to keep a balance of water in its body.

Around the head and vital organs, an arthropod's cuticle grows thick and hard. In the areas surrounding the joints, however, the cuticle is thin and flexible to allow movement. Inside the exoskeleton, muscles attach to various parts of the inner skeletal surface. Contraction of these muscles causes movement of the flexible joints.

There are some drawbacks to an exoskeleton. For example, having an exoskeleton limits the size that arthropods can attain. The giant insects that are so popular in horror movies are a physical impossibility. Over a certain size, the exoskeleton becomes so bulky that the muscles cannot move it. The strength of the joints also limits an insect's size. For a giant insect to support its weight, its joints would need to be harder than diamond and yet still flexible. Neither the cuticle nor any other known substance is so strong.

Another serious disadvantage of having an exoskeleton is apparent during growth. In the process of growing to full size, an arthropod must periodically shed and recreate its exoskeleton. This shedding of the cuticle is called molting and can take several hours to complete (see MOLTING). Molting is a dangerous time for an arthropod. After the old cuticle is shed, it takes some time for the new one to harden. The soft new shell affords very little protection and is not a firm support for the muscles, the result being that the newly molted arthropod may have trouble moving. Although it may seem inefficient to have a skeleton that requires periodic replacement, arthropods have not suffered from a lack of success—they outnumber every other type of animal on Earth.

Many mollusks, such as clams, oysters, scallops, and mussels, have an extremely hard exoskeleton that is composed largely of calcium carbonate (limestone; see MOLLUSKS). These soft-bodied sea creatures are called bivalves because their hard exoskeletal shells form two parts, called valves.

A hinge of flexible ligament connects the two halves. One or two large muscles, called adductor muscles, open and close the two halves of the shell. Scallops have such strong adductor muscles that they are able to evade predators quickly by clapping together the two halves of the shell. This clapping motion forces water out of the shell and jet-propels the scallop along the sea bottom.

Unlike arthropods, bivalves do not need to molt their shells. As a bivalve grows, it gradually enlarges its shell by adding calcium carbonate to the outer edges. Snails also gradually enlarge their shells. As the snail's body grows, the shell grows with it, coiling around itself in a widening spiral. Other mollusks, such as slugs, have no shell at all.

A coral reef is a cluster of many exoskeletons (see CORALS). Each coral animal, called a polyp, secretes calcium carbonate from its skin, gradually forming a hard, rocklike tube, which connects with the tubes of other coral polyps in the colony. The soft polyp uses this tube for support and protection. The polyp usually partially extends its body and tentacles from

*The outer protective and supportive surface of members of the phylum Arthropoda is called the cuticle. This extracellular layer may be thin and flexible or thick and rigid.*

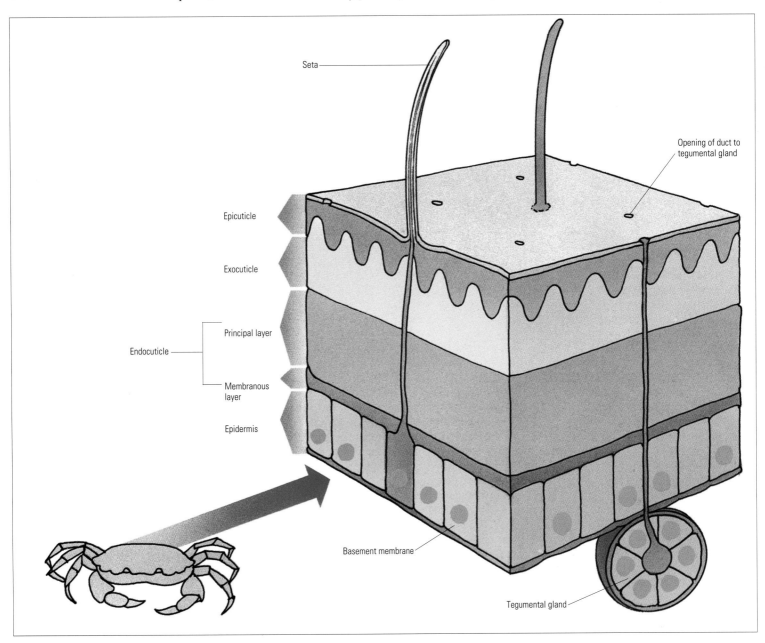

*The mode of growth of some species of coral varies tremendously, flat or rounded skeletal masses or upright and branching growth forms, for example.*

the mouth of the tube to catch microorganisms for food. However, it can contract its body into the tube completely if threatened by predators. Since each generation grows on the skeletons of the old generation, coral reefs can grow to be enormous underwater structures. Coral reefs play an important role because they provide habitats for a wide variety of marine life (see CORAL REEF BIOMES).

## ENDOSKELETONS

An endoskeleton is a hard, supportive structure that is present within the soft flesh of an animal. The principal advantage of an endoskeleton is that it does not require periodic molting because it grows along with the animal. In general, because endoskeletons are lighter than exoskeletons, animals with endo-skeletons are able to grow to larger sizes. The most serious disadvantage of an endoskeleton is that it leaves the soft body tissues relatively exposed. An endo-skeleton can be made of silica (the main component of sand and quartz), calcium carbonate, cartilage, or bone (see BONE; CARTILAGE). Animals with endo-skeletons can be divided into two categories: those without a backbone, called invertebrates, and those with backbones, called vertebrates (see INVERTEBRATES; VERTEBRATES).

### Invertebrates

Sponges are invertebrates with an endoskeleton (see SPONGES). They commonly live on ocean floors and can range in size from less than 1 inch (2.5 cm) to more than 6 feet (1.8 m) in length (see OCEAN FLOOR). A sponge is a filter feeder, obtaining

## SKELETAL ADAPTATIONS

What does a bat have in common with a gorilla? A lot more than one might think. Give or take a few finger bones, ribs, and vertebrae, the two skeletons have all the same elements. The skeleton of most vertebrates follows a very similar pattern. What accounts for the differences in size and shape between the many vertebrates is the size and shape of each individual bone.

For example, all mammals (with the exception of sloths and manatees) have seven vertebrae in their neck. It might be hard to believe that a giraffe has the same number of bones in its neck as a human, a mouse, and a whale, but the difference in appearance is connected to the shape of the bones. A giraffe has highly elongated vertebrae in its neck. By contrast, the neck vertebrae in a whale are short and wide to withstand the huge forces on the body.

Hands are a part of the skeleton that frequently show high degrees of adaptation. A bat has four fingers and a thumb, just as humans do, but a bat's hand is adapted to support a wing membrane. A bat's fingers are longer than its arm bones, whereas the short and delicate human fingers are adapted for grasping and manipulation. In a horse, the finger bones are fused together to form a single hoof, both strong and light, which is appropriate for an animal that gallops at great speed. Sloths have highly modified hands and feet that terminate in long, hooklike claws, which help the sloth to hang beneath tree branches.

Birds have adaptations related to flight (see BIRDS; FLIGHT). Many of a bird's bones are hollow; within them are thin supports that function like girders to strengthen the bone, while adding very little weight. Some hollow bones contain air sacs, extensions of the lungs. Likewise, bird skulls are unusually delicate and full of holes; in the process of evolving from their reptile ancestors, birds have also replaced heavy teeth with lighter, horny beaks (see JAWS).

The skull is another part of the skeleton that varies widely in shape between species. The shape of an animal's skull can reveal a great deal about how the animal lives, what it eats, whether it hunts or is hunted, and at what time of day it is most active. Carnivores typically have a prominent jaw and enlarged canine teeth for piercing prey. A bird's skull ends in a pointed beak for plucking seeds and insects out of tight places. An anteater's skull is unusually long to house its formidable tongue, which can extend up to 2 feet (0.6 m).

The skull of an antelope has a pair of ringed horns to help defend it from predators. Just like deer, bison, and other grazing animals, antelope have their eye sockets on either side of their head to enable them to keep a better watch for predators. Predators, such as lions and owls, have their eyes situated on the front of the face to improve depth perception, which is important for hunting. Animals that are active at night have larger eye sockets to hold the larger eyes needed for good vision when light is scarce.

### A CLOSER LOOK

particles of food by straining water through the many tiny pores in its body. A sponge is covered by a thin layer of cells called epithelial cells, which control the closing and opening of the pores.

Underneath the epithelial cells, the sponge is supported by a skeleton of tiny needles called spicules. Spicules are made of minerals such as calcium carbonate and silica. There may also be a component of the skeleton made of a tough, fibrous protein called spongin. The mineral endoskeleton is hard and forms a lattice pattern, whereas the spongin endoskeleton is soft and flexible. Sponges with a solely spongin skeleton are sold commercially as bath sponges.

Another group of invertebrates that has endoskeletons is the echinoderms, such as starfish, sand dollars, sea urchins, and sea cucumbers (see ECHINODERMS). At first glance, the spiny body of an echinoderm such as a sea urchin might seem to be an exoskeleton. However, the spines of a sea urchin are extensions of a ball-shaped endoskeleton that lies just beneath the skin. Likewise, the spines on the surface of a starfish are protrusions of the internal skeleton. A starfish's skeleton consists of calcium-containing plates that are connected by skin and muscle tissue. None of the echinoderms are particularly flexible; most walk slowly along the seafloor on tiny appendages called tube feet. The tube feet have no rigid skeleton but are moved with a hydrostatic system similar to that of the tentacles of coral polyps.

Squid and octopuses, members of the cephalopod (meaning "head-foot") class of mollusks, are invertebrates with endoskeletons. Attached to their large head are a number of muscular tentacles—8 in the octopus and 10 in the squid. In both types of animals, the head is supported by an internal braincase made of cartilage, although squid also have a small internal support that is made of the same calcium carbonate as are the external shells of other mollusks. Cartilage, a tough but flexible material that contains the protein collagen, provides sufficient support for these animals because the body is already partially supported by the surrounding water. The extra support provided by water enables marine animals to grow larger than they could if they lived on land. For example, a giant squid found dead in New Zealand measured 55 feet (16.8 m) in length.

Both squid and octopuses propel themselves much as animals with hydrostatic skeletons do. Each creature has a mantle cavity—a hollow space in the body that can be filled with water. By expelling water from the mantle cavity in powerful spurts, the squid or octopus can propel itself with surprising speed. The water is expelled through a tube-shaped structure called a siphon. As the siphon can be turned in almost any direction, the animal is able to move wherever it chooses.

## Vertebrates

Although arthropods may be the most numerous type of animal in the world, vertebrates include the largest and the most intelligent animals. Vertebrates have a backbone that consists of elements called vertebrae. The term *backbone* is somewhat deceptive, however, because some vertebrates do not have a single bone in their body. These vertebrates have endoskeletons made entirely of cartilage (see CARTILAGE); they are still grouped as vertebrates, although their vertebrae are not made of bone.

The most primitive of the cartilaginous vertebrates are jawless fish. Jawless fish were the first animals to develop vertebrae. Fossils show that many early jawless fish were covered by bony plates—evidence that endoskeletons may have evolved after exoskeletons. The descendants of these early vertebrates are today's jawless fish, which include the sea lamprey (*Petromyzon marinus*) and the hagfish (*Eptatretus burgeri*). The mouthparts of jawless fish do

*The sea urchin* Echinus esculentus, *shown below, is roughly spherical in shape. This shape is supported by the presence of an endoskeleton composed of circular calcareous plates bearing movable spines.*

*Sharks, such as the gray nurse shark (Eugomphodus taurus) shown above, are vertebrates that possess an endoskeleton composed entirely of cartilage.*

not have hinges and therefore do not form jaws (see JAWS). Lampreys have a mouth resembling a round, toothy sucker, which they use to attach themselves to the bodies of other fish and suck their blood.

Sharks and rays are another group of fish with an endoskeleton made of cartilage. Although sharks are powerful swimmers, their cartilaginous endoskeletons are not particularly mobile. For example, a shark's pectoral fins barely move at all. By contrast, bony fish can often execute a delicate paddling motion with their pectoral fins. While some bony fish swim mainly by flipping their tail, a shark swims by wagging its entire body back and forth. In general, because cartilage is more flexible than bone and provides less support, fish with cartilaginous endoskeletons are constrained to move with smooth, broad motions.

## Structure of bone

For most vertebrates, bone is the primary material of the endoskeleton. Unlike the chitin of an arthropod's exoskeleton, bone is a living material. Within a bone are bone-making cells called osteocytes. The bone that osteocytes make is composed of the protein collagen and the mineral calcium phosphate. In contrast, cartilage is not mineralized and contains just collagen. The addition of calcium

phosphate to bones makes them harder and more rigid than cartilage, although bones retain some of the flexibility associated with collagen.

In a typical bone, the osteocytes are arranged in units called Haversian systems. At the center of each Haversian system is a blood vessel that brings oxygen and nutrients to the nearby bone cells. Surrounding the central blood vessel are concentric layers of bone called lamellae. Part of what makes bones so strong is the arrangement of the Haversian systems. The long Haversian canals are arranged parallel to the direction of greatest stress in the bone, and thus, the bone is strongest where strength is most needed (see BONE).

Most bones are hollow and have a spongy tissue called marrow in the central core. Marrow has several functions; some marrow is simply a repository for energy in the form of fat, while other marrow produces red and white blood cells and antibodies for the immune system. Bones themselves function as a repository for calcium, a mineral that is necessary for the proper functioning of cells throughout the body (see CALCIUM). If calcium intake is low, the blood borrows calcium from the bones.

Most bones are formed first as cartilage tissue. These bones are called endochronal bones. Since cartilage grows faster than bone, vertebrate embryos in the early stages of development have cartilage skeletons until bones gradually develop and replace the cartilage. Some of the cartilage remains as cushioning at the ends of each bone.

A functioning vertebrate endoskeleton cannot consist only of bone. Connective tissue is required to connect and support the bones and to attach muscles to the bones. Cartilage is a form of connective tissue, serving to fill the space between bones and to prevent them from scraping against each other. Meanwhile, bones are connected to one another across joints by fibrous bands called ligaments. Muscles are connected to bone by connective tissue called tendons. Muscle contractions cause the bones to move at the joints (see MUSCULAR SYSTEMS).

There are seven types of moving joints in vertebrate skeletons: ball-and-socket joints, gliding joints, pivot joints, saddle joints, hinge joints, ellipsoid joints, and condyloid joints. Each type of joint allows a particular kind of motion. The joint that connects human legs to the hips is an example of a ball-and-socket joint. The rounded end of the leg bone fits into a round cavity in the pelvis, permitting a wide range of movement.

Other joints restrict motion to a single plane. Hinge joints, such as those found in human fingertips, bend only in one direction. A saddle joint, such as the joint in the thumbs, permits motion in two directions, but does not permit rotation. Rotation is accomplished by pivot joints. Pivot joints in the forearms make it possible for humans to turn doorknobs. In all types of joints, glands called bursae secrete a lubricant called synovial fluid that makes joint motion easier and reduces wear on the surrounding cartilage.

## Structure of a vertebrate skeleton

Vertebrate skeletons consist of three distinct components: the dermal skeleton, the visceral skeleton, and the somatic skeleton. The dermal skeleton, also called the membrane skeleton, originally formed a protective, bony layer around the body of early vertebrates. In almost all vertebrates, the dermal skeleton has dwindled in the process of evolution. Bones that are part of the dermal skeleton grow within membranes and are not preceded by cartilage, as are most other bones. In humans, the only remnants of the dermal skeleton are the collarbone and certain bones in the skull.

The visceral skeleton consists of bones that originally functioned to support the gill arches in fish. All vertebrates are descended from primitive jawless fish, and although many vertebrates do not have gills and thus do not have gill arches, gill arches can be seen in the early stages of development of all vertebrate embryos, even human ones. In vertebrates other than mammals, the bones of the visceral skeleton have become part of the jaw. In

*The bony skeletal system of birds is well adapted for flight. Adaptations include a reduction in the weight of the bones, partly through the evolution of bones that are hollow.*

## BONES OF CONTENTION

An important part of any medical student's schooling is the study of human anatomy—specifically the study of the human skeleton (see ANATOMY). With over two million people in the United States dying every year, it might be imagined that teaching material would not be hard to find. However, human skeletons have become an increasingly rare commodity since 1986, when India banned their export. Before then, India had run a bustling business in human remains, exporting as many as 15,000 skeletons and 50,000 skulls each year to medical schools around the world. The ban was ordered by the Indian government in response to unconfirmed rumors that people were being murdered for their skeletons. Outside India, there are not many companies that prepare human skeletons for sale, so skeletons are now more difficult to come by. In the mid-1980s, a human skeleton could be had for a few hundred dollars; by the mid-1990s an assembled human skeleton could easily cost a few thousand dollars.

Part of what makes human skeletons so expensive is the complicated process of preparing them. Human skeletons are surprisingly fragile, and the flesh must be removed very carefully. The simplest but most labor-intensive way to remove the flesh is by hand, although there are also chemicals that can dissolve the flesh away. An ecologically sound alternative is to use ants or beetles to pick the skeleton clean. Afterward, the bone must be degreased and bleached, a process that helps to preserve it against decay. By any method, the process of curing a skeleton is painstaking. There is an alternative—a plastic model made from a cast of a real skeleton. Plastic skeletons are cheaper and more durable than real skeletons, but they are not fully satisfactory substitutes. Plastic fails to convey the density and remarkably fine structure of real bone; for example, details such as the delicate honeycomb texture or the paper-thin bones of the nasal cavity are not rendered well by plastic.

Another alternative is the use of computer models. Technological advances have made it possible for students to view computer images of real human specimens. These models are generated by modern scanning techniques, such as magnetic resonance imaging (MRI; see MAGNETIC RESONANCE IMAGING) and computer tomography (CT). Computer models are able to show not just bone structure but also the arrangement of tissues and organs. However, a computer is unable to convey properties such as weight, texture, and true color. Where skeletons are concerned, there is no match for the real thing.

## SCIENCE AND SOCIETY

# SKELETAL DISORDERS

The human skeleton is an amazing structure, but it is subject to problems, just as any other tissue in the body. One of the most common skeletal complaints is backache. Most people experience pain in the their back at some time, and this pain has partly to do with having an upright posture. Human quadrupedal ancestors walked on all fours with their backs oriented horizontally. Their vertebrae had only to support the abdomen, and this weight was distributed evenly among the vertebrae. Being bipedal, humans walk with their back oriented vertically, and the vertebrae must support not only the abdomen but the head, shoulders, and arms, too. Since the vertebrae are stacked on top of each other, the weight they bear is distributed unevenly, with increasing amounts of pressure on the lower vertebrae. The *S*-shaped curve of the human spine helps to distribute the weight more evenly, but pain is still most common in the lower back.

The lower back is also the most likely location for a slipped, or prolapsed, disk. The human spine is constructed of more than 30 vertebrae, and between each of these bones is a disk of gel-like material in a fibrous outer covering. These disks help separate the vertebrae and absorb shock. With excessive back strain, the pressure of the vertebrae can cause the outer disk covering to rupture and the gel to be squeezed out, a problem called prolapsing. Without the cushioning of the disk, the vertebrae can exert painful pressure on the surrounding nerves, and in serious cases, the unsupported vertebrae can damage the spinal cord and lead to paralysis.

Arthritis is a skeletal disorder that affects one in every seven people in the United States. It occurs when membranes that surround a joint become inflamed and swollen. This problem can cause other parts of the joint to become swollen in turn, the result being joints that are stiff and painful to move. Persistent arthritis can cause the bones to thicken and distort, and thus, further restrict movement. The small joints in the hands and feet are most often affected and sometimes develop a gnarled appearance. Arthritis can be caused by a microbial infection but is most often caused by the deterioration of the cartilage between bones, a condition associated with old age.

Osteoporosis is a disease that causes bone to deteriorate and become brittle. Bone is a living tissue, and within each bone, there is a continual process of renewal. Some cells break down old bone, while other cells create new bone; it is estimated that the human skeleton is replaced completely every two years by this renewal process. In osteoporosis, the breakdown of old bone occurs faster than bone replacement, and the result is a loss of bone mass. Osteoporosis weakens bones and makes them more prone to fracture. More than 600,000 bone fractures each year in the United States are attributed to osteoporosis.

Women are particularly susceptible to osteoporosis. After menopause, women experience a drop in the level of estrogen, a hormone that contributes to bone maintenance. This drop in estrogen can cause the bones to deteriorate. Being of slighter build to begin with, women generally have less bone mass to spare. For this reason, some doctors prescribe estrogen to postmenopausal women to prevent the onset of osteoporosis. However, many doctors

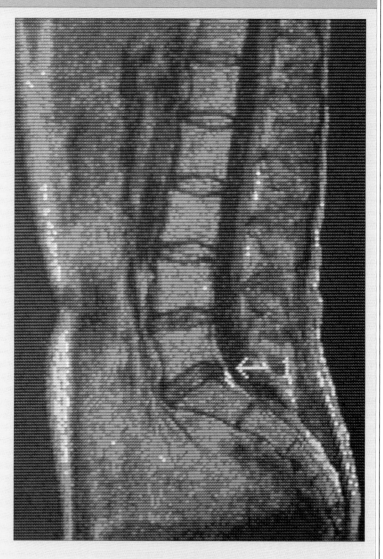

*A slipped disk, a common back complaint, shown in the picture above, results from excessive pressure on the vertebrae.*

believe that osteoporosis can best be prevented by a calcium-rich diet and exercise, both of which strengthen bone.

A related bone disease is osteomalacia, also called rickets. Rickets is a softening and weakening of the bone that results from vitamin D deficiency. Vitamin D plays a critical role in the maintenance of the skeleton, as it enables the body to absorb calcium from food. Calcium is the principal strengthening agent in bone. If insufficient calcium is deposited in the bones, they can grow weak, tender, and painful. Extreme rickets can result in curvature of the bone, making walking difficult. Rickets was once a common childhood disease, but it can easily be prevented by a diet rich in calcium and vitamin D.

## AT RISK

mammals, the bones of the visceral skeleton have transformed into the auditory ossicles, the tiny bones in the inner ear that help transmit sound.

The somatic skeleton is the largest component of the vertebrate skeleton. It is subdivided into an axial and an appendicular skeleton. The axial skeleton was the first part of the somatic skeleton to evolve. Included in the axial skeleton are the bones of the head, the backbone, the ribs, and the tail. The appendicular skeleton includes the limb bones and the girdles that attach them to the backbone.

The basic form of a vertebrate skeleton is remarkably similar for a wide variety of vertebrate animals. All bony vertebrates have a skull and a

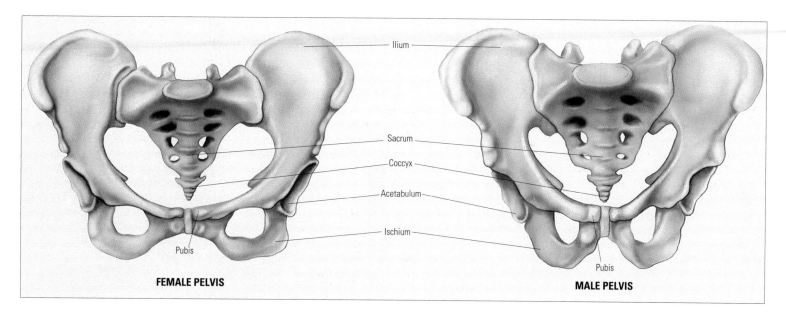

Ilium

Sacrum

Coccyx

Acetabulum

Ischium

Pubis

**FEMALE PELVIS**

Pubis

**MALE PELVIS**

number of vertebrae that connect the skull to the rest of the skeleton. Vertebrates can have forelimbs, hind limbs, neither, or both. Snakes have neither forelimbs nor hind limbs, while manatees, whales, and some salamanders have only forelimbs.

The forelimbs are attached to the backbone by the pectoral girdle. In mammals, the pectoral girdle is formed by two shoulder blades, or scapulae. The human forelimb contains an arm bone called the humerus, which fits into a cavity in the scapula to form a ball-and-socket joint. At the other end, the humerus connects to the forearm bones called the radius and the ulna. At the far end of the radius and the ulna, wrist bones (carpals) connect the forearm to the hand, which consists of five bones called metacarpals. The finger bones are called phalanges. There are two phalanges in the thumb and three in each of the four fingers.

The hind limbs are attached to the backbone by the pelvic girdle. In humans the pelvic girdle is formed by three bones that are fused together: the ilium, the ischium, and the pubis. Together, these three bones form a cavity into which fits the ball end of the leg bone (femur). In women the pelvis is wider to allow passage of a baby during childbirth.

Each hind limb consists of a femur and two shin bones called the tibia and the fibula. The front bone, the tibia, bears almost all of the body's weight. The role of the fibula is to anchor the muscles that move the foot and toes. The tibia and fibula are supported by anklebones called tarsals. Metatarsals and phalanges make up the bones in the feet. In humans the number of phalanges in the feet is identical to the number in the hand: two in the big toe and three in each of the other toes.

## Upright posture

Even though the basic structure of the skeleton may be similar for all vertebrates, each animal has unique adaptations to its skeleton. Most of the adaptations of the human skeleton are associated with an upright posture. Although some other animals are able to walk on two legs for limited periods,

few mammals other than humans are adapted for a permanently bipedal (using two feet for standing and walking) lifestyle.

Upright posture has resulted in changes in the shape of the human backbone. In quadrupedal animals, or animals that walk on four legs, the backbone is either straight or it forms a single arch. In humans, the backbone is S-shaped. This shape helps to cushion the weight that the vertebrae must support. If the vertebrae were simply stacked one on top of another, the shock of motions such as running and jumping would be more likely to jar the body and cause injury. The gentle S-shaped curve of the backbone helps it flex to absorb this shock, as a spring does.

Another adaptation associated with upright posture is the unique shape of the human pelvic girdle. In the primate relatives, the pelvic girdle is longer and cocked at an angle, and the legs are roughly perpendicular to the backbone. The long, angled pelvic bone provides a point of attachment for the muscles that move the legs. In humans the legs are roughly parallel to the backbone. The human pelvic girdle is shorter and rounder and oriented vertically. This arrangement balances the weight of the upper body directly over the legs.

Human hands and feet are also different from those of primate relatives (see FEET; HANDS). In other primates, the hands and feet are often similar because they share the same functions; for example, both appendages participate in the tasks of weight bearing and grasping. Human hands and feet are specialized. The only job of the human foot is to support the weight of the body, and therefore, human feet are larger and sturdier than human hands, with longer bones to serve as levers. Freed from the necessity of bearing the weight of the body, human hands have developed into highly precise gripping instruments. Part of what makes the human hand so dexterous is its long and mobile thumb. A human thumb is able to touch each of the fingertips. The thumb of a close human relative, the chimpanzee, is much shorter and less mobile.

*The structure of the pelvic girdle and its vertical orientation are two important human adaptations that enable bipedalism and an upright posture. The female pelvis is wider than the male pelvis to ease childbirth.*

# THE ELEPHANT MAN

The skeleton of Joseph Carey Merrick—the Elephant Man—stands alone as the most extreme example of human skeletal deformity in modern history. Merrick was born a seemingly normal child in 1862, in Leicester, England, but by the age of 18 months, he began to show signs of a growing deformity. A bony lump appeared on his forehead, his skin grew loose and rough, and his feet and right arm grew disproportionately large.

These deformities worsened as the years wore on. Merrick's head grew enormous, to a circumference of 3 feet (1 m). Tumorous growths of bone and flesh distorted his skull and face so that speech and facial expression were almost impossible (see below). Although his left arm was perfect, his right arm hung like a useless club, three times as large as the left arm and measuring 12 inches (30 cm) around at the wrist. Folds of cauliflower-textured skin hung from his body.

Unable to work, Merrick earned money by exhibiting himself in a freak show as the Elephant Man. This show attracted the attention of a London physician, who eventually had Merrick admitted as a permanent resident of the London Hospital. Merrick's disease mystified medical science, and absolutely nothing could be done to help him. He died of suffocation in his sleep at the age of 28; the weight of his giant head caused the collapse of his windpipe.

In the years after Merrick's death, doctors thought he had suffered from a disease called neurofibromatosis. Mild forms of neurofibromatosis occur quite commonly, affecting an estimated 100,000 Americans. In most cases, the only symptom of neurofibromatosis is coffee-colored splotches on the skin called café au lait spots, but in more serious cases, the disease causes the growth of tumors throughout the body and can lead to irregular bone development. However, neurofibromatosis is not known to cause deformities as severe as those of Joseph Merrick, and he did not have the café au lait spots that are present in 95 percent of people with neurofibromatosis.

Specialists now think that Joseph Merrick more likely suffered from an extremely rare genetic disorder called proteus syndrome. The cause of proteus syndrome is unknown, but the disease is characterized by excessive growth of the bones and flesh, excessive growth of the head, and severe curvature of the spine. Even now, there is no treatment for this rare and poorly understood disease.

The human skeleton is a walking testimony to the advantages of not specializing. The human skeleton is not adapted for excellence in any particular skill. Fish are better swimmers, antelopes are better runners, groundhogs are better diggers, and monkeys are able to climb trees with much greater agility. However, by being able to carry out all of these activities to some degree, humans as a species have managed to be extremely successful.

P. TESLER

**See also:** ANATOMY; ANNELIDS; ARTHROPODS; BIRDS; BONE; BRAIN; CALCIUM; CARTILAGE; CONNECTIVE TISSUE; CORAL REEF BIOMES; CORALS; ECHINODERMS; EVOLUTION; FEET; FLIGHT; HANDS; INVERTEBRATES; JAWS; JELLYFISH, SEA ANEMONES, AND HYDRAS; MAGNETIC RESONANCE IMAGING; MOLLUSKS; MOLTING; MUSCULAR SYSTEMS; OCEAN FLOOR; SHARKS; SPONGES; VERTEBRATES.

**Further reading:**
Brusca, R.C., and G. J. Brusca. 2002. *Invertebrates.* 2nd ed. Sunderland, Mass.: Sinauer Associates.
Hildebrand, M., and G. E. Goslow. 2001. *Analysis of Vertebrate Structure.* 5th ed. New York: John Wiley.
Manohar, M., P. Panjabi, and A. White. 2000. *Biomechanics in the Musculoskeletal System.* London: Churchill Livingstone.

# SKIN

**Skin, the protective outer covering of vertebrates, connects and protects but also performs numerous functions**

Bird feathers, fish scales, and insect cuticles are all products of specially adapted skin. Every living creature is covered in an outer garment, a continuous layer that holds together body fluids and organs, serves as a protective barrier against the outside world, and allows the organism to survive in and communicate with its surroundings. This body covering—the integument in invertebrates and the skin of vertebrates—consists of cells that combine to form a tissue called epithelium. Epithelium that forms the outermost layer is called epidermis.

## CORE FACTS

- All creatures have an outer covering that holds together their body tissues and organs, protects them, and communicates changes in the environment. In vertebrates, this covering is called skin.
- The invertebrate epidermis is usually only one cell deep; vertebrate skin has many layers.
- Secretory cells in invertebrate epithelium produce a protective cuticle, lubricant, or adhesive; different types of secretory glands in the vertebrate epithelium produce sebum, sweat, and in the case of female mammals, milk.
- The skin is the human body's largest and heaviest organ.

## Invertebrate integuments

In most invertebrates the epidermis is a single layer of epithelial cells. These epithelial cells secrete a noncellular cuticle. The cells are tall and stand side by side, with their long axes perpendicular to the cuticle. Some of these cells are sensory (sensitive to touch, pain, and temperature), some are glandular (secreting substances), and some have stinging properties; others produce bristles, ridges, or other growths. The cuticle secreted by this layer serves many functions but it is mainly a barrier or protective armor. In insects and crustaceans, it acts as an exterior skeleton (see SKELETAL SYSTEMS).

Insects have the most elaborate cuticle of all invertebrates. Their exoskeleton is a tough, hard integument made of fibers of chitin, a substance secreted from the epidermis. The chitin is embedded in a network of protein and stiffened (sclerotized) into a type of natural plastic. It is shaped into rigid plates covering each body segment and linked to neighboring segments by flexible fibers. In addition to acting as an outer skeleton to which muscles are attached, the insect cuticle is a waterproof covering that contains the body fluids and prevents drying. Ducts opening out onto it allow epidermal glands to discharge waterproofing and lubricating secretions. The insect cuticle contains cells capable of producing

*A fingerprint, the pattern of ridges and furrows in the skin's epidermal layer on the surface of the fingertips, is thought to be unique to each person.*

## CONNECTIONS

- The skin of many **MAMMALS** is covered by a protective layer of **HAIR**.

- Dark skin is less likely to be damaged by **ULTRAVIOLET RADIATION** from the Sun.

- **MOLTING**, or the shedding of old skin, takes place in some **REPTILES**.

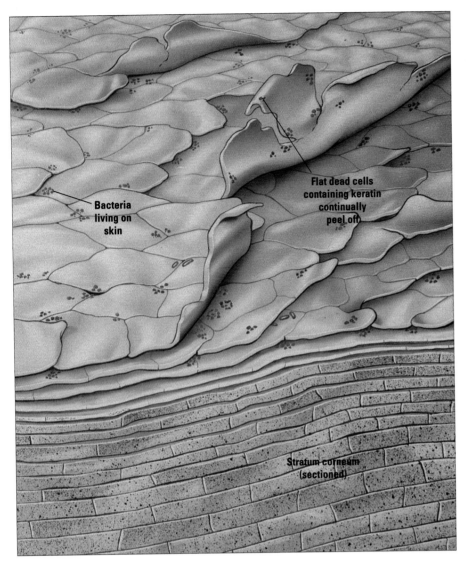

**Bacteria living on skin**

**Flat dead cells containing keratin continually peel off**

**Stratum corneum (sectioned)**

*The outer layer of skin in most vertebrates is composed of dead or dying cells. These cells are usually shed and replaced in a continuous process, the new cells rising from the lower epidermis to replace those that have fallen away.*

intervals, depending on the species, and replaced by new cells rising from the lowest epidermal level, just above the dermis. In humans the epidermis renews completely every 28 days. The new epidermis is identical to the old, with its unique wrinkles, lines, and imperfections. The dermis, which is highly developed in mammals, consists mainly of collagen and other fibrous tissue richly supplied with blood and lymph vessels, nerve endings, fat globules, glands, and smooth-muscle cells. It supplies the epidermis with nutrients and enables it to respond to environmental signals, such as temperature, injury, or moisture changes.

One major function of skin is physical protection: the intact epidermis prevents foreign bacteria or viruses from infecting or growing on the organism, keeps out other foreign materials, and keeps in body moisture and vital fluids. Another function is temperature regulation, alerting mammals and birds to the need to raise or lower their body temperature and informing reptiles, amphibians, and fish (which rarely regulate their body temperature by metabolism; see METABOLISM) to move to colder or warmer surroundings. The skin acts as a surface from which heat may be obtained or dumped into the surrounding air or water. Birds have feathers, which form in much the same way as hairs do but provide much more effective insulation than fur. Reptiles have dry, scaly skin that is composed of dead, dry cells containing keratin. Because the skin is thick and dry, water does not evaporate easily from its surface, so reptiles are able to preserve water and heat. Some reptiles have a set of scales hard enough to be considered armor, which protects them from predators. Some skin, such as that of certain tropical frogs, has poison glands as added protection.

Skin not only separates and protects the organism from the environment but also interprets and communicates changes in that environment. It is not surprising, therefore, that the process of evolution has produced dramatic differences in the skin of different classes and orders of vertebrates, depending on their different habitats.

## Mammalian skin

A distinguishing characteristic of mammals is their hair, produced from follicles in the dermis and consisting of a form of keratin (see HAIR). Keratin is also present in the dead cells of the outer epidermis, where it serves as a barrier to water loss and the invasion of foreign chemical substances and organisms.

The mammalian dermis has many different glands. Hair follicle glands secrete the materials needed to produce and sustain individual hairs as well as oils that keep the skin waterproof. Human sweat glands provide an effective cooling system, and similar glands control temperature in horses and cattle. Cooling occurs when sweat evaporates. Evaporation requires energy, which is supplied in the form of body heat. Dogs have few sweat glands, so they pant, releasing body heat by the evaporation of saliva in the mouth or tongue. Insulation is a problem

bristles, scales, claws, or wing structures, depending on the species. The insect cuticle is shed periodically to allow the insect to grow a new replacement. As its body grows, it will again molt the old cuticle.

After insects, mollusks are the second largest class of invertebrate animals, including clams, oysters, mussels, snails, squid, and other soft-bodied animals, usually with a hard external shell. The molluskan epidermis often secretes a mucous slime that defends against predators. The shell is made from other secretions combined with minerals, as are the pearls present in oysters. Other epidermal cells secrete threads that enable some mollusks to anchor themselves to the seafloor.

### Vertebrate skins

All vertebrates have two skin layers: the relatively thin epidermis and the far thicker, tougher underlying dermis. The epidermis is several cells thick, arranged parallel to the outer layer of skin. This outer layer consists of dead cells composed chiefly of keratin, the protein present in hair, nails, claws, beaks, feathers, scales, and quills. The skin of land-dwelling vertebrates of all types—mammals, birds, and reptiles—is far more complex than that of water-dwelling vertebrate species. The outer layer of dead or dying cells is shed, or molted, at various for polar aquatic animals. They lose heat extremely quickly in cold water. This problem is overcome by the production of a layer of blubber in the dermis. Most mammals have dermal glands that produce odors essential for sexual communication.

## Human skin

Very fine but plentiful body hair is a distinctive feature of human skin, the largest (about 18 square feet, or 1.67 m$^2$) and heaviest (about 9 pounds, or 4 kg) organ in the human body. Human skin changes over time; there is minimal hair growth, sweating, and sebaceous gland activity in infants and children, which increase at adolescence and decline with age.

As skin ages and is affected by exposure to the wind and Sun, it becomes drier, less elastic, more loose, flabby, and wrinkled. Thickness of skin varies far more widely in humans than it does in other mammals, from 1/16 inch (1.6 mm) on the soles of the feet, to 1/40 inch (0.6 mm) on the eyelids. There is also variation in hairiness, most hair being on the head, eyebrows, armpits, and pubic areas and none on the lips, forehead, and upper cheeks.

## Epidermis

The epidermis contains melanocytes, cells that produce a dark pigment called melanin, which, when combined with the reddish tinge of blood from

vessels in the dermis, produces the skin surface coloring (see PIGMENTATION). Melanin protects the skin from the Sun's ultraviolet radiation; it is absent in the hereditary condition albinism.

Coloring differences between individuals and between members of different human races is caused by the activity of their melanocytes—that is, the amount of melanin the body produces.

## SKIN GRAFTS

The skin is a vital organ that protects the body from infection, and thus, loss of significant amounts of epidermis through burns or disease can be very serious. The exposed dermis must be covered by a new epidermis, and this is achieved through skin grafting, the transplanting of new epidermis from one part of the body to another or from one person (a donor) to another. Generally, a donor graft will be unsuccessful unless the donor is an identical twin, although incompatible skin grafts will last a few weeks, providing temporary protection. Surgeons also use artificial skin grafts made of animal fibers and silicon plastic as a temporary measure. The problem of skin graft rejection by the patient's immune system might be overcome by a promising but still experimental approach, in which samples of the patient's uninjured skin are used to grow sheets of genetically identical epidermis. The discovery of a substance called epidermal growth factor (EGF) has made this technique possible. This chemical is placed in cell cultures with the patient's normal epidermal cells to promote growth. At present, this procedure is restricted to patients with life-threatening skin problems.

*This cross-section of mammalian skin shows the relative positions of the structures within the dermis and the epidermis.*

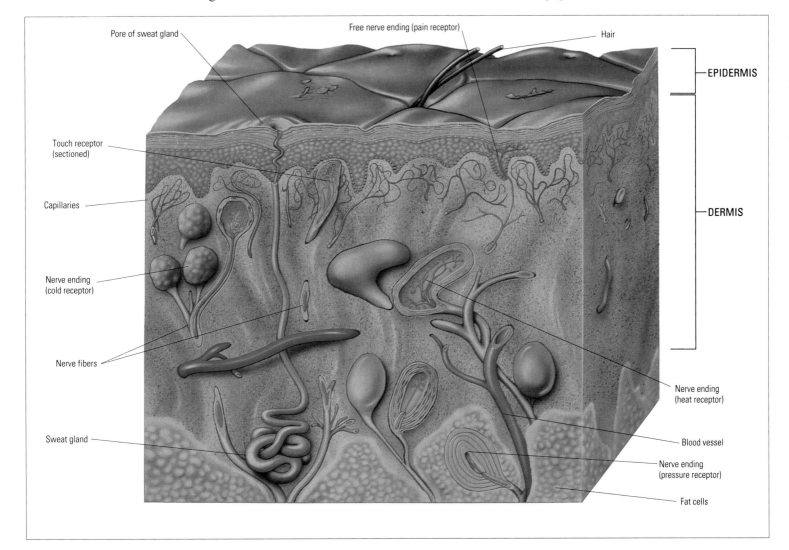

Pore of sweat gland

Free nerve ending (pain receptor)

Hair

EPIDERMIS

Touch receptor (sectioned)

Capillaries

Nerve ending (cold receptor)

Nerve fibers

Sweat gland

DERMIS

Nerve ending (heat receptor)

Blood vessel

Nerve ending (pressure receptor)

Fat cells

## SKIN COLOR

Differences in skin color and other racial characteristics probably arose as a result of the geographical isolation of large populations of early humans in widely varying climatic regions. Some of these differences may have had adaptive value and were therefore favored by evolutionary selection. For example, dark skin protects against ultraviolet radiation in tropical areas, while fair skin is less likely to suffer frostbite in cold regions. Fair skin also enhances vitamin D synthesis when sunlight is less intense at high latitudes in winter.

The isolation of early humans led to the concentration of some distinctive characteristics within Asian, African, European, and other populations. However, in recent centuries, geographical isolation has broken down to a large extent, and humans have interbred extensively so that the genetic makeup of fewer and fewer groups can be called pure. Of the 30,000 to 50,000 genes in the human species, there is no single one for skin color, hair type, or facial contours. The visible differences between the races, including skin color, are the result of the interactions of many genes, and thus, children of a white European parent and a black African parent usually have intermediate skin coloring.

### A CLOSER LOOK

The epidermis also contains the pores, or surface openings, of sweat glands and hair follicles.

Scientists have learned that immunological and metabolic activity take place in the epidermis. Epidermal cells manufacture thymopoietin, a hormone that helps in the formation of disease-fighting white cells, which are abundant in the skin. Epidermal cells also produce interleukin-1, a protein needed for the normal functioning of T-cells, a type of cell in the immune system (see IMMUNE SYSTEMS; IMMUNOLOGY).

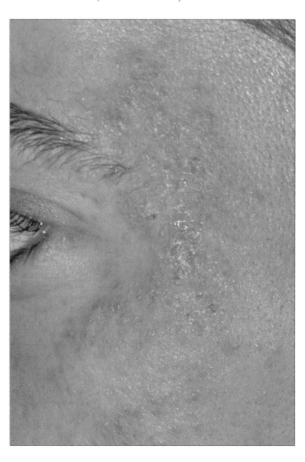

*An individual with eczema may develop a rash, accompanied by small blisters that become crusted. Eczema is an inflammation of the skin, the cause of which is often unknown, although it sometimes results from an allergy.*

Although the sweat glands lie deep in the dermis, the tubes through which they discharge water to cool the skin lie within and are made by the epidermis. The greatest number of sweat glands are present on the palms and soles; the back has the fewest. The lower epidermal layers contain nerve endings and sensory receptors that are capable of perceiving touch, cold, warmth, and pain.

### Dermis

The dermis is thicker and more complex than the epidermis. It consists of a matrix of collagen and other fibrous tissue and contains hair follicles, blood and lymph vessels, nerves, fat globules, and sebaceous glands, which supply the living epidermis that lies above with nutrients, disease-fighting properties, and sensory perception. Scientists believe that human skin is more sensitive than other mammalian skin. The sebaceous glands produce sebum, a fatty substance that is released into the hair follicles and discharged onto the skin surface and thus helps keep it moist, soft, and supple.

### Ecology of skin

The healthy skin surface is home to billions of microscopic organisms, mostly bacteria and some fungi. Almost all are harmless; some are even helpful because they compete with and usually prevent the growth of harmful, disease-causing bacteria. Intact skin is usually a mechanical barrier against infection. Ordinary washing temporarily removes most microorganisms from the skin, but an absence of washing does not result in an increase in their numbers. Overuse of antibiotic medications can kill these harmless bacteria, leaving the body more prone to attack by harmful disease-causing ones.

### Skin and disease

The skin itself is subject to disease, which can be caused by an injury from heat, cold, sunlight, or chemicals; an infection; an allergy or autoimmune disease; cancer; or abnormalities of body chemistry, the nervous system, or the emotions. Acne is probably the most common skin disease. It almost always begins at puberty, when the hair follicles and sebaceous glands are stimulated by the sudden increase in the production of sex hormones. Overproduction by these glands and follicles and the presence of certain bacteria result in the development of the distinctive pimples of acne.

R. STILLER

**See also:** ANEMIA; IMMUNE SYSTEMS; IMMUNOLOGY; METABOLISM; PIGMENTATION; SKELETAL SYSTEMS; TRANSPLANTS.

### Further reading:
Callen, J. P., K. E. Greer, A. F. Hood, A. S. Paller, and L. J. Swinyer, eds. 1997. *Color Atlas of Dermatology.* Philadelphia: Saunders.
Mackie, R. M. 1999. *Healthy Skin: The Facts.* New York: Oxford University Press.

# SLEEP

**Sleep is a natural state of lowered consciousness and reduced metabolism during which the body rests**

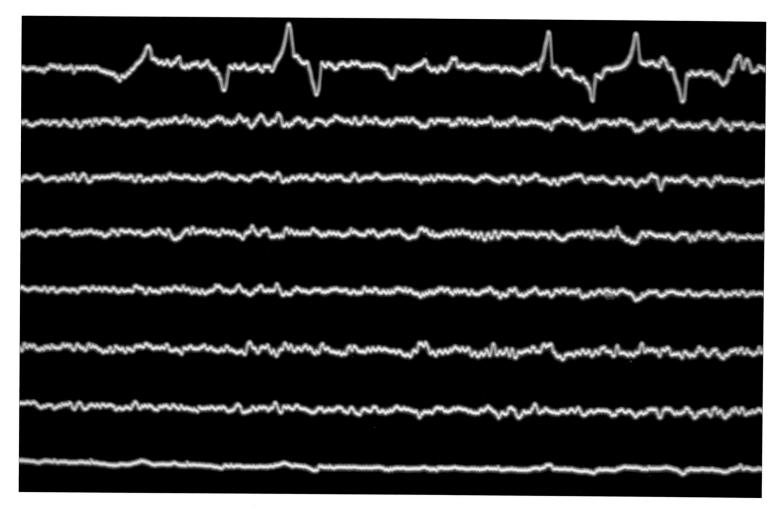

Many people think that when they sleep their body is at rest. However, although sleep certainly provides rest for the physical body, taking up about one-third of an average person's life, the brain is far from resting during the hours of sleep. The brain is highly active, although the activity is different from the type of activity that goes on during waking hours. The brain is so important in controlling sleep that scientists believe that sleeping occurs only in more highly evolved vertebrates with fairly well-developed cerebral cortices (the outer parts of the cerebrum; see BRAIN).

Scientists still do not know exactly what the brain does during sleep, but most speculate that it uses the time for some form of reorganization, or "housekeeping." Some scientists also believe sleep evolved as an energy-conservation mechanism because during sleep the muscles relax, the heart rate and respiration slow down, and the body temperature falls. Sleep can also help animals avoid extremes of temperature. Many desert animals, for example, sleep out of the Sun during the day when it is too hot to feed.

Whatever sleep is for, humans cannot do without it. Volunteers have stayed awake for up to six or seven days without irreversible effects, but in laboratory experiments, mammals that are not allowed to sleep eventually die.

All animals pass through two distinct types of sleep: deep, or quiet, sleep and active sleep. In humans, scientists have identified four levels, or stages, of sleep by measuring brain electrical activity using an electroencephalograph (EEG), a device that detects tiny electrical currents in the brain using electrodes attached to the scalp.

*This electroencephalogram (EEG) shows electrical activity in several areas of the brain, the heart, and facial muscles of a subject in REM sleep.*

## CORE FACTS

- The brain is highly active during sleep; its activity can be measured using an electroencephalograph (EEG), which detects electrical currents in the brain.
- There are four stages of sleep, ranging from Stage I (light sleep) to Stage IV (deep sleep), and sleepers move through the cycle three or four times a night.
- Stage I sleep, with its fast, active brain waves, is accompanied by rapid eye movement (REM).
- People tend to move back and forth between REM sleep, during which they dream, and non-REM sleep.
- Sleepers do not move about during REM sleep, because motor signals from the brain to the muscles are interrupted by the brain stem.

## CONNECTIONS

- Sleep is the most profound change in **ANIMAL BEHAVIOR** that most **VERTEBRATES** regularly experience, during which the body's **METABOLISM** slows down.

- To avoid **PREDATION** by daytime hunters, many **MAMMALS** adopt a **NOCTURNAL LIFE**.

## SLEEP DEPRIVATION

Experts believe that millions of Americans are getting too little sleep. The problem is the same in all industrialized nations but more so in the United States than in Europe. Only in Japan, where 12-hour workdays are common, is the sleep problem worse.

Evidence for insufficient sleep includes the fact that, according to the U.S. Department of Transportation, 20 percent of all drivers have dozed off at least once while driving, and at least 200,000 traffic accidents a year may be sleep related. Thousands of industrial accidents can also be blamed on drowsy workers, and overworked hospital interns make disastrous mistakes with their patients. Teachers report an increasing number of students nodding off in class; those who stay awake often suffer from reduced attention span and have difficulty remembering information taught during their lessons.

The problem began with the invention of the electric light, which enabled people to stay up after sunset. It has grown worse with the advent of movies, radio, video games, computers, and especially, television, with late-night talk shows and all-night movies. In two-career families, parents stay up later to have time with their children and thus keep the children up later in the process. Teenagers may be more sleep deprived than adults because they need more sleep: nine-and-a-half hours compared with eight hours for adults.

Daytime drowsiness is the most obvious symptom of a lack of sleep. Other signs include not being able to wake up without an alarm clock or falling asleep the moment one's head hits the pillow.

### SCIENCE AND SOCIETY

When a person is awake with his or her eyes open, the EEG records a very rapid, low-voltage wave pattern because many brain cells are firing action potentials (see NERVOUS SYSTEMS). The voltage is low because the cells in different parts of the brain are firing at different times. When the eyes are closed, the pattern changes to a regular wave (alpha wave), rising and falling about 8 to 12 times per second. The voltage is higher because many brain cells are firing at the same time.

### Sleep stages

It usually takes about 15 minutes to fall asleep. The sleeper first enters a light sleep called stage I, in which the EEG records a wave (theta wave) that has a frequency of four to eight cycles per second. Stage II sleep follows very quickly, with the appearance of spindle waves, a short burst of faster waves occur-

*The diagram below shows the likely movement between different stages of sleep during a normal sleep cycle.*

ring every so often. In stage III sleep, the theta-wave frequency slows to two to four cycles per second, with an occasional spindle. Stage IV sleep shows a frequency of between 0.5 to 2 cycles per second.

A sleeper usually descends rapidly through these stages in the first 30 minutes after falling asleep because the slowing down of brain waves is fairly continuous. Stage IV sleep, the deepest sleep, lasts for about an hour. Someone awakened during this period of sleep is usually groggy and needs several minutes to become fully alert.

After stage IV sleep, the sleeper slowly moves back through the stages, usually to stage I, then after 30 minutes or so, down again to stage II or stage III. The cycle repeats three or four times during the night. After the first descents to stages III and IV, the sleeper spends little time in deep sleep, spending the rest of the night moving between stages I and II.

After the first descent, stage I sleep changes in a very important way. Each time stage I sleep occurs during the rest of the night, the brainwaves are fast and active, very much like the waking pattern, and are accompanied by rapid eye movement (REM). Electrodes attached to the corners of volunteers' eyes measure the electrical signals to the muscles that move the eyes. People move back and forth between REM and non-REM sleep throughout the night, each cycle taking about 90 minutes.

During sleep a person's breathing and heart rate slow down and the blood pressure drops compared with waking levels. However, all of these indicators increase slightly during REM sleep. People awakened during REM sleep usually report that they have been dreaming; if they are awakened during non-REM sleep, they do not report dreaming.

Time-lapse photography of sleeping volunteers shows the greatest amount of body movement just before and after REM sleep but very little during it. A mechanism in the brain stem (the part of the brain that connects to the spinal cord) cuts off motor signals from the brain to the muscles; thus, people do not usually act out their dreams.

Both REM and non-REM sleep appear to be essential. If volunteers in sleep laboratories are awakened whenever they go into either REM or non-REM sleep, they eventually spend many extra hours

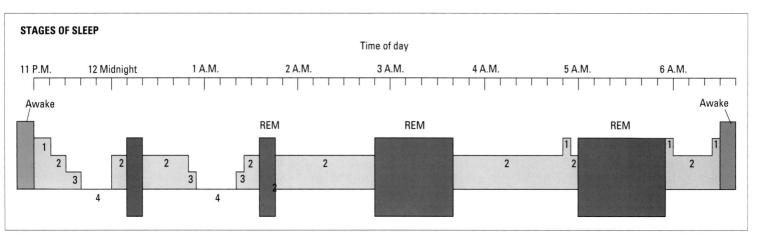

**STAGES OF SLEEP**

in either REM or non-REM sleep, respectively, to make up for the loss. Birds and mammals pass through the same stages of sleep as humans and show the characteristic brain-wave patterns; just as humans do, they pass through a period of REM sleep.

## Length of sleep

The sleep cycle changes through life. Younger people generally need more sleep than older people, although some young people can sleep very little and suffer no ill effects. Newborn babies sleep for about 16 or 17 hours a day, waking and sleeping on a 90-minute cycle; about half of each sleep period is REM sleep.

During the first few months of life, these short cycles combine until at about age four months, a baby sleeps for eight hours, with a few daytime naps. By one year, the baby sleeps for about 12 hours per day, one-third of which is REM sleep. Adults aged 20 to 40 generally need about eight hours of sleep a night; teenagers need about nine and a half hours.

The length and depth of sleep decrease with age; people over 60 sleep as little as five or six hours a night. Scientists do not know whether this situation is a natural result of aging or because of a sedentary lifestyle. Older people sleep more lightly and are less likely to go into stage IV sleep, so they may be more likely to awaken before they have slept as long as they need to.

A trace of a baby's original 90-minute cycle remains in adulthood. It forms the basis of the REM and non-REM sleep cycle, the rising and falling patterns of which are controlled by a biological clock in the pons, a section of the brain stem. Nerve fibers from the pons extend upward into the cerebral cortex and apparently send signals that set cortical neurons firing in unison at regular intervals and thus launch an episode of REM sleep.

Most vertebrates and almost all mammals and birds sleep, although there is considerable variation in the amount of time spent sleeping. Shrews, for example, take minute-long naps, while sloths can sleep for 20 hours. Animals such as dolphins, rabbits, and horses divide their sleep into naps rather than sleeping for one extended time each day. This behavior may be necessary if an animal cannot store enough energy to stop feeding for long, or if a long sleep would make the animal more vulnerable to predators than when it is awake. Sleep differs from hibernation in that it occurs daily at regular intervals rather than seasonally and involves a less drastic reduction in metabolism (see HIBERNATION).

## The circadian rhythm

The brain stem also controls the daily 24-hour cycle (or circadian rhythm; see BIORHYTHMS) of sleeping, waking, and core body-temperature variation. Temperature and alertness rise in the morning and fall toward evening, reaching the lowest point during deep sleep. Because there is usually a dip in the early afternoon, some people like to take afternoon naps, but the cycle can vary markedly from one person to another.

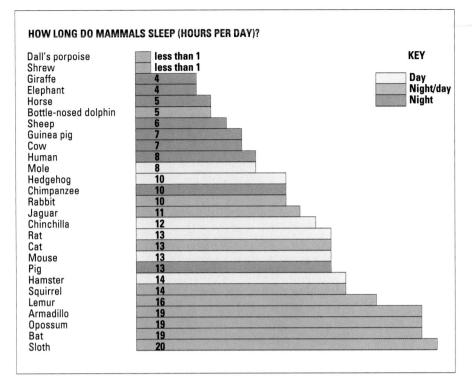

**HOW LONG DO MAMMALS SLEEP (HOURS PER DAY)?**

| Mammal | Hours | Key |
|---|---|---|
| Dall's porpoise | less than 1 | |
| Shrew | less than 1 | |
| Giraffe | 4 | |
| Elephant | 4 | |
| Horse | 5 | |
| Bottle-nosed dolphin | 5 | |
| Sheep | 6 | |
| Guinea pig | 7 | |
| Cow | 7 | |
| Human | 8 | |
| Mole | 8 | |
| Hedgehog | 10 | |
| Chimpanzee | 10 | |
| Rabbit | 10 | |
| Jaguar | 11 | |
| Chinchilla | 12 | |
| Rat | 13 | |
| Cat | 13 | |
| Mouse | 13 | |
| Pig | 13 | |
| Hamster | 14 | |
| Squirrel | 14 | |
| Lemur | 16 | |
| Armadillo | 19 | |
| Opossum | 19 | |
| Bat | 19 | |
| Sloth | 20 | |

KEY
- Day
- Night/day
- Night

The word *circadian* comes from the Latin words meaning "approximately" and "day." The word *approximately* is important because when left to itself, the body's internal clock runs longer than 24 hours. Volunteers living in isolation with no clocks or cues to indicate day or night adopt a day lasting 26 to 30 hours, during which they sleep up to 10 hours and stay awake up to 20 hours. The same free-running clock is seen in blind laboratory animals.

*The diagram above shows the approximate number of hours' sleep different mammals have each day.*

## SLEEP DISORDERS

Nearly everyone experiences occasional insomnia, or lack of sleep. There are two types of insomnia: inability to fall asleep and a tendency to wake up frequently and be unable to get back to sleep. Insomnia occurs when the portions of the brain involved in active thought refuse to turn off. This problem may be caused by anxiety or excitement, caffeine or other stimulants, or prescription drugs given for asthma or high blood pressure. Narcolepsy is a disorder that causes people to fall asleep without warning at any time during the day. It can be treated with stimulant drugs.

Many people have physical ailments that interfere with sleep. Sleep apnea occurs when the breathing passage collapses (perhaps several hundred times a night) and the sufferer, gasping for breath, wakes up. The sufferer will not remember the brief awakenings but will be drowsy during the day. This problem occurs most often in overweight men and snorers. The primary treatment is losing weight, but drugs and sometimes surgery are also used.

Myoclonus is the formal name given to involuntary twitching of the leg muscles that can keep people (mainly elderly men) awake for the first hour or two after going to bed. Sleepwalking, teeth grinding, and talking during sleep occur most often in children but are usually quickly outgrown. They occur during sleep stages III and IV, possibly because of a disconnection between the upper part of the brain involved in thinking and the lower part controlling motor activity. This disconnection also seems to cause night terrors in children, who wake from stage III or IV sleep with a rapid heartbeat and fast, shallow respiration and a physical feeling of fear without any obvious cause. Sometimes in adults the mechanism that turns off motor activity during REM sleep fails, and sleepers act out their dreams (sleepwalk).

## A CLOSER LOOK

Thus, it is the alternation of daylight and darkness that resets the clock to a 24-hour day. This clock has been traced to two small clusters of neurons, the suprachiasmatic nucleus, located atop the hypothalamus in the brain directly above the optic nerves, to which they are connected. Studies show that during exposure to bright light, this structure sends signals that cause the secretion of the hormone melatonin, a sufficient buildup of which causes sleepiness.

All mammals experience sleep that fluctuates on a circadian rhythm under the control of the suprachiasmatic nuclei. In all cases, the body clock is synchronized with the daily routine of night and day. Most birds fly only in daylight, and so they sleep at night. Most reptiles need the Sun's warmth to be fully active, and they also sleep at night. To avoid daytime predators, such as birds of prey, small mammals sleep by day and feed by night. Some animals, such as rabbits and foxes, sleep for part of the day and part of the night. In contrast, the periods that many marine animals sleep, especially coastal ones, such as sea lions, are determined by the daily cycle of tides.

## Dreaming

Apparently everyone dreams during REM sleep, although people do not remember all of their dreams. Those that are remembered probably occur during the last cycle of REM sleep before waking.

There are two schools of thought about whether dreams have meaning. Freudian psychologists believe that dreams represent thoughts and desires the conscious mind cannot handle. During sleep, the barriers that keep these thoughts hidden break down and let them through, but the mind manages to disguise them and hide their real meaning.

However, after studying the physiological events that trigger dreaming, many other psychologists say that dreams result from a random firing of neurons. Each time a neuron is stimulated, it calls up whatever stored memories or thoughts are linked to it, and the mind simply does its best to make up a story that fits the collection of ideas. Often the things people experience during the previous day turn up in their dreams, perhaps because the brain is organizing and storing the day's experiences during sleep.

Laboratory experiments on mammals suggest that, for them, REM sleep is a time of processing the previous day's information and experiences (see ANIMAL EXPERIMENTATION); it is not known whether these animals dream in the same way as humans do.

W. STEELE

**See also:** ANIMAL EXPERIMENTATION; BIORHYTHMS; BRAIN; HIBERNATION; MEMORY; NERVOUS SYSTEMS.

## Further reading:

Empson, J., and M. Wang. 2002. *Sleep and Dreaming.* New York: Palgrave MacMillan.
Hobson, J. 2002. *Dreaming: An Introduction to the Science of Sleep.* New York: Oxford University Press.
Jovet, M. 1999. *The Paradox of Sleep: The Story of Dreaming.* Cambridge, Mass.: MIT Press.

# SLEEPING PILLS

Many insomniacs, individuals who are unable to obtain sufficient sleep, turn to sleep-inducing drugs. Over-the-counter nonprescription sleep aids usually contain antihistamines, which are taken typically to relieve cold or allergy symptoms. Most aids also cause drowsiness, but the U.S. Food and Drug Administration (FDA) has found three to be safe, effective sleep aids: diphenhydramine hydrochloride, diphenhydramine monocitrate, and doxylamine succinate.

Some people believe an alcoholic drink before bedtime helps them sleep. Alcohol does help one fall asleep, but it also causes wakefulness a few hours later, so the person does not get a good night's sleep. It also suppresses REM sleep.

Older prescription sleeping pills contained either chloral hydrate or barbiturates, overdoses of which could be fatal. Physicians now prescribe benzodiazepines (librium, valium, or halcion) as tranquilizers. In a few isolated cases, benzodiazepines have caused hallucinations and violent behavior.

Most sleep drugs have one problem in common; after a week or two, the patient becomes accustomed to them, and larger and larger doses are needed to bring on sleep. Eventually, patients can become addicted to the drugs, being unable to sleep at all without them. Also, nearly all sleep drugs suppress REM sleep. It is also very dangerous to combine a sleeping pill with any other prescription drug or with alcohol.

There are also drugs that keep people awake. The best known is caffeine, present in coffee, tea, cola drinks, and over-the-counter stay-awake pills popular with long-haul truck drivers and students cramming for exams. People vary widely in their sensitivity to caffeine; some can drink a dozen cups of coffee without much effect on sleep, while others stay awake all night after one cola.

Amphetamines have a stronger effect than coffee. They are often abused because they create a brief feeling of alertness and strength (and are sold on the street as uppers or speed). Besides keeping people awake, caffeine and amphetamines can make them nervous and jittery and long-term use can damage the heart as a result of overstimulation.

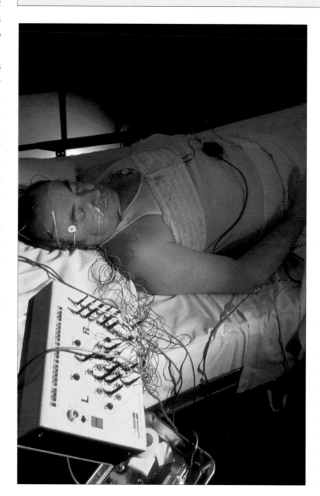

*Sleep research provides scientists and doctors with a better understanding of the structure and function of sleep, by determining the level of activity in different parts of the brain, while monitoring other physiological processes, such as heartbeat, breathing, and body movements.*

# SMALLPOX

**Smallpox is a contagious and sometimes deadly viral disease characterized by pus-filled pimples**

Smallpox, once one of the world's most feared diseases, killed hundreds of millions of people and scarred and blinded millions more. However, the last naturally occurring case of smallpox was in 1977, and in 1980 it became the first disease to be eradicated (wiped out) by humans following a worldwide program of vaccinations. Almost 200 years earlier, smallpox was also the first disease to be targeted by a vaccine (see INFECTIOUS DISEASES; IMMUNIZATION).

## Symptoms

Smallpox is caused by a virus that is carried in the air. People with the disease spread it by breathing or sneezing out virus-laden droplets. Cross-infection occurs when another person breathes in these droplets. Between 10 and 12 days later, the disease symptoms appear. At first, the sufferer develops aches and a fever. After a few more days, a rash of small pimples appears on the face and spreads to other parts of the body. The pimples gradually fill with pus over the next week. Scabs then form over the pimples, which fall off three or four weeks later, leaving behind scars.

Before doctors could treat smallpox, one in five sufferers died; survivors were at least scarred and at worst blinded by the disease, but they became immune to the virus and could not get the disease again.

During the Middle Ages, smallpox was so common that almost everyone had it at some time. Epidemics frequently swept across Asia, Africa, and Europe. During the wars of the time, more soldiers were often killed by smallpox than by enemy action. Before Europeans reached the Americas, the native people had never suffered from smallpox. Their arrival brought the virus and deadly smallpox epidemics that killed millions of Native Americans.

## Prevention

In the 18th century, European doctors learned that people in Turkey were successfully protecting themselves against smallpox by injecting the pus from a sufferer's pimples. Many of these people went on to develop a dangerous case of the disease, but a few had only a minor bout of sickness and then appeared to be immune to it. In 1796 British physician Edward Jenner (1749–1823) took this idea a stage further (see JENNER, EDWARD). He noticed that people who had suffered from cowpox, a similar although less deadly disease, did not catch smallpox. Using the pus from cowpox sores, Jenner developed the world's first vaccine; it gave people cowpox but protected them against smallpox.

Smallpox vaccine is now manufactured from a similar virus called vaccinia virus. Although effective, this virus is not completely harmless and a few vaccinated individuals develop life-threatening encephalitis (inflammation of the brain). Thus, some controversy exists about mass vaccinations of populations antici-

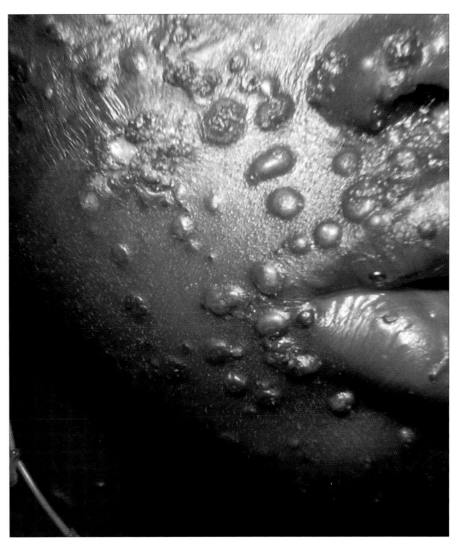

pating the use of smallpox as a terrorist bioweapon (see BIOLOGICAL WARFARE). Despite vaccines being available, the disease continued to exist almost everywhere until the 1940s, when it was eliminated from Europe and North America. Until 1971 U.S. children were vaccinated as infants. After that time, only people traveling in areas where smallpox still existed were given the vaccine. In 1967 the World Health Organization (WHO) began a program to rid the world of smallpox; sufferers were isolated, and every contact was vaccinated against the disease. The last known case of naturally occurring smallpox was found in Somalia in October 1977. In May 1980 WHO declared that smallpox had been eliminated.

T. JACKSON

**See also:** BIOLOGICAL WARFARE; IMMUNIZATION; JENNER, EDWARD; MICROBIOLOGY.

## Further reading:

Hopkins, Donald. 2002. *The Greatest Killer: Smallpox in History*. Chicago: University of Chicago Press.
Ridgway, Tom. 2001. *Smallpox*. New York: Rosen.

*The familiar rash of pus-filled pimples, characteristic of smallpox infection. In 1978 two British laboratory workers caught the disease after the virus they were studying was released accidentally.*

## CONNECTIONS

● The causative agent of smallpox is a **VIRUS**.

● Vaccines can sometimes be used to control **INFECTIOUS DISEASES**, such as smallpox.

# SMELL

**Smell is an important sense, enabling individuals to perceive and recognize specific chemicals**

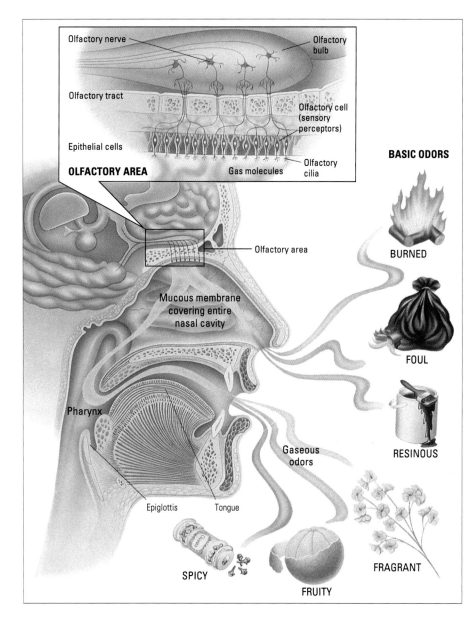

## Ability to smell

Olfaction, or the ability to smell, is an ancient, essential tool that as long as 3.5 billion years ago (in a more basic form) enabled early life-forms to find food and avoid predators. The primitive chemical receptors that helped these creatures survive eventually evolved into the human's highly complex brain (see BRAIN). The cerebral hemispheres of the human brain, in which abstract thought takes place, developed from tiny buds atop primitive olfactory stalks. The olfactory bulbs, which are connected with the ability to detect odor, remain closely linked with the part of the brain called the limbic system, the source of powerful emotions, and the hippocampus, which controls memories. These links help explain why smells can evoke strong memories and emotions.

The human olfactory apparatus brings molecules of odorous substances straight into contact with smell receptors. At the visible end of the apparatus is the nose, where air is breathed in (inspired). As the air reaches the upper end of the passage above the nostrils, it passes over the olfactory membrane, an inch-square patch of skin that contains a dense web of different types of cells, including from 6 to 10 million cells capable of sensing smells. The tips of these receptor cells consist of cilia, tiny threadlike extensions that reach out into the air to catch odorous molecules. Each cilium has receptors along it into which odorous molecules fit. The cells involved in sight and hearing are never replaced once they lose function or are damaged, but these receptor cells are replaced every five to six weeks.

## Lock-and-key theory

Olfaction is not completely understood, but the most accepted theory describes receptors as locks into which odor molecules fit like keys. A smell is

---

*Inhaled air passes into the nasal cavity, where chemicals are detected by olfactory (sensory) cells.*

## CONNECTIONS

● **SNAKES** detect odors using their tongue and a chemical detector in the mouth.

● The smell of nectar, which is produced by plants, aids **POLLINATION**.

Some people say that of the five human senses—sight, smell, hearing, touch, and taste—smell is the least significant. Yet, like most other animals, humans depend on the sense of smell to orient them toward the world. Although humans may not be aware of it, they use odors to identify close relatives, sort out edible from inedible foods, and help them avoid certain dangerous situations.

Odor plays an important role in human development, assuring bonding between family and group members, enhancing the pleasures of eating, and warning if something that is about to be eaten is bad or poisoned. Human babies learn to recognize their mother by odors emitted around her breasts within three days of birth, and mothers can recognize their own infant by smell the day after birth. Among some cultures, for example, Aleut, Filipino, and Maori, people sniff each other's faces or rub noses, smell being a factor in recognition.

## CORE FACTS

■ A lock-and-key theory explains the ability to detect smells; receptor cells in the nasal passage have "locks" into which odor molecules fit like "keys," firing off nerve signals to the brain.

■ Smells often trigger strong memories and emotions because the olfactory bulbs are very closely linked with the brain's limbic system (the source of emotions) and the hippocampus (responsible for memories).

■ Humans have a limited sense of smell as opposed to most other animals; dogs can detect some scents that are nearly one million times too faint for humans to notice.

■ The sense of smell can be damaged by brain injury and smoking and temporarily impaired by colds or allergies.

■ One of the first associations a baby makes is with its mother's smell.

sensed when a particular molecule fits a particular receptor or a combination of receptors. The information passes from the receptor(s) along the axon (a nerve strand extending from the receptor cell; see NERVOUS SYSTEMS), through a bony plate, and directly into one of the two olfactory bulbs in the brain, where the smell is then identified.

Most people can detect a tiny amount of any odorous substance, which travels on air currents in streams, or plumes. As few as eight molecules of a substance can trigger an impulse in a nerve ending, but at least 40 nerve endings must be stimulated for a smell to be perceived. The highly sensitive cells that make up the olfactory apparatus allow most humans to distinguish as many as 10,000 different smells. However, humans can smell substances only from which molecules are escaping into the air; substances that do not evaporate at room temperature, such as stone or glass, cannot be smelled.

Many other mammals have more acute abilities to sense smells than humans. Dogs may have as many as 300 million receptor cells in their olfactory membranes, which spread over an area 50 times larger than those of humans. The structure of the nasal area also varies among animals, allowing dogs, for example, to pass much more of the air they breathe over their olfactory membrane. Snakes and lizards have highly developed scent-sensing organs called Jacobson's organs, which are used to smell odors brought in on the tongue (see SNAKES).

## Scent-detecting organs

Many animals, such as fish and amphibians, have scent-detecting organs all over their body, which alert the animal if it comes into contact with dangerous substances. Bees emit odors from glands at various points on their body, particularly the abdomen, that enable them to identify fellow hive members from nonmembers.

The olfactory organs of ants are in their antennae and, like bees, they can recognize colony members by their smell. Researchers have found that they can make a foreign ant acceptable to any colony by swabbing it with the scent of that colony. Ants with a foreign scent, however, will be attacked. Insects have specialized scent receptor cells capable of recognizing only sex-attractant scents, while other receptor cells can perceive a variety of odors.

## Messenger pheromones

Animals communicate with one another using messenger substances, or scents, called pheromones (see PHEROMONES). These substances are emitted from the body and elicit specific actions when detected by another animal. There are two categories of pheromone: primary and releaser. Primary pheromones govern the general physiological state of the animals receiving the messenger chemical. They include the substance emitted by a queen bee that prevents other females in the hive from developing into rival queen bees. The second type of chemical messenger,

### PERFUME

Perfumes, mixtures of essential oils of fragrant plants, fixatives such as resins and animal secretions, and alcohol, have been made since 1370, when the perfumers of Queen Elizabeth of Hungary came up with the recipe for "hungry water." Elizabeth's perfumers realized that by diluting oils and fixatives in alcohol, they could mellow the heady odors of the musk and ambergris and preserve the fleeting plant fragrances for a long time. Earlier perfumers—at least as far back as ancient Egypt—had made scented oils and over the centuries devised many other innovations, including the distillation of essential plant oils, which made perfumes less costly. When the Crusaders returned to Europe from the East, they brought this knowledge back with them in the form of samples of Arab essences.

Sixty thousand flowers, leaves, fruits, seeds, woods, barks, resins, and roots contribute the essential oils that are the basis of perfumes. Widely used scents include bitter orange blossoms, jasmine, rose, and citrus oils. These scents are combined with fixatives such as balsam (a resin from plants and shrubs), civet (from the scent glands of the African civet cat), castor (from glands in the groin of the beaver), and ambergris (a fatty substance from the intestines of the sperm whale). In their pure form, these fixatives can have very strong, unpleasant smells, but when diluted in alcohol, they become much less intense and bind the various fragrance elements together. After perfumers select and blend a scent's ingredients, they chill and filter the product and age it for up to a year.

Chemists have been devising new scents and copies of natural scents in the laboratory for some time, and they have even been able to create the scents for flowers that do not have oils of their own, including lily of the valley and gardenia. By growing certain cells of fragrant plants on synthetic membranes and collecting the essential oils from the solution in which the membrane is bathed, perfume manufacturers are now able to harvest essential oils even more effectively.

### A CLOSER LOOK

releaser pheromone, causes immediate and obvious changes in behavior. For example, an injured minnow releases a chemical telling its fellow minnows that they, too, may be in danger, and they flee.

Through pheromones, animals broadcast several types of messages. They can guide a predator to its next meal or, conversely, warn prey of a nearby predator. Strong odors, such as the skunk's distinctive scent, can deter predators. Odors also act as signposts to show animals the way home (see INSTINCT). Salmon are guided upstream to spawning

*Snakes have a very distinctive method of detecting smells. By waving the tongue in the air, snakes collect chemical molecules, which are then passed into the mouth and onto the sensory organs.*

## SMELLING SALTS

Female characters in 19th-century novels sometimes faint, and when they do, they are often revived with smelling salts, or sal volatile. Smelling salts are mixtures of ammonium carbonate or ammonium bicarbonate and perfume. When held under the nose and inhaled, the fumes emitted by smelling salts irritate nerve endings in the mucous membranes of the nose, palate, and mouth. As these nerves become irritated, they stimulate medullary reflexes in the brain that, in turn, stimulate breathing. Physicians are now more aware of the potentially injurious properties of high concentrations of ammonia vapor and use smelling salts very rarely, but they are sometimes used to revive athletes who have fainted.

grounds by pheromones, and just as ants mark the path to a meal for their fellow ants, so other animals use pheromones to show other group members where to find food. Pheromones also signal when members of a species are ready to mate, and because animals respond physiologically to pheromones, they ensure that both the male and female of the same species are ready to breed.

In mammals, these signals are often contained in urine, and the range of messages conveyed can be quite complex. They can tell other members of the species about the age, social status, sex, reproductive condition, family membership, and territory occupancy of the emitter. The messages may also contain warning, alarm, and distress signals.

### Disorders of smell

Sometimes something goes wrong with people's sense of smell. Anosmia (from the Latin and Greek words meaning "without smell") describes the disorder suffered by people who have lost some or all of their ability to smell and taste. Anosmia can be

*When threatened by a predator, a skunk may expel a fine spray of foul-smelling liquid. The odor from this liquid is very strong and may persist for days.*

permanent or temporary, depending on its cause. In the common cold, for example, the nose becomes blocked with mucus, and the sufferer is temporarily unable to smell (see COLD, COMMON).

The disorder can arise following a head injury in which the connection is severed between the brain's olfactory bulb and the receptor cells inside the nose. The connection can sometimes be reestablished if the nerves grow back. Anosmia can also be caused by brain tumors, genetic defects, exposure to toxic chemicals, and allergies (see ALLERGY).

A sense of smell plays a crucial role in the sense of taste, which is simply the ability to detect four flavors: sweet, sour, salt, and bitter (see TASTE). All of the other sensations humans describe as taste are derived from the movement of food molecules into the back of the mouth and into the passage connecting the mouth and nose, where they collide with the olfactory epithelium.

### Synesthesia

In the condition called synesthesia, two or more senses—sight and hearing, taste and movement (considered a sense in this context)—converge. People with synesthesia, who are called synesthetes, experience the stimulus of one sense as perception in another; they may perceive sounds as colors, for example, or tastes as shapes. synesthesia is extremely rare: only 10 people in 1 million have the condition. The most common type of synesthesia is chromesthesia, or colored hearing.

Synesthetic experience is involuntary, lasts throughout the synesthete's lifetime, and remains characteristic; for example, if a person perceives a dog's bark as the color blue, he or she will always do so. The condition also usually operates only in one direction, for example, from sound to smell, but not the reverse. Synesthetic evocations are not complex as are hallucinations or dreams (see HALLUCINOGENS; SLEEP) but consist simply of colors, tastes, textures, and simple shapes.

Scientists are still unsure of the origin of synesthesia. Psychologists and neurologists (who study the physical structure of the brain) debate whether synesthesia has a physiological basis in the brain or an emotional basis in the mind.

B. HANSON

**See also:** ALLERGY; BRAIN; COLD, COMMON; EMOTIONS; HALLUCINOGENS; INSTINCT; NERVOUS SYSTEMS; PHEROMONES; SLEEP; TASTE.

### Further reading:
Classen, C., D. Howes, and A. Synnott. 1994. *Aroma: The Cultural History of Smell.* New York: Routledge.
Finger, T. E., D. Restrepo, and W. L. Silver, eds. 2000. *The Neurobiology of Taste and Smell.* Hoboken, N.J.: Wiley-Liss.
Watson, L. 2001. *Jacobson's Organ and the Remarkable Nature of Smell.* East Rutherford, N.J.: Plume Books.

# SNAKES

**Snakes are limbless, scaly, elongated reptiles, some of which are highly venomous**

*The rat snake (Elaphe obsoleta), shown above, is well adapted to a predatory existence. It possesses needle-sharp teeth, which it uses to capture and kill rodents and other prey.*

Snakes provoke a range of emotional reactions in people, but because some can kill humans, they tend to be feared or revered wherever they occur. Snakes are the most recently evolved of the larger groups of reptiles, appearing in the lower Cretaceous period (about 135 million years ago) and probably evolved from lizards. They belong to the class Reptilia, order Squamata, and suborder Serpentes. However, because snakes and lizards have so many features of their structure in common, herpetologists (scientists who study reptiles and amphibians) increasingly do not use the suborder but simply place all lizards and snakes in the order Squamata.

## CORE FACTS

- Snakes are some of the most successful reptiles and live on every continent except Antarctica.
- As cold-blooded animals, snakes are ectothermic; that is, they depend on an external heat source to maintain their body temperature.
- Some snake species are venomous. Their venom is often introduced into prey species through large, sharp fangs, which in some cases are also hollow.

Snakes are particularly successful reptiles. They can adapt to many different niches within the environment. There are about 3,000 species of snakes. They live on every continent except Antarctica, and their range extends south from Canada and northern Sweden (some have been reported a few degrees from the Arctic Circle) into the tropics. The relatively few places that contain no snakes include Ireland, New Zealand, and some Polynesian islands.

### Physical characteristics

Snakes are vertebrates and are limbless. Most are distinguished from legless lizards by their very mobile skull, which can rotate and expand to allow an enormous gape. Not all snakes have such a skull, however. Snakes have ears, but they cannot receive airborne sounds because they do not have an external and middle-ear cavity. They do, however, have an inner ear, which enables them to detect ground vibrations. Thus, cobras do not move to the snake charmer's music; in many cases, the snakes are attracted only to the movement of the snake charmer's pipe.

Snakes have no eyelids. Instead, their eyes are protected by a transparent scale called the spectacle, or brille—hence, the famous glassy stare of a snake.

## CONNECTIONS

- Although they are limbless, snakes are **VERTEBRATES** with an elongate **SKELETAL SYSTEM**.

- Snakes have specialized **JAWS** and **TEETH**, which are used for attacking and killing both predator and prey species.

## RECORD-HOLDING SNAKES

The Asiatic reticulated python (*Python reticulatus*) is the snake with the greatest confirmed length, recorded at about 33 feet (10 m) long. The South American green anaconda (*Eunectes murinus*) occasionally grows to comparable lengths, but its girth is much greater, and it may reach an estimated 500 pounds (230 kg) in weight. Slender blind snakes (family Leptotyphlopidae) are the smallest known, the smallest species measuring on average 5 inches (13 cm) in length.

The Asian king cobra (*Ophiophagus hannah*) and the Australian taipan (*Oxyuranus microlepidotus*) are among the most venomous snakes in the world. The king cobra is the largest poisonous snake known, measuring nearly 20 feet (6 m) long. Its venom is so powerful that a human can die within 15 minutes if there is no appropriate antivenin on hand. One of the most threatening venomous groups of snakes, the saw-scaled vipers (*Echis* spp.), lives in West Africa, India, Sri Lanka, and the Middle East, most often near populated areas. These aggressive snakes have enough venom to kill about 10 adult humans, but they are outclassed in this respect by the cobras. A single cobra can store as much as 1/10 ounce (2.8 g) of venom, and just over 1/25 ounce (1.1 g) of dried venom can kill about 150 people.

One of the fastest snakes, which also happens to be venomous, is the feared black mamba (*Dendroaspis polylepis*). It moves at close to 6 miles per hour (10 km/h), with its head and the front part of the body held high in the air.

Snakes do sleep, but it is difficult to tell when. When the snake sheds it skin, the scale on the eye is also shed. Most diurnal snakes, such as racers (*Coluber constrictor*), have round pupils, while the pupils of most nocturnal snakes are vertically elliptic (oval).

A snake's skin is divided into hard plates called scales. Each scale has layers of keratin (a water-resistant hard protein) on the outside. The skin eventually dies and, in a process called molting, is replaced by a new skin that grows beneath the old one. Most snakes go through such molts (see MOLT-ING), literally crawling out of their skins, unlike birds and mammals, which lose skin cells one at a time.

Because snakes have elongated bodies, most of their internal organs are also elongated. All snakes except pythons have only one lung, which may extend almost the length of the body. The paired organs, such as the kidneys and testes, lie one in front of the other, instead of side by side, as in most other vertebrates. Snakes have good eyesight and a highly developed sense of smell (see SMELL). Like lizards, snakes have a Jacobson's organ, a chemical detector in the roof of the mouth. A snake's tongue samples its environment by picking up airborne particles; the tongue carries them to the Jacobson's organ to be "smelled."

Some species, such as pit vipers, seek their prey in the dark. They have heat-sensitive organs in pits located in the upper jaw. Signals from these organs are sent to the same part of the brain as the signals from the eyes. When a snake "sees" the thermal (infrared) image of its prey, it is sensing the animal with the pit organs. When the snake attacks, secondary heat sensors in the mouth take over to allow the snake to continue to target the prey.

### Overcoming prey

Catching prey and feeding differs between species. Some snakes, such as pythons and boa constrictors, grab prey in their mouth and kill the victim by constriction. Even with prey many times the size of the snake, constriction causes suffocation and the rupture of major blood vessels. Like most other snakes, constrictors have a loosely jointed jaw structure, in which the elastic hinges of the jaw dislocate in order to accommodate larger prey during feeding.

Other snakes, such as rattlesnakes, use venom to subdue prey. Snake venom may be neurotoxic, killing prey by affecting the nerves (as with cobras), or it may be hemotoxic, killing prey by breaking down the red blood cells (as happens with vipers). The method of delivery of venom also differs between species. Back-fanged snakes, such as the African boomslang (*Dispholidus typus*), have short solid fangs along the surface of which venom drips as the snake bites its prey, but most venomous snakes, such as cobras and rattlesnakes, have hollow front fangs that rotate forward when attacking and deliver venom directly into the victim.

### How snakes move

Although snakes have no limbs, they can move because they have an unusual skeleton and muscles. Their backbones have an unusually high number of vertebrae (up to 400 in the python), which are linked together by complex ball-and-socket joints. The vertebrae also give support to the ribs, which are attached to powerful muscles.

Snakes move in a variety of ways: by forming the body into a series of S-shaped loops, producing both a sideways and a backward thrust; by sidewinding, with the main thrust sideways instead of backward; by a concertina movement, coiling close together and then stretching out; by rib walking, involving the lengthwise wave motion of the ribs and belly scales; and when faced with a burrow or tight space, by pressing the belly scales against the ground. Some snakes also use the enlarged scales on their bellies to help them to climb.

*The boa constrictor (*Boa constrictor*) has vertically elliptical pupils (as do many nocturnal snakes), which can open very wide in dim light.*

Certain climbing snakes, such as the American tree boa (*Corallus* spp.), use their strong prehensile tails to grasp branches and climb trees. Two species of long, slender "flying" snakes make a rapid series of S-shapes when gliding; by flattening the body to increase the surface area, sufficient lift to glide to a nearby branch is created.

## Mating and reproduction

In North America, courtship and mating occur in the spring, shortly after the snakes emerge from hibernation. In the tropics, snakes do not hibernate, however. Courtship and mating rituals vary between species. For example, vine snakes and garter snakes congregate in large numbers, with many males attempting to mate with a small number of females. Other snakes meet in pairs, the males weaving themselves against the female. Mating occurs when the male snake inserts one of a pair of reproductive structures (hemipenes) into the female's cloaca (common urinary and reproductive opening). The male's sperm fertilizes the egg internally.

Depending on the species, a female snake either lays eggs or gives birth to live young. If eggs are laid, they usually develop in the soil or beneath decaying vegetation. Usually, after laying the eggs, the parents abandon the area, although some snakes protect and warm the eggs by coiling their bodies around them.

## Primitive snakes

Blind snakes are very primitive small snakes that have vestiges of upper hind leg bones. Some scientists believe they are more like certain lizard species than snakes. Blind snakes include the Mona blind snake (*Typhlops monensis*), Schlegel's blind snake (*Rhinotyphlops schlegeli*), a large African species, and the tiny flowerpot snake (*Rhamphotyphlops braminus*), which lives in many parts of the tropical world.

There are numerous families of primitive snakes, all with their own characteristics. For example, pipe snakes, such as the coral pipe snake (*Anilius scytale*), have more prominent scales than blind snakes but not to the extent of more-advanced species. They also have vestiges of hind legs on either side of the anal opening. Sunbeam snakes reach a maximum length of about 3¼ feet (1 m) and have a noticeably rounded body. Scientists continue to speculate as to why their scales shimmer with rainbow colors, because sunbeam snakes are nocturnal burrowers. When excited, the snakes vibrate the tail much as rattlesnakes do.

Pythons (of the family Pythonidae) and boas (also called boids; of the family Boidae) include several well-known snakes, such as the Indian and brown pythons, boa constrictors (*Boa constrictor*), and anacondas (*Eunectes* spp.).

Boids include the largest snakes alive today, although many species are small to medium sized. Their belly scales are large, the pupils of the eyes are vertical, as with most snakes, and they are among the only snakes with a pair of lungs. Boids are also the only large animals on Earth that are mute

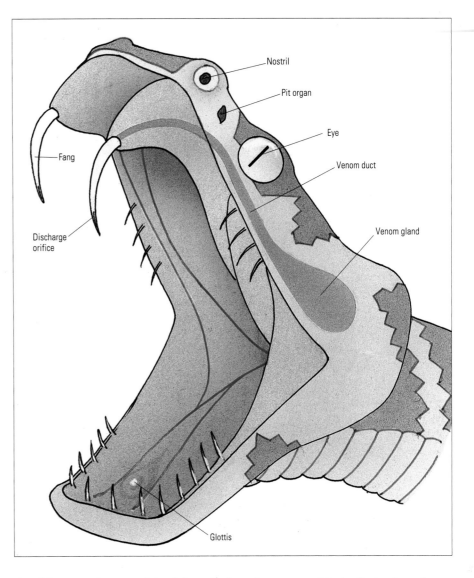

(unable to make sounds), although they do occasionally hiss. Most pythons and boas kill their prey by constriction, using large, powerful muscles in the body. The biggest boids have been known to consume animals as large as a goat or an antelope.

## Advanced snakes

Over 80 percent of all snakes belong to the advanced families. More than half of all snakes—at least 1,700 species—belong to the Colubridae family.

*The tooth structure of many venomous snakes, particularly rattlesnakes and cobras, has evolved to provide a means of injecting the venom through the fangs directly into the snake's victim.*

## THE RATTLER'S SECRET

Rattlesnakes rattle their tails when threatened. The tail consists of hard, bell-shaped, interlocking segments. Each time the rattlesnake sheds its skin, a new rear segment, or rattle, is formed. However, instead of the old segment dropping off with the rest of the skin, it remains loosely attached to the new segment. When the snake feels threatened, it contracts its muscles, causing the tail to vibrate and the loose segments to rattle against each other.

### A CLOSER LOOK

snake bites. Instead, they are fixed to the upper jaw-bone, as are all the other teeth. When the mouth is closed, the fangs lie protected in grooves in the lower jaw. The familiar hood in cobras is an effect achieved as the snake spreads its neck ribs.

Depending on the species, cobras and their relatives either lay eggs or bear living young. They are venomous snakes (as opposed to constrictors). Most of these snakes are active at dusk and night, avoiding bright sunlight. The cobra family also includes the feared black mamba of Africa (the largest venomous snake on the continent; *Dendroaspis polylepis*), American coral snakes, and Australia's death adder (*Acanthophis antarcticus*).

Sea snakes are related to cobras, but because they never venture onto land, they possess physical characteristics that reflect their aquatic life. These features include a laterally compressed tail that acts like a paddle and dorsally located nostrils that can be sealed. The scales of sea snakes are generally the same size all over the body.

Vipers share a common ancestor with pit vipers and are considered very advanced snakes. A viper's fangs contain tubes that transmit venom to the snake's victim—much like a hypodermic needle would. It has smaller scales on its head than on its body, and the fangs are very long. Each upper jaw has a joint that allows the fangs to rotate through 90 degrees—a way of quickly activating or retracting the fangs. Vipers are compact snakes, and their head tends to be rather pointed at the front, giving it a triangular appearance. True vipers live only in Europe, Asia, and Africa.

Pit vipers are successful mainly because they have pit organs—heat-sensitive structures that help them detect warm-blooded prey or cold-blooded prey, such as lizards, that have warmed themselves up in the sunshine. The fangs of pit vipers often fall out after attacking prey and may be replaced two to four times a year. Pit vipers include cottonmouths, or water moccasins (*Agkistrodon bilineatus*), copperheads (*Agkistrodon contortrix*), and 30 species of rattlesnakes (*Crotalus* spp.), including eastern and western diamond-backed rattlesnakes and the sidewinder (*Crotalus cerastes*).

P. BARNES-SVARNEY

**The desert-dwelling sidewinder (Crotalus cerastes) is well known for its distinctive means of locomotion, which enables it to move across soft sand while keeping much of its body off the hot surface.**

The North American colubrid snakes include the ring-necked, water, smooth, and king snakes. Among the better-known species found throughout the United States are garter snakes (*Thamnophis* spp.), small, slender snakes that bear live young and feed mainly on earthworms.

Cobras and their relatives are often large snakes, and because they are highly venomous, they are widely feared. Their fangs, unlike those of vipers, cannot be erected so that they point forward as the

**See also:** COLD-BLOODED ANIMALS; LIZARDS; MOLTING; REPTILES; SMELL.

**Further reading:**
Green, H. W. 1997. *Snakes. The Evolution of Mystery in Nature*. Berkeley, Calif.: University of California Press.
Heatwole, H. 1999. *Sea Snakes*. 2nd ed. Malabar, Fla.: Krieger.
Stafford, P. 2000. *Snakes*. London: Natural History Museum / Washington D.C.: Smithsonian Institution Press.
Thorpe, R. S., W. Wüster, and A. Malhotra. 1997. *Venomous Snakes: Ecology, Evolution, and Snakebite*. Oxford, U.K.: Clarendon Press.

## SNAKE ENEMIES

Even though snakes seem to have everything in their favor, there are times when they are not on the winning side. In temperate climates, many snakes are especially vulnerable on cold mornings, when they must warm themselves in the sunshine. Snakes are also vulnerable when they are shedding their skin.

There are animals that attack snakes. For example, mongooses of all species kill snakes, and some, such as the Indian gray mongoose (*Herpestes edwardsi*), a small, 32-inch (81 cm) long solitary carnivore, live almost exclusively on them. The mongoose's success lies in its agility, timing, and speed, as well as the protection afforded by its thick coat of fur. The Javan gold-spotted mongoose (*Herpestes javanicus*) was introduced to Hawaii to kill rats and some parts of the West Indies to control snakes. Eagles and hawks also prey on snakes, swooping down and using their strong talons to sieze the snake as close to the head as possible to prevent it from turning and biting its attacker.

# SOCIAL ORGANIZATION

**Social organization is the pattern of relationships between individuals of a species**

*Social groups range from two individuals to large groups, such as the flock of Canada geese (*Branta canadensis*) shown above.*

## CONNECTIONS

● **SOCIOBIOLOGY** tries to explain social organization in terms of **EVOLUTION**.

● Social organization is often important for **MATING** and **REPRODUCTION**.

● Social **INSECTS** such as **TERMITES** and **ANTS** live in complex societies.

● Social **ANIMAL BEHAVIOR** relies on **COMMUNICATION**.

There are many ways in which animals can form social groups. These groups range from the complex societies of bees, often swarms of thousands of individuals, through schools of fish, to the simple pairing of male and female geese. Other examples of such groups include herds of as many as 100,000 zebras (*Equus burchelli*) that migrate annually across the Serengeti Plain in Africa and flocks of thousands of Canada geese (*Branta canadensis*) that fly to their breeding grounds in the Arctic.

At first, these aggregations of animals may seem to be unstructured and random; however, many if not most animals have very highly defined social systems. For example, a herd of zebras is composed of thousands of family units, or harems, each with one male, several females, and their offspring. The swarm of bees is the beginning of a new hive, in which one female, or queen, produces all the eggs, while thousands of sterile worker bees fly out, collect food, and rear the young produced. The geese land, whereupon pairs separate, make their nests, and raise their goslings on their own.

## Safety in numbers

Scientists regard social behavior as a characteristic of animals that is acted on by natural selection. In this view, genes influence social behavior, and social behavior is likely to be adaptive (see ADAPTATION) and

heritable, through the behavior genes. This evolutionary approach to studying social behavior is sometimes called sociobiology (see SOCIOBIOLOGY).

The way in which social behavior is adaptive is not always obvious. Female lions (*Panthera leo*) form social bonds that are vital for hunting in groups. However, they may also live in groups to protect their cubs from aggressive adult males. Similarly, female African kobs (*Kobus kob*), a species of antelope, gather with the adult males to avoid the attentions of young inexperienced males.

Nevertheless, the costs and benefits of social organization often fall into two areas, namely, antipredator behavior (to avoid being eaten) and foraging behavior (the finding, catching, and defending of food supplies).

### CORE FACTS

■ Societies may range from a small group of individuals, such as a pride of lions, to a large group of thousands of individuals, such as a swarm of bees.

■ Social groupings may at first appear to be random and unstructured but are often very complex, with a clear hierarchical structure.

■ There are both benefits and costs to animals living in large social groups.

In any group of animals, the more animals there are around, the less likely it is that a predator will make a successful attack on any single individual. Antipredator behavior can be relatively uncoordinated or highly coordinated. For example, in a large flock of geese or a herd of zebras, the mere fact that there are a large number of animals and hence a large number of eyes looking around makes it very hard for a predator to approach the group undetected. Social birds, such as swallows and bee-eaters, may clump their nests together and thus protect their chicks from attacks by snakes and birds of prey.

However, it is animals that form small groups that have evolved the most effective antipredator behavior. In general, the tighter the bonds that hold a group together, the more coordinated their antipredator behavior. For example, in a group of social mongooses, such as the meerkats (*Suricata suricatta*), individuals take turns scanning the sky for eagles so that the others can feed efficiently and safely.

Forming groups to avoid predators is not without its costs. While animals in the middle of a large herd are at a lower risk of attack, those on the edge of the herd may be at a greater risk than if they were on their own.

Even the active antipredator behavior exhibited by individuals in highly structured social groups can work against other group members. For example, many animals that live in groups make alarm calls to warn other members of their group that a predator is near. For many years, scientists thought that alarm calls were the ultimate sacrifice of a single individual for the good of the group (see ALTRUISM).

However, such behavior can benefit the individual, sometimes at the expense of other members of the group. The call alerts the predator that it has been sighted. As a result, if the predator chooses to attack the group, more often than not it will ignore the individual that has been making the alarm calls and attack less wary members. In this way, the animal raising the alarm avoids being attacked.

## Communal feeding

As well as forming to defend against predators, social groups also develop when animals feed together. Typical communal feeders are the social carnivores, such as hyenas, wolves, and wild dogs. These animals live in closely bonded social groups composed of near relatives—brothers, sisters, aunts, and uncles. They hunt as a team, and by coordinating their efforts, they are able to kill animals up to 10 times larger than themselves.

The passenger pigeon (*Ectopistes migratorius*) once flew in huge flocks across the American plains, searching for groups of trees, such as oaks, that were masting. Masting trees are those producing a rare abundance of fruit. Because masting trees are so rare, the passenger pigeons would at times spread out into a single line of thousands of birds, flying next to one another in a ribbon several miles wide to search for their food source.

Some biologists now think that the passenger pigeon ultimately became extinct because, as their numbers declined because of habitat loss and hunting, they reached a stage where they could no longer search for food efficiently.

*Carnivorous predators, such as gray wolves (Canis lupus), often live in closely bonded social groups consisting of dominant and subdominant animals. Below, a subdominant animal adopts a submissive posture on the ground to avoid aggression from more-dominant animals.*

## Defending food supplies

In addition to catching or finding food, social groups of animals may be important in defending food from competitors. For example, fruit is an important part of the diet of many tropical birds and monkeys. However, in most tropical rain forests, only a few fruit trees in any particular area will produce food at any given time. By joining together in a group, monkeys may be able to defend a fruit tree against other members of their own species, other species of monkeys, or even large fruit-eating birds, such as hornbills.

Such communal defense of food sources is not limited to monkeys. The social organization of the red fox (*Vulpes vulpes*), a common species in Europe, changes radically as the food supply increases or decreases. When food sources are abundant and concentrated (for example, in garbage dumps), foxes band together, just as fruit-eating monkeys do, to defend their food. However, when food is highly dispersed and no advantage is gained by group defense, foxes are most likely to live in pairs.

The flexibility in the social organization of the fox illustrates a more general principle—living in groups can have benefits in terms of food defense, but it also has costs because any food found or defended must be shared. Thus, the group size reflects a balance between the advantages of communal feeding and food defense and the costs of increased competition for food within the group.

## Dominance

Within any social group, there is almost always a hierarchical structure; some particular individual is the head of the group, exerting dominance over other individuals and controlling their behavior in some way. These animals in turn may dominate others farther down the chain.

The concept of dominance was first put forward in 1922 by Norwegian scientist T. Schjelderup-Ebbe, who observed a pecking order in domestic chickens. In chickens, pecking is a form of aggression. The dominant bird, which can be of either sex, pecks at all the others in the flock. The next bird down in the pecking order pecks all except the dominant bird, and so on down the social structure.

There are many other examples of hierarchical dominance. The vervet (*Cercopithecus aethiops*), a variety of South African monkey, shows a linear hierarchy, in which one animal dominates another, which dominates the next, and so on. Even sea anemones have been reported to live in dominance hierarchies. However, some scientists have argued that because much of the work on dominance hierarchies has been carried out in zoos and other enclosed establishments, hierarchies may be produced largely by stress as a result of captivity.

## Keeping it in the family

The smallest unit of social structure is a pair of unrelated animals of opposite sex who come together to breed and raise their offspring. This group, the

### THE NAKED MOLE RAT: A MAMMAL BEHAVING LIKE A SOCIAL INSECT

In mammals, the most extreme form of sociality is found in naked mole rats (*Heterocephalus glaber*, below). Naked mole rats live in underground colonies, similar to those of ants, of between 40 and 300 individuals. The colonies live in a maze of tunnels with separate chambers for breeding, food storage, and waste products. Only the dominant female, or queen, breeds. She mates with up to three breeding males, who are usually her brothers or her sons. As a result of this close inbreeding, all the offspring are very closely related, sharing on average 85 percent of their genes. The queen suckles all the young pups, but worker mole rats tend them and clean them and bring them food when they reach weaning age. The pups grow up to become new workers. The workers perform all activities except breeding. This cooperative breeding behavior arises through the evolutionary process of kin selection, which acts on the genes shared by the entire colony. Every individual acts in the interest of the genes it shares with its brothers and sisters. The responsibilities of workers differ according to size: smaller animals act as sweepers, keeping the tunnels and chambers clean, and do most of food collecting. Larger workers make up the defense force of the colony.

### A CLOSER LOOK

monogamous pair, can be expanded into a larger social group in many ways. The most common way to increase group size is for several unrelated females to join up with a single male. This system is often called polygyny, or harem breeding. Harems formed by plains zebras or gorillas (*Gorilla gorilla*) are examples of such social groups. In both these species, all the adult females in the group are usually unrelated, and the harem male is unrelated to each female.

Groups can also form from monogamous pairs if offspring from one year stay on to help their parents raise their brothers and sisters in the following year. In most species, the young leave their parents before the next set of offspring is born. However, in a variety of mammal species, young animals may stay with their parents for one year or even two.

There are a number of reasons why these young mammals might delay their own breeding. In some cases, there may be no open territories available; thus, the helpers lose nothing by assisting their parents. In other cases, the experience and skills gained while helping the parents may benefit the helpers

## SOCIAL CNIDARIANS

Cnidarians (sea anemones, corals, jellyfish, and relatives; see CORALS; JELLYFISH, SEA ANEMONES, AND HYDRAS) are remarkable examples of animals with intimate social organization. Depending on the species, complex colonies of cnidarians may be formed from related or unrelated individuals.

The basic unit of the colony is the zooid. It is an animal formed from two layers of cells, with a central mouth surrounded by tentacles. The zooids have different duties; in the genus *Obelia*, some zooids reproduce and others feed and defend the colony with stinging cells called nematocysts. Some other cnidarians have three forms of zooids, concerned with feeding, reproduction, and defense.

One of the most remarkable cnidarian colonies is the Portuguese man-of-war (*Physalia*). Its central body is up to 12 inches (30 cm) across, but its tentacles can reach 70 feet (21 m) in length. In most ways, the colony functions as an individual. All of its zooids come from a single fertilized egg and are produced by asexual budding. Nevertheless, they develop into four different types: three zooids are concerned, respectively, with feeding, reproduction, and defense, and the fourth forms the large gas-filled sail that has given the animal its name (man-of-war is an old name for a warship, from the days of sail).

## A CLOSER LOOK

*Honeybees (Apis mellifera), of the order Hymenoptera, live in large, complex social groups. The queen bee controls the activity of all the worker bees in the nest by means of a pheromone.*

when they breed in the future. Alternatively, the helper may also stand a chance of inheriting the breeding territory or part of it from its parents.

Generally, however, some individuals give up breeding and help relatives raise their offspring, an evolutionary process called kin selection (see ALTRUISM; SOCIOBIOLOGY). In some societies, kin selection leads subdominant animals (animals lower on the dominance hierarchy) to give up breeding altogether. In a pack of wolves (*Canis lupus*) or African wild dogs (*Lycaon pictus*), for example, only the dominant male and dominant female breed, but the other members of the pack help raise the puppies. As a result, these animals have evolved to produce large litters; thus the chance of many offspring surviving increases.

Social insects in the order Hymenoptera (ants, bees, and wasps) have taken sociality to its extreme, with most individuals being sterile. The sterile individuals are workers and are often divided into strict castes, with each caste devoting itself to a particular task, such as defense of the nest or collection of food.

### Social problems
Animals that tend to live in large social groups, such as cliff-nesting swallows, are much more likely to contract diseases than closely related species that nest separately (see NESTING). They often carry a larger number of parasites, such as ticks and fleas. Diseases and parasites are more easily transmitted in dense groups, but the problem is also due to the difficulty that socially nesting species have in finding good nesting sites. In the case of cliff-nesting swallows, because cliffs that can be excavated easily to make nest holes are rare, these socially nesting birds tend to use the same nest holes every year and thus collect an increasing number of parasites through time.

### Communication
All forms of social behavior rely on communication between the members of the group. The means of communication can take many forms. It can be vibration, as in the dance of the worker bee (see COMMUNICATION; WASPS AND BEES), the change in direction of a school of fish, or the vibration of a moth's antennae. The means of communication can be visual, as in the white undertail of a rabbit or rump of a deer, which signals the approach of a predator. It can be auditory; nearly all mammals and birds communicate using a wide variety of calls. Alternatively, communication can be based on pheromones, chemical substances secreted by organisms to bring about a response from other organisms of the same species.

Humans are animals, and their behavior has been subject to natural selection much as the behavior of other animals has been. What goes on in the school playground, on the playing field, at home, in the workplace, and in the military is similar in some ways to what researchers have observed in nature. The realization that there is a component of human social behavior that is genetic inspired the science of human sociobiology (see SOCIOBIOLOGY).

J. GINSBERG/B. INNES

**See also:** ADAPTATION; AGGRESSION; ALTRUISM; CORALS; ETHOLOGY; EVOLUTION; JELLYFISH, SEA ANEMONES, AND HYDRAS; NATURAL SELECTION; NESTING; POPULATION; SOCIOBIOLOGY; WASPS AND BEES.

### Further reading:
Bennett, N. C., and C. G. Faukes. 2000. *African Mole Rats: Ecology and Eusociality.* New York: Cambridge University Press.
Gadagkar, R. 2001. *Survival Strategies: Cooperation and Conflict in Animal Societies.* Cambridge, Mass.: Harvard University Press.
McGrew, W. C., ed. 1996. *Great Ape Societies.* New York: Cambridge University Press.

# SOCIOBIOLOGY

**Sociobiology is the study of animal behavior from an evolutionary viewpoint**

Sociobiologists assume that an animal's behavior has the same biological basis as the color of its fur or the size of its teeth. Thus, as with an animal's physical features, its behavior also results from an interaction between its genetic makeup and the environment in which it is raised. Unlike psychologists, who want to understand how mental processes cause animals to behave in different ways, sociobiologists want to understand why the behaviors evolve in the first place and how they help an animal to survive, reproduce, and pass on its genes to future generations (see EVOLUTION; EVOLUTIONARY PSYCHOLOGY; GENETICS; HUMAN EVOLUTION; PSYCHOLOGY).

## The beginnings of sociobiology

The birth of sociobiology as a recognized scientific subject came in 1975 when U.S. biologist Edward O. Wilson (b. 1929) published a book entitled *Sociobiology: The New Synthesis*. For most of the book, Wilson explained how evolutionary theory could account for the behavior of animals as different as ants, monkeys, and seagulls, inspiring many scientists to start sociobiological studies of their own.

However, Wilson's last chapter, on humans, caused him a great deal of trouble. Wilson himself could see nothing wrong with looking at human behavior from a sociobiological angle; if evolution can explain the behavior of all the other animals on Earth, he reasoned, why could it not also explain that of humans?

Following this logic, Wilson went on to illustrate how human behavior has a biological, genetic basis, just as the behavior of blackbirds and baboons does. As a result of this single chapter, Wilson outraged large sections of the scientific community, most notably Harvard paleontologist Stephen Jay Gould (1941–2002). Many people simply refused to accept that human behavior could be linked to genetic makeup, because as they saw it, this connection

indicated that humans had no control over their own behavior and were driven by their genes.

No single behavior is purely the result of genes alone, however; the environment plays a very important role in determining how genes express themselves (the so-called nature-nurture debate). However, the damage was done, and almost overnight, sociobiology became a dirty word. The scandal that has surrounded human sociobiology ever since has overshadowed the fact that sociobiology in its broader sense—the study of the biological basis of animal behavior—has helped solve some of the most puzzling problems in biology, problems that baffled even English naturalist Charles Darwin (1809–1882; see DARWIN, CHARLES).

## Selfish animals

When Darwin's theory of evolution was first applied to animal behavior, people assumed that animals behaved in ways that were good for the species as a whole. For example, lionesses (female lions) that suckled young cubs that belonged to other females in their pride were assumed to do so to ensure there would be plenty of lions in the next generation and that the species would not become extinct.

*Lionesses in a pride often suckle one another's cubs, a behavior called kin selection, in which an animal helps promote the survival and reproductive success of its relatives.*

## CORE FACTS

- Sociobiologists believe animal behavior, including that of humans, is directed by both genetic makeup and by the environment.
- Sociobiologists point out that evolution depends on genes and that a behavior can evolve only if the genes that cause it are passed on to future generations.
- According to sociobiological theory, animals should be selfish; their behavior should be directed at passing on their own genes.
- Altruism can evolve if the individuals that benefit are relatives.
- Kin selection is a type of behavior in which animals promote the survival and reproductive success of their relatives.

## CONNECTIONS

● The idea that the human brain and behavior as well as the body have evolved over millions of years is the basis of **EVOLUTIONARY PSYCHOLOGY**.

● **ETHOLOGY** is the study of animal behavior under natural conditions.

However, it was difficult to use this argument to explain why a male lion entering a pride for the first time very often killed all the young cubs, a behavior most unlikely to prevent the species from becoming extinct. This example and others like it created a problem for animal behaviorists.

Sociobiology solved this problem by pointing out that evolution depends on genes and that a behavior can evolve only if the genes that cause it get passed on to future generations and become more common. Thus, an animal cannot behave for the good of the species but must always behave in ways that are good for it as an individual, even if these behaviors are harmful to other members of the species. For example, imagine an animal that, when a lion appeared, would throw itself at the lion to be eaten so that all the other members of its group had time to run away to safety. While this behavior would certainly be good for the species, it could never become a common behavior in future generations. It could not evolve because individuals who carried the genes for the behavior would be very likely to die without having any offspring to carry the genes—and if the genes do not get passed to future generations, neither does the behavior. Instead, the genes for running away from lions would be passed on because all the animals that exhibited this behavior would be very likely to survive and reproduce. The genes promoting the self-sacrificing behavior that was good for the species would soon be outcompeted by genes that promoted running away from lions.

*A common vampire bat (Desmodus rotundus) taking blood from a roosting hen. Some vampire bats exhibit a rare form of behavior called reciprocal altruism; a well-fed bat will regurgitate some of its meal to a second bat that had been unable to feed, but only if that second bat had previously provided a meal to the first.*

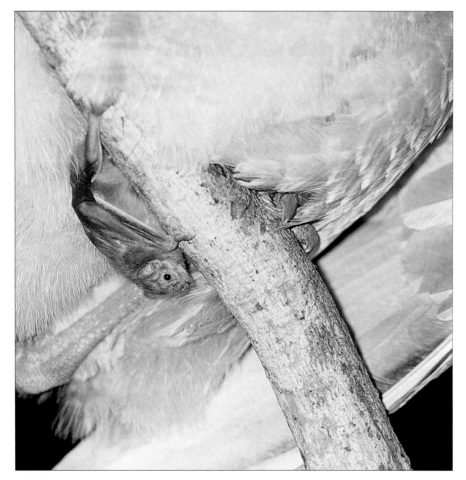

In evolutionary terms, the fitness of running genes (the number passed on to future generations) would be very much higher than the fitness of the sacrificing genes. Thus, according to sociobiological theory, animals should be selfish; in this biological sense, their behavior should be directed at passing on their own genes and not helping to pass on the genes belonging to other members of their species.

The notion of animals behaving selfishly provides a perfect explanation for the male lion's behavior. When a male enters a pride for the first time, he kills the cubs because they are unrelated to him and do not share any of his genes. If he helped care for them and raise them, he would be helping another animal (the cubs' father) pass on its genes rather than his own. By killing the other male's cubs, he has more time and energy to put into producing his own cubs, and so his own genes will be passed on; he also ensures that there are fewer of the other male's genes around to compete with his own.

## The problem of altruism

If behavior is always to the advantage of the individual rather than the species, why should a lioness suckle the cubs of other mothers and help promote their genes at the expense of her own? Such behavior, where one animal provides a benefit to another at a cost to itself, is termed *altruism* (meaning unselfish) and, according to sociobiological theory, should not occur (see ALTRUISM). The problem of altruism thus became the central issue that sociobiologists had to solve if their theory was to stand the test of time.

In 1964 British biologist William D. Hamilton pointed out that altruistic behavior could evolve if the individuals that benefited from the behavior were relatives, because close relatives share many of their genes; two sisters share 50 percent of their genes, while two cousins share 12.5 percent. Thus, if a lioness has a gene that causes her to help raise her sister's cubs, there is a good chance that the gene will be passed on even if that female has no offspring of her own; her sister is likely to contain an identical copy of that gene, which she then passes on to her offspring.

As far as evolution is concerned, it does not matter whose body the gene is in, providing it gets passed on. Thus, the lionesses in a pride feed one another's cubs because they are sisters. Far from behaving unselfishly, female lions are helping themselves—or more exactly, their genes—by helping other animals. In cases such as these, altruism is not really altruism at all; the behavior is just as selfish as committing infanticide. This type of behavior in which animals help to promote the survival and reproductive success of their relative is called kin selection.

However, there are also examples of altruistic behavior between animals that are unrelated to each other, and thus, kin selection is not involved. One striking example of this behavior occurs in colonies of vampire bats. Every night the bats fly out from their colonies and feed on the blood of large animals, such as cattle. Not every bat is successful, however, and

*Argentine horned frogs (Ceratophrys ornata) of South America mating. Female frogs choose their mates carefully after listening to the males croaking, to ensure that the male has good-quality genes to pass on to any offspring.*

some return to the colony without having been able to get a blood meal. A serious problem arises for the bats because they are very small animals with a very fast metabolism, and if they do not feed, they could die from starvation overnight. To prevent this critical situation from occurring, the hungry bats beg from well-fed bats, which regurgitate some of their blood meal and prevent the hungry bats from starving. Feeding another bat helps that animal to survive, but the behavior puts the feeder bat's life at risk because giving away blood increases its own chances of starvation. Kin selection cannot explain this behavior because the bats are unrelated. So, how could this behavior have evolved? With no shared genes in common, the feeding bat would be helping another animal's genes to survive at the expense of its own and so would be expected to die out very quickly.

In 1971 U.S. sociobiologist Robert Trivers proposed a solution. He argued that it would be an advantage for animals to help nonrelatives if they could be sure that the favor would be repaid at a later date. In this way, the benefits would balance out. This idea works only if animals recognize each other and interact with the same individual each time so that the benefits are swapped fairly.

Scientists found that this was exactly what the vampire bats were doing. Bats would give blood only to those hungry bats that had previously given blood meals to them. As with the lionesses, the bats were behaving in a self-interested way, giving a meal away to ensure that they themselves would get one when they were in danger of starving. This behavior, called reciprocal altruism, occurs much more rarely in the animal kingdom compared with kin selection because, when benefits are exchanged

in this way—with a delay between one animal giving the benefit and the other returning it—it is very easy for the second animal to cheat and take the benefit without repaying it when the time comes. Behavior systems based on reciprocal altruism are therefore much harder to establish than those based on kin selection.

## Mating behavior

Although altruism is an important topic, sociobiologists are also interested in studying other behaviors that help an animal survive and reproduce. One large area of research concerns how animals choose their mates. Selecting a good mate is crucial for an animal because the offspring produced will inherit half its genes from the mate. A mate with poor-quality genes will lead to poor-quality offspring that are unlikely to survive, the result being that, in turn, an animal will fail to pass on its own genes. Mate selection behaviors therefore allow animals to avoid poor-quality mates and to get hold of the best-quality mate that they can. The female of the species is often the more choosy sex because her eggs are very expensive to produce in terms of energy, and thus she cannot afford to waste any of them on an inferior male.

Female frogs show very interesting mating behavior that allows them to select a good-quality male. In the mating season, male frogs come together at a pond, where they spend the evenings croaking. Females come to the pond and, after listening for a while, go directly to a particular male and mate with him. Studies of this behavior have shown that the females choose males based on what they sound like. In some species females prefer males who can croak at high speeds, while in others

*A bighorn sheep has large, powerful horns. The males fight each other for the right to mate with females by running at each other and banging together their horns. The strongest sheep wins the battle, mates with a female, and is thus more likely to pass on his genes to the next generation.*

they prefer males with a very loud or deep croak. In each case, the croaks tell the female about the quality of the male. Males who croak at high speed are showing that they are of good quality because they have lots of energy to spare and are good at getting food. In the same way, a deep voice tells a female that the male is large, his size indicating that he is also good at getting food. A large frog is also an older frog, and so the female knows that he is good quality because his skill has enabled him to survive long enough to grow to a large size. Females that choose such males stand a better chance of having surviving offspring, because the offspring will inherit some of their father's qualities. Since a male cannot cheat—a poorly fed male simply cannot keep up a high rate of calling for long—these calls' attributes are called honest signals.

As well as competing with each other for a female's attentions, male animals also compete directly with each other. In bighorn sheep, for example, males fight for the right to mate by running at each other and banging together their large and powerful horns. The winning male is then able to mate with the female sheep and is much more likely than the other males to father offspring. Although this fighting behavior indicates that females do not get any choice as to which male they mate with, they benefit in much the same way that female frogs do, because their offspring inherit the genes that made their fathers such good-quality competitors (see COMPETITION).

## Human sociobiology

In recent years the scandal surrounding human sociobiology has died down, and it is clear that, as elsewhere in the animal kingdom, sociobiological theories can provide an insight into human behavior. For example, just as a lioness cares for her sister's cubs, the Ye'kwana women of Venezuela are much more likely to provide care for another woman's child if she is related to them than if she is just a friend, and they are more likely to help close relatives, such as sisters, than more-distant relatives, such as aunts. A similar study of 300 Los Angeles women also found that close relatives were more likely to provide help when it was needed than unrelated friends. In both studies, if women looked after unrelated children or helped out their unrelated friends, they tended to do so in a reciprocal manner, taking turns to look after each other's children, just as vampire bats take turns giving blood meals.

In all, it seems fair to say that sociobiology revolutionized the study of animal behavior by providing clear evolutionary explanations for a wide range of phenomena and increasing immeasurably humans' understanding of the living world. Sociobiology has also given rise to new and more focused areas of study, such as behavioral ecology and evolutionary psychology, both of which have benefited from the evolutionary insights of sociobiological theories. After a very shaky start, sociobiology is now well established.

L. BARRETT/S. P. HENZI

**See also:** ALTRUISM; ANIMAL BEHAVIOR; COMPETITION; DARWIN, CHARLES; EVOLUTION; GENETICS; HUMAN EVOLUTION; PSYCHOLOGY.

## Further reading:
Alcock, J. 2001. *The Triumph of Sociobiology.* New York: Oxford University Press.
Dawkins, Richard. 1996. *The Blind Watchmaker: Why the Evidence of Evolution Reveals a Universe without Design.* New York: W. W. Norton and Company.
Dawkins, Richard. 1990. *The Selfish Gene.* 2nd ed. Oxford: Oxford University Press.
Laland, K., and G. Brown. 2002. *Sense and Nonsense.* Oxford, Oxford University Press.
Wilson. E. O. 2000. *Sociobiology: The New Synthesis.* 25th anniversary ed. Cambridge, Mass.: Harvard University Press.

# SOIL ECOLOGY

**Soil ecology refers to the relationship between the organic and inorganic parts of the soil**

Take one measure of pulverized rock and organic matter, including the decaying plants and animals, and then add liberal quantities of bacteria, fungi, earthworms, insects, and tiny plants, and air and water. The result is soil—a complex, dynamic, living system that covers most of the terrestrial surface of Earth, without which there would be no life. More animals live in soil than in all the other environments of Earth put together.

Soil is essential for life on land. It is the medium in which plants grow, supporting their roots and providing them with nutrients for growth. Soil collects and stores precipitation; water filters through its many layers until it recharges the aquifers and groundwater reserves from which many people draw

water. Soil also holds air in its pores, and thus provides oxygen to plant roots and the billions of other organisms that live in soil. The decay process is a large feature of soil and ensures that organic matter is available for living organisms to use.

Over time, as rocks have eroded and living organisms have died and their remains decayed, soil has built up on the solid rock layer of Earth's crust, called the bedrock. There are many different types of soils, depending on the soil's constituents, but its basic character depends on the underlying bedrock.

## Soil formation

Soil is continually being formed. Wind, rain, and extremes of temperature all work on the parent rocks to break them down little by little. Water collects in rock cracks, freezes and expands continually, and gradually exposes more rock surface to erosive forces. Tree roots grow down into cracks in rocks and splits them apart. Ocean waters rub pebbles against each other as the waves rush on and off the beaches. Ice, water, and wind carry rock particles that scour rock surfaces.

The chemical reactions that take place on exposed rock surfaces are even more destructive to rock. Water-borne acids react with elements in the rock and slowly change them into other materials. Some rocks are broken down relatively easily.

*The diverse environmental influences on soil produce different soils. In tropical rain forests, vegetation decays quickly, but soils are thin because nutrients are taken up immediately.*

## CONNECTIONS

● Nutrients and water are removed from the soil by the **ROOTS AND ROOT SYSTEMS** of plants.

● The soil ecology in **WETLANDS** is very different from that in **DESERT BIOMES**.

● Human influence on soil ecology ranges from **AGRICULTURE** to large-scale **POLLUTION**.

### CORE FACTS

- A soil's chemistry and composition depend on its bedrock, but soil itself varies enormously according to the shape of the landscape, vegetation, and climate, for example.
- Human activities, such as farming, can accelerate soil erosion.
- Numerous microorganisms in soil help decompose dead and decaying matter and aid the recycling of nutrients.
- Earthworms help aerate the soil. Adequate soil air is essential for plant and animal respiration.

For example, some minerals, such as feldspars and micas, turn into clay. Harder materials, such as quartz, break down into sand and silt.

### Soil profiles and horizons

When people dig down into the earth or when natural forces such as earthquakes shift earth around, soils that lie below the surface are often exposed. In these cross sections of soil, called soil profiles, many different horizontal layers, or horizons, of soil that have built up and changed over long periods of time can be seen. These horizons are bands of varying thickness and color. The properties of different types of soil horizons vary widely, and soil scientists have given each type of horizon an identifying letter.

On the surface of the earth is the top horizon, called the O horizon, which may be a thin layer composed of plant residue. Below this horizon is a layer of rich, dark, organic material, called the topsoil or A horizon. Next is the subsoil, the B horizon, which is likely to contain high levels of clay. Beneath these layers is the C horizon, one that is so far below the surface that it contains little organic matter and is close in composition to the parent rock.

### Soil character and plants

Because weather conditions and types of rocks and organisms vary around the globe, soils also differ from place to place. Plants have adapted to these varying soil conditions and can grow in almost every habitat. Plants need rainfall, carbon dioxide from the air, and certain chemical nutrients from the soil. Some soils contain more plant nutrients than others, and certain soil characteristics affect how well plants will be able to absorb those nutrients.

In desert regions, which are present in large areas on most continents, the soils are derived mainly from sandstone and shale parent rocks. These soils are low in humus (organic matter) because the sparse rainfall limits plant growth. The soils may also contain high levels of mineral salts that discourage crop growth.

On the great flat plains of the midwestern United States and of other regions in South Africa, Russia, and Canada are deep layers of black soil lying above a limestonelike layer. These plains receive just enough rainfall to support grasses but not trees.

The most productive soils for agriculture are present alongside rivers and at their mouth, where floods have deposited sediments containing sand, silt, and clay onto the surrounding land. These areas are young soils with a high mineral content.

The oldest soils are present in countries of tropical regions. They are often deep red because they contain high levels of iron. Most of the nutrients have been washed out of these soils because of heavy rainfall, but tropical soils can support rich, dense forests because dying vegetation decays quickly and provides nutrients for new growth.

### Soil erosion

When tropical forests are cleared, soil erosion occurs because there are no tree roots to hold it all together (see DEFORESTATION). Leaching, in which valuable nutrients are washed from the topsoil, is accelerated, and the soil's organic content decays quickly in the hot sunlight, leaving very poor soil for cultivation.

*A woman harvests peanuts from the roots of a peanut plant in Mauritius. While most agricultural crops grow better in soils with a neutral pH and do not survive in acidic conditions, peanuts grow well in acidic soils.*

The loss of fertile topsoil through soil erosion is a worldwide phenomenon; scientists believe around 25 billion tons (22.7 billion metric tons) of topsoil are lost every year. Annual erosion rates are 18 to 100 times greater than the annual renewal rate (the rate at which soil is reformed). Although erosion of topsoil occurs naturally through wind and water, human activities can greatly accelerate it. Poor land management is partly to blame; large areas of fertile farmland are being lost to the construction of new buildings or as a result of overgrazing of livestock.

## Soil pH

One soil property that concerns farmers and gardeners is pH, the measure of acidity. A soil's pH shows the balance between concentrations of two types of ions, particles that carry an electrical charge. Hydrogen ions ($H^+$) are positively charged and react with negatively charged molecules, and hydroxyl ions ($OH^-$) are negatively charged and react with positively charged molecules.

Alkaline soils contain more hydroxyl ions, while acidic soils contain more hydrogen ions. Soils that are neutral (having equal quantities of hydroxyl and hydrogen ions) have a pH of 7, the center of the pH scale, which runs from 0 to 14. A pH of less than 7 is acidic and a pH of more than 7 is alkaline.

A soil's pH is an important determinant of how well it releases nutrients to plant roots. When many hydrogen or hydroxyl ions are in the soil (when the soil has a very low or high pH, respectively), the ions react with ions of opposite charge, some of which are substances needed by plants. Because these nutrients are bonded with an ion with an opposite charge, they are in a form that the plant cannot absorb.

In the United States, much of the land east of the Mississippi River tends to be acidic, while soil in the hot, dry region of the southwest is alkaline. Plants have adapted to all these conditions, but crop plants generally prefer more neutral soils; the most productive agricultural soils have pHs between 5.5 and 8.3. Farmers with acidic soils can add finely pulverized lime (an alkali) to bring soil pH closer to neutral. However, some crops grow well in acidic soils: for example, peanuts in the southern United States.

## Life in the soil

All soils teem with different life-forms; more creatures live below the surface of Earth than above. The chemistry and composition of soil determines the life it supports. For example, wet, acidic soil contains relatively few living organisms, while alkaline soil tends to be rich in minerals that support many different types of life.

Bacteria are the most abundant life-form in most soils and are responsible for the decay of crop residues. Among these bacteria are microscopic organisms called saprophytes, which help decompose dead and decaying matter, by secreting enzymes on the material and then absorbing what has been digested (see SAPROPHYTES). The end product of this decomposition is humus, the organic component of soil.

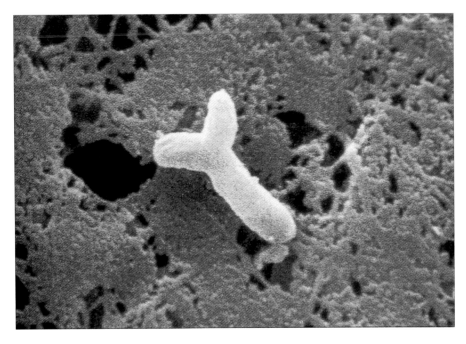

*Bacteria, such as this nitrogen-fixing bacterium (Rhizobium leguminosarum), often occur in large numbers in the soil.*

Some bacteria help to recycle nutrients. For example, some organisms help recycle carbon; during the process of decomposition, bacteria and fungi release carbon dioxide. Others help recycle nitrogen; the roots of leguminous plants, such as peas, have swellings, called root nodules, which contain bacteria that convert nitrogen from the atmosphere to ammonia. Ammonia is also produced by bacteria that live in the soil. This substance is then converted to nitrates and taken up by plants.

Other microorganisms are also present in the soil, including algae and various fungi, which range from organisms composed of single cells to large wild mushrooms. The number of these small organisms in the soil is vast. A peanut shell filled with soil may contain between several hundred million to a few billion microorganisms. The importance of their actions to soil health is very great.

Slightly larger than microorganisms are nematodes (see NEMATODE WORMS). These eel-shaped, colorless worms are abundant in most soils; one acre of soil (0.4 ha) may host a million nematodes. Most of these worms eat dead plants, but some are parasites, eating the roots of live plants (see PARASITES). Ants also abound in soil and tunnel everywhere,

## SOIL AND DISEASE

Soil supports huge numbers of beneficial microorganisms as well as those that are dangerous to humans and animals. Anthrax and tetanus are both diseases caused by bacteria that reside in the soil until they find a new host (see ANTHRAX). They often kill the host animal as they multiply within its body. During this process, the bacteria form spores that are capable of withstanding extreme climatic conditions. These spores are released when the dead host, an anthrax-infected sheep, for example, is buried in the soil and can remain dormant there for long periods. Tunneling creatures, such as earthworms, can bring these spores to the soil surface, where humans and other animals may breath them into their lungs. The spores may also infect people and animals by entering the body through wounds. Either way, the bacterial life cycle continues.

*Soil provides a home to many different organisms, including mammals, such as Richardson's ground squirrel (Spermophilus richardsonii), shown above, which lives in burrows in predominantly dry areas.*

constructing mounds and in the process bringing up subsurface soil. They also gather vegetation into their mounds, which then become rich in organic matter. Every 10 to 20 years, when an ant colony's queen dies, the ants abandon the colony and establish a new one nearby. By burrowing and recolonizing, ants can eventually rework the soil covering an entire prairie.

Earthworms do an essential job by aerating the soil and mixing organic materials with minerals as they go. They collect their food by eating soil and digesting the nutrients it contains. The rest of the soil passes through their bodies and either fills the tunnels as they move or is brought to the surface. The tunnels aerate the soil and help rainwater to drain away. Some earthworms pull leaves from the forest floor into their burrows; these piles of leaves, or middens, enrich the soil. Through their burrowing, the 4,000 or so worms that inhabit an acre of soil can bring between 7 and 18 tons (6.4 to 16.3 metric tons) of soil to the surface each year.

Soil also houses larger animals, including moles, which tunnel just below the surface, eating earthworms, grubs, and plant roots and loosening the soil and making it more porous. The size of a mole's burrow depends largely on the richness of the soil. In an old pasture full of earthworms and insects, moles do not have to burrow very far to find food; in sandier or stonier soil, the burrows may be very deep. Burrowing mice, ground squirrels, marmots, and prairie dogs bring tons of subsoil to the surface.

## Soil aeration

Aeration of the soil is essential for the survival of plants and other organisms. Between 30 and 60 percent of the soil is occupied by space, part of which is filled with soil air. The amount of air filling these spaces can affect the rate at which plants uptake minerals, because plant roots use oxygen for respiration. Other organisms living in the soil need oxygen for respiration. Plants living in swamps and marshes have adaptations that enable them to survive in anaerobic soil, such as large air spaces within plant tissues. They may also have adapted roots; trees, for example, may develop dozens of prop roots that sprout downward from the stem and exist half in the air and half in the waterlogged soil.

## Soil contamination

Farming can contaminate the soil. Pesticides are common culprits (see PESTICIDES). In the 1940s, the pesticide DDT was considered revolutionary because it killed insects quickly. However, widespread use was also killing off eagles and other fish-eating birds (see CARSON, RACHEL LOUISE; DDT). The pesticide percolated through the top layers of soil and entered the food chain through rainwater runoff from sprayed farmland. There is still concern about the health effects of many pesticides still in use.

Toxic waste from industry can also contaminate soil. Every year the United States produces nearly 300 million tons (272 million metric tons) of hazardous waste. Buried industrial chemicals made headlines in 1978 when New York's Love Canal community was abandoned in the wake of an unusually high number of cancers and birth defects. These problems were traced to 44,000 tons (40,000 metric tons) of chemicals that had been buried there 30 years earlier by the Hooker Chemical Company (see POLLUTION), some of which had leaked through the landfill and contaminated the soil and water in the region.

B. HANSON

**See also:** ANTHRAX; BACTERIA; CARSON, RACHEL LOUISE; DDT; DEFORESTATION; DESERTIFICATION; FUNGI KINGDOM; NEMATODE WORMS; PARASITES; PESTICIDES; SAPROPHYTES; SYMBIOSIS.

## SOIL AND CONSERVATION

Peat bogs form as the edges of ponds and lakes fill in with nutrients from higher areas. These nutrients encourage aquatic plants, such as lilies and pondweeds, to grow. As they die, the plants sink into the water and build up at the bottom. The pond or lake becomes shallower, and cattails and reeds take over. When the organic matter reaches the level of the water, sphagnum mosses may begin to grow. These layers of organic matter may reach as deep as 50 feet (15.3 m). In many countries, including the Netherlands, these wetlands are cleared, drained, and used for agriculture because the resulting soil contains a great deal of organic matter, although it is highly acidic and so has to be treated with chemical fertilizers. However, as it dries, the soil becomes loose and powdery and is easily removed by the wind and rain. In dry weather, the soil can catch fire and burn out of control for months, probably destroying its organic layer in the process. After being drained, bog lands settle and can sink well below their original levels, the scientific explanation being that some organic matter decomposes after being exposed to aerobic (oxygen-loving) microorganisms.

**AT RISK**

## Further reading:

Hassett, J. J., and W. Banwart. 1997. *Soils and Their Environment.* Englewood Cliffs, N.J.: Prentice Hall.
Lavelle, P., and A. V. Spain. 2002. *Soil Ecology.* New York: Chapman and Hall.

# SPACE MEDICINE

**Space medicine is the science of preserving or restoring the health or physical condition of astronauts**

As space flights become longer and increasingly common, more and more attention must be paid to the health and overall well-being of the astronauts who make journeys into space. The environment in space is very different from that on Earth, and the physiological processes inside the body of astronauts have to adapt to these changes. Astronauts have suffered a number of medical conditions over the years as a result of space travel because their bodies were not well prepared beforehand. Doctors now thoroughly examine each crew member with care for any signs of health problems when they return to Earth, no matter how long or short the space flight.

## Space maladies

The most common illness experienced by astronauts in space is space sickness, which causes sweating, nausea, vomiting, and cold fingers in as many as two-thirds of space crew members on their first space journey. Space sickness is related to motion sickness and arises because the body's balance system becomes disoriented by weightlessness—the absence of gravity. Without the pull of gravity, tiny calcium crystals in the inner ear move in unusual ways, sending nerve impulses to the brain that contradicts what the eyes and ears sense about the position of the body (see BRAIN). Symptoms occur either because these mixed signals trigger the brain's vomiting response center or because they mimic the action of certain toxins, which the body feels it must eliminate through vomiting.

Astronauts also frequently complain of having a fat face or feelings of fullness in the head, stuffiness in the sinuses, and puffy eyes. These symptoms result from a shift in the pooling of body fluids from the legs and lower body (which occurs because of the influence of gravity on Earth) to the more even distribution of fluids to the upper extremities occurring in space. The fluid redistribution causes no real difficulties in space, but when astronauts return to Earth, changes in blood pressure induce dizziness or fainting when they try to stand up or

*An astronaut unpacks supplies from the medical kit on space shuttle Discovery. In 2001 space shuttles started to transport astronauts to the International Space Station, where a permanent human presence maintains an ongoing space-medicine research program.*

move suddenly. The change in fluid distribution also leads the body to believe it has excess liquid in the tissues, which must be eliminated through increased urination (see EXCRETORY SYSTEMS).

Weightlessness reduces the demands made on the circulatory system (see CIRCULATORY SYSTEMS). As a result, the heart relaxes, slows down, and shrinks. The size of the heart usually returns to normal, however, within about two months of reexposure to Earth's gravity.

In space astronauts have no need to lift their body weight and are able to move without exerting much effort. As a result, their leg muscles begin to waste away. Astronauts on *Skylab 2* lost 11 percent of the volume and 25 percent of the strength in their legs after just under a month in space. However, the astronauts quickly regained both the size and tone of the muscles after resuming their normal activities on Earth.

The most serious potential problem of long-term space travel is the loss of bone (see BONE). On Earth, human bones completely renew themselves about every six months. In zero gravity, however, while the bone is lost at the same rate as on Earth, it is renewed at a much slower rate. Thus, over time, the astronaut's skeleton becomes brittle, a condition called osteoporosis. Osteoporosis may begin after only four to eight months of weightlessness; after prolonged exposure, the bone loss may be permanent. To reduce the risk of developing osteoporosis or muscle wastage, astronauts must exercise for several hours a day while in space.

---

## CORE FACTS

■ Space motion sickness, bone loss, and shifts in fluid balance are the results of spending periods of time in space, which is not subjected to Earth's gravity.

■ Astronauts must train before their flights and, once in orbit, wear suitable clothing and do vigorous exercises to maintain their health and well-being.

■ Low temperatures in space, combined with performing missions outside the spacecraft in direct sunlight, test the skills of astronauts, spacesuit engineers, and space scientists.

---

## CONNECTIONS

● The weightlessness associated with being in space upsets the balance of signals sent by the **EYES** and **EARS**.

● The lack of gravity in space has a considerable effect on the **MUSCULAR SYSTEMS** of astronauts.

*A spacesuit maintains a safe pressure on an astronaut's body of around one-third atmospheric pressure, without which the astronaut's blood would boil and he or she would quickly die. A space suit also protects an astronaut from radiation and from temperature extremes.*

## Space flight and medicine

In the early days of space exploration, astronauts relied on space suits to relieve the problems caused by the absence of atmospheric pressure. The first space suits were made of 15 layers of material and were so heavily pressurized that they forced the fingers to extend straight out.

Shuttle spacecraft now have the same atmospheric pressure as Earth. Crew members need wear only lightweight flight suits during liftoff and reentry; they must wear pressurized space suits only when they carry out extravehicular activities (EVAs). Space suits are now reinforced to withstand the vacuum of space by maintaining pressure at 4 pounds per square inch, which is less than a third of Earth's atmospheric pressure at sea level of 14.7 pounds per square inch. Astronauts cannot survive breathing ordinary air at such a low pressure; thus, the suits circulate pure oxygen, which is then filtered to remove the carbon dioxide that the astronauts breathe out (see RESPIRATORY SYSTEMS).

Space suits are also adjusted to temperature. The temperature in space is very low, ranging from -418 to -454 °F (-250 to -270 °C), but astronauts typically perform EVAs in direct sunlight. The suits must therefore have a cooling system to reduce the effects both of the heat from the Sun and the astronaut's own body heat. Another advance in flight gear includes a piece of equipment called the lower body negative pressure device—a pair of vacuum trousers that counteract the fat-face syndrome.

Space flyers routinely undergo training to desensitize themselves to space motion sickness. Some astronauts-in-training learn how to alter their physical responses to motion sickness by consciously controlling their breathing and muscle movements. Other astronauts prepare for the weightless environment in the Vomit Comet, a military cargo plane that flies in such a way as to produce forces that fluctuate between zero gravity and 1.8 gravity (Earth's gravity is 1.0).

During long space flights, loss of bone and muscle tissue is kept in check by in-flight exercise programs using a treadmill equipped with bungee cords to make the muscles work harder. One astronaut who exercised for four hours a day had only 7 percent bone loss after 184 days in space.

Space medicine is becoming increasingly important as long stays in space become more common. Space medicine specialists must now prepare astronauts for such missions as a three-year trip to Mars or prolonged duty on the space station *Freedom*. Space scientists at the University of Texas, Dallas, are experimenting with an inflatable collar that may prevent the loss of body fluids during space flight. Engineers at Massachusetts Institute of Technology, Cambridge, are testing a rotating bed as a way of reproducing gravity so it can act as an onboard centrifuge and provide astronauts with periodic exposure to simulated gravity identical to that on Earth.

K. SANDRICK

**See also:** BONE; BRAIN; CIRCULATORY SYSTEMS; EXCRETORY SYSTEMS; PHYSIOLOGY; RESPIRATORY SYSTEMS.

**Further reading:**
Evans, C., and J. Ballard. 2001. *Safe Passage: Astronaut Care for Exploration Missions.* Washington, D.C.: National Academy Press.
Pool, S., and A. E. Nicogossian. 2002. *Space Physiology and Medicine.* 4th ed. Philadelphia: Williams and Wilkins.

## ANIMALS IN SPACE

Laika, a female dog, lived in a cylindrical chamber for seven days on the satellite *Sputnik 2* in 1957, proving for the first time that living creatures could survive orbital flight. She was euthanized (put to death painlessly), however, before the satellite burned up on reentry to Earth.

The use of animals by space agencies has also included monkeys and apes. The chimpanzee, Ham, sent into orbit by NASA in 1961, showed that animals could not only survive but also perform various tasks in space. Also, two weeks before the *Apollo 11* voyage (the first manned voyage to land on the moon), the flight of the mission's spacecraft was cut short because its passenger, a small monkey, became ill and died as a result of body fluid loss. This led space doctors to delay the Moon shot until they could protect their astronauts from similar problems.

## A CLOSER LOOK

# SPECIAL EDUCATIONAL NEEDS

**Special educational needs describes a variety of problems and disorders that affect a person's ability to learn**

## CONNECTIONS

● Special educational needs include **AUTISM**. Some needs affect the speed of **CHILD DEVELOPMENT**, and all have an impact on **LEARNING**.

● The most serious conditions covered by the term *special educational needs* are the result either of **BRAIN** damage and lower **INTELLIGENCE** or physical disabilities, such as impaired **VISION** or **HEARING**.

The term *special educational needs* was coined in the late 1970s to group together the many different types of difficulties and disabilities that can affect learning. People with special educational needs have requirements beyond those provided by the normal system of education. The term is sometimes also used to describe extremely bright or gifted pupils, but for the most part and in this article, it is taken to mean those people who encounter difficulty with learning.

## Slow learners

Slow learners include all children or teenagers who demonstrate difficulties in various aspects of learning. Those with the most complex needs, often accompanied by genetic or medical disorders, are said to have severe learning difficulties. Many children with severe learning difficulties are taught in separate schools or specialist units, although moves toward increased inclusion have seen a greater proportion of this population educated in mainstream schools. While these children have difficulties with learning, educators now recognize that they can make progress with structured teaching approaches, although at a generally slower pace.

*Young people with special educational needs often have trouble with memory. Some conditions may be linked to phobias and difficulty in expressing emotions.*

Pupils with moderate learning difficulties make up the majority of the special needs population. Moderate learning difficulties may include a wide range of recognized problems, such as dyslexia, dyspraxia, and attention deficit disorder. Unlike severe

### CORE FACTS

■ People with special educational needs have requirements for learning that are not provided by conventional teaching or systems of education.

■ People with special educational needs may have mental or physical disabilities that make it harder for them to learn, or they may have a condition that prevents them from learning certain skills by traditional methods.

■ People with severe or moderate learning difficulties or emotional and behavioral problems have special educational needs. Moderate learning difficulties include dyslexia, dyspraxia, and attention deficit disorder (ADD).

# DYSLEXIA

Dyslexia is one of the most common of all special educational needs. Scientists estimate that there are as many as 40 million dyslexic children and adults in the United States. The word *dyslexia* comes from two Greek words: *dys*, meaning "impaired" and *lexia*, "word." Dyslexic children usually have difficulty with spelling and often get letters confused. The greatest confusion occurs between letters that are mirror images of one another, such as *b* and *d* or *p* and *q*. Another symptom of dyslexia is jumbled spelling; words are written out with all the correct letters present but in the wrong order.

Dyslexia can affect more than just spelling, however. Many dyslexic children mix up left and right and have trouble with directions. They may also find it difficult to follow instructions with two or more parts, such as "Go to the store cupboard, get a board rubber, and take it to Mr. Brown."

A major feature of dyslexia is difficulty with sequencing (putting things in order). This inability, combined with a tendency to write numbers backward (14 instead of 41, for example), can also cause problems with math.

The exact cause of dyslexia is not understood properly, although it is more common in children who have a history of learning difficulties in their family than those who do not. What is clear is that dyslexic people are no less intelligent or less able than anyone else. Many dyslexic people display compensating strengths for the weaknesses caused by their condition. Dyslexic children and teenagers are often more creative and better physically coordinated than their peers, for example, while dyslexic adults include some of the world's most successful and famous people, including actor Tom Cruise, entrepreneur Richard Branson, and artist Pablo Picasso, to name but three.

## A CLOSER LOOK

*Some underachievers at school have emotional or behavioral problems rather than specific learning difficulties. These young people are withdrawn, aggressive, or disaffected (disinterested in any aspect of school life).*

learning difficulties, moderate learning difficulties are not always linked to intelligence (see INTELLIGENCE). Many students with moderate learning difficulties are just as bright as their classmates but find it harder to learn by conventional methods.

At the other end of the spectrum from children with severe learning difficulties are those children of below-average ability who have always been taught in mainstream schools. Many children with Down

syndrome have learning difficulties, although individuals demonstrate a range of levels of need and ability. It is important not to stereotype pupils ar have low expectations of a pupil who has Down syndrome or emotional or behavioral difficulty.

## Types of learning difficulties

There are a variety of conditions that can affect learning ability. Some difficulties have a general effect and make it harder for a person to learn any new subject. Other conditions are more specific and cause problems only in certain areas.

Dyslexia is the best-known type of learning difficulty. People with dyslexic display a wide range of symptoms (see the box on the left), but most have trouble with reading and spelling. Dyslexia affects a huge number of people but until fairly recently was not properly understood or acknowledged. The major turning point came in 1968, when the World Federation of Neurology defined dyslexia as "a disorder in children who, despite conventional classroom experience, fail to attain the language skills of reading, writing, and spelling commensurate with their intellectual abilities." Before this time, many obviously bright dyslexic students had been dismissed as simply being lazy.

Dyspraxia, a difficulty with coordinating muscles and movement, is less widely known. The problem is caused by the system in the brain responsible for sending messages to the body being underdeveloped (see BRAIN). Dyspraxia occurs in 2 percent of the population and is more common in boys than girls. The effects of dyspraxia vary depending on how pronounced the condition is. At its most severe, it can cause problems with speech, short-term memory, and the ability to read and write (see MEMORY; SPEECH). The difficulty with coordinating muscles can make it hard for children to hold a pencil or pen or participate in basic physical activities.

Attention deficit disorder (ADD), or attention deficit hyperactivity disorder (ADHD), is one of the most common of all problems affecting learning. Between 3 and 5 percent of all school-aged children are believed to have ADD. As with dyslexia, ADD is not linked to intelligence and can affect children of any level of intellectual ability. The main symptoms are a short attention span, forgetfulness, failure to finish tasks, reluctance to begin tasks that require sustained mental effort, carelessness, and difficulty following instructions. The majority of children with ADD also exhibit signs of hyperactivity, and one-third have another related condition. Three-quarters of all children with ADD are boys. Attention deficit disorder can be treated with a combination of medication and therapy or counseling. The medication helps to normalize brain activity. The most commonly prescribed drugs for this condition are Ritalin, Dexedrine, and Adderall.

Another widely known about but rarely understood condition affecting learning is autism (see AUTISM). Autism is four times more common in boys than girls and ranges from profound learning difficulty to slight impairment of social skills in people of normal intelligence. The mildest form of autism is called Asperger syndrome. Children with Asperger syndrome generally have above-average intelligence but have difficulty in communicating.

Autistic children have little understanding of the thoughts, feelings, and needs of others. They often seem indifferent to the world around them and do not return affection. Autism can affect a child's ability to learn language, and when they do, they may use limited, repetitious phrases or talk about the same thing all of the time. Teaching a child with autism is often extremely difficult, not because of lack of intelligence but because of his or her apparent lack of motivation. Autistic people also have a strong dislike of change and may react with tantrums if introduced too suddenly to something new.

## Emotional and behavioral problems

Some children and teenagers who do not have specific learning difficulties may still underachieve in school because of emotional problems or difficulties in managing their behavior (see EMOTIONS; LEARNING). Most children with emotional and behavioral difficulties fall into one of three categories: withdrawn, acting out (aggressive), or disaffected.

Withdrawn children are usually quiet and passive and often underreact to situations. They may have low self-esteem and appear unhappy. The cause of withdrawal may be clinical depression or a history of abuse, although it is often difficult to identify causal factors. Symptoms include oversensitivity to criticism, a lack of interest in work, inability to form close relationships, and anxiousness to conform. Withdrawn pupils often go unnoticed, although their needs are as great as those of any other child or teenager who has problems with learning.

By contrast, students who act out are hard to miss. Often overindulged or poorly disciplined at

*A deaf student and his teacher use a combination of hearing aid, sign language, and lip reading to help overcome learning difficulties. Deafness is one of the most common physical problems that can affect an individual's capacity to learn.*

## DEAFNESS AND LEARNING

Being deaf has no effect on a person's intelligence but it can have a major effect on his or her ability to learn (see HEARING; LEARNING). This situation is particularly true in classes where children with normal hearing are taught alongside a child or children with hearing difficulties. In this sort of environment, most of the information transmitted from teacher to pupil is done by voice. Unless the teacher is aware of a deaf or partially deaf student's disability and needs, that student will have trouble following a lesson.

Very few people with hearing disabilities are profoundly deaf (unable to hear anything at all). Most people can hear some sounds but not others. There are two main types of hearing loss: conductive and sensorineural. Conductive hearing loss is caused by interference in the transmission of sound from the outer to the inner ear. This problem may be the result of blockage or physical damage to the middle ear. People with conductive hearing loss simply hear everything much more quietly. Loud voices sound like whispers,

while quiet voices may not be heard at all. Sensorineural hearing loss is rarer but more likely to be permanent. It is caused by damage to the inner ear and usually results in sounds becoming distorted. In the most common form of sensorineural loss, high-frequency sounds are cut out, with the overall effect that vowels are clearly audible but most consonants cannot be heard. Hearing aids can help with conductive hearing loss, but people with sensorineural loss find learning to speak difficult if not impossible.

Just as children with normal hearing learn the sounds of words, so most deaf children learn to lip-read. Teachers can take a few simple measures to improve a deaf student's chances of learning, such as sitting the student at the front of the class and near a window so that the teacher's face is well lit, and cutting down on background noise. In addition, the availability of cochlear implants and high-technology hearing aids can greatly improve the access of some deaf children to learning.

**A CLOSER LOOK**

## Physical and sensory impairments

Special educational needs covers all types of problems with learning. These problems include difficulties caused by physical disabilities. One of the most common physical impediments to learning is deafness (see the box on page 1537), which makes it hard for students to follow any type of teaching by voice (see HEARING). The use of signing or symbol representation in teaching is commonly seen as an essential element of enabling such pupils to learn. Visual impairment (partial or complete lack of vision in both eyes) causes another set of problems (see VISION). Visually impaired children have no trouble following a teacher's voice, but they are generally unable to use conventional books or visual aids. Those children with a partial loss of vision may be able to make use of this equipment with some type of additional aid, such as a handheld magnifier. Alternatively, they might be able to use large-print books or materials that have been printed out larger by their teachers.

Students with no vision in either eye require specialized equipment to learn, such as books written in Braille. Invented by a 15-year-old French boy, Louis Braille, in 1824, Braille uses patterns of raised dots to represent letters. Books or worksheets written in Braille are read using the tip of the index finger. Contracted words, such as *HM* for him, are sometimes used to speed up the reading process. Just as raised dots are used in Braille to represent letters, so raised shapes can be used on specially produced worksheets for diagrams. As with deafness, visual impairment has no impact on a child's intelligence, and with these aids a blind or partially sighted child can learn just as effectively as one with normal vision.

There is a wide range of other physical disabilities that may affect a child's ability to learn. Conditions such as cerebral palsy, spina bifida, and muscular dystrophy impact on coordination and movement, and affect the student's ability to write and sometimes to speak. With the correct equipment and assistance, however, these conditions can be at least partially bypassed and need not prevent anyone with them from learning.

D. GILPIN

**See also:** ANXIETY; COGNITION; EMOTIONS; MEMORY; PERSONALITY DISORDER; PHOBIAS; SPEECH; STRESS.

## Further reading:
Batshaw, M. L. 2002. *Children with Disabilities.* Baltimore: Paul H. Brookes Publishing.
Knight, P., and R. Swanwick. 1999. *The Care and Education of a Deaf Child.* Tonawanda, N.Y.: Multilingual Matters.
Mesibov, G., and M. Howley. 2003. *Accessing the Curriculum for Pupils with Autistic Spectrum Disorders.* London: David Fulton Publishers.
Riddick, B., J. Wolfe, and D. Lumsdon. 2002. *Dyslexia: A Practical Guide for Teachers and Parents.* London: David Fulton Publishers.

*A teacher helps a young blind student use a book written in Braille. Blind students are another group who have special educational needs.*

home, they can be extremely disruptive and cause problems for other students as well as for themselves. Aggressive children, usually noisy and disobedient, disregard the needs of others and are often either bullies or the victims of bulleying. The learning problems of aggressive children stem from poor concentration and a confrontational attitude to authority and rules. Aggressive children make it hard for teachers to teach them and go out of their way to avoid being taught; many aggressive children are truant, for example.

Disaffected students tend to be teenagers. For them school and the subjects taught there are irrelevant. The disaffected student shows no interest in schoolwork and lacks motivation. He or she may have little consideration for others, be unimpressed by school rules, and be truant. As with withdrawn and aggressive children, the best solution is closer personal attention from the teacher, although it is not always possible owing to the needs of other students in the class.

# SPECIES

The basic unit of classification is species (see TAXONOMY). By counting the number of species present in an area, scientists get an idea of its biodiversity. However, there is no single definition of species that is satisfactory to all biologists. Most biologists agree that a species is a group of individuals that can interbreed to produce fertile offspring. This concept is the biological species definition. In practice it is rarely possible to establish when interbreeding cannot occur, and thus many biologists group species simply on physical similarity, although members of breeding populations can vary in appearance. The biological concept cannot be used for species that reproduce asexually or fossil species.

A species is a subdivision of a genus, which is a subdivision of a family. Thus, wolves, dogs, and coyotes are species of the genus *Canis*, of the family Canidae. This hierarchical classification system was developed by the 18th-century Swedish botanist and taxonomist (classifier) Carl von Linné. Von Linné is better known by his latin name, Carolus Linnaeus. In Linnaeus's binomial (two-name) system, the first name (capitalized and, after its first mention, abbreviated) expresses the genus, a group of species that are similar or related. The second, usually a descriptive or geographic adjective, denotes the species. Thus, the wolf, dog, and coyote are named, respectively, *C. lupus, C. familiaris*, and *C. latrans*.

## Early ideas about species

Systematic classification of organisms began with Greek philosopher Aristotle (384–322 BCE), who categorized them by their physical similarities. This system persisted for about 2,000 years, until the scientific revolution of the 1600s inspired a more detailed examination of nature.

The concept of the biological species has its origin in the work of English botanist John Ray (1627–1705). The first stage in the development of any science is the observation and classification of its

*Greek philosopher Aristotle (384–322 BCE) proposed the first classification of organisms, based on their physical similarities.*

phenomena. Ray classified and catalogued plants according to their seeds, which he considered to be invariable and therefore the best basis for a natural taxonomy. He published his three-volume *Historia Plantarum*, an encyclopedia of all known plants, between 1686 and 1704. Some 50 years later, Linnaeus organized all known plants and animals into hierarchies of class, order, genus, and species, assigning *C. lupus* to the order Mammalia (mammals) and class Carnivora (carnivores). He named the human species *Homo sapiens*, meaning "thinking human."

## Limitations

Until the emergence of English naturalist Charles Darwin (1809–1882) and other 19th-century evolutionists, it was accepted, at least publicly, that all forms of life were fixed unchangeably as God had created them. Thus, by biblical authority, species could not change, and new species could not be created. A requirement of evolutionary theory, however, is that species do change and that new species arise through speciation. Biologists now define species of sexual organisms not as fixed entities but as populations of breeding individuals isolated reproductively from other breeding populations. This definition is called the biological species concept.

Classification based on physical similarities has limitations. It does not allow for individuals from the same species who do not seem to resemble each

## CORE FACTS

- A species is the basic classification unit of biodiversity.
- Species are populations of breeding individuals reproductively isolated from other breeding populations.
- Isolation of breeding populations makes possible the evolutionary divergence of species.
- Species change over time, and new species can arise through evolutionary speciation.
- Species can be isolated reproductively and geographically.
- The mass creation of new species has always been accompanied by the mass loss of existing species.
- There are estimated to be 10 million species on Earth, and more than 10,000 become extinct each year.

## CONNECTIONS

- The concept of "species" helps scientists describe and understand **BIODIVERSITY**.

- **EVOLUTION** by **NATURAL SELECTION** leads to change within species and the creation of new species, while others become extinct.

- Many **BIRDS OF PREY** are now **ENDANGERED SPECIES**.

*The mule is a hybrid, the result of a male donkey mating with a female horse. Like many hybrids, it is sterile, so it cannot produce offspring that are part donkey and part horse. Horses and donkeys, therefore, are preserved as discrete species.*

other. In some cases, apparently similar organisms reveal wide individual differences on closer examination. In others, related species that by definition do not normally interbreed may do so under changed circumstances, including artificial environments.

Despite these difficulties, the biological species concept works well when classifying living, sexually reproducing organisms. Difficulties multiply, however, when biologists classify fossils of extinct organisms. Not only do they know little of the organisms' method of breeding, but fossilized organisms lived at different times in Earth's history. Species change over time and can become reproductively isolated or reunited at different times. Biologists must classify fossil species without knowledge of reproductive isolation and according to a different species concept that uses physical similarities only.

Even some living organisms, those that reproduce only asexually, such as some bacteria, some corals, and some plants, provide problems for the biologi-

cal species concept. They do not form breeding populations, so their criteria for species are again limited to physical similarities—in structure, chemicals, physiology, and genes.

## Reproductive isolation

Reproductive isolation is the crucial step in speciation, the formation of a new species. If one asks how a species, such as *C. lupus*, originated, essentially one is asking how at some earlier period wolves were isolated reproductively from other carnivores.

The mechanisms by which species become isolated reproductively are either prezygotic (occurring before fertilization) or postzygotic (occurring after fertilization). Most mechanisms are prezygotic, interfering to keep members of different breeding populations from mating (see MATING). This interference can be ecological (connected with timing), mechanical (associated with the nature of the respective sperm or eggs), or behavioral.

Ecological isolation occurs when breeding populations live in the same area but in different habitats and so do not meet and therefore cannot breed. Some monkeys living in mangroves spend all their life in treetops eating fruit. They do not encounter monkeys of another species that live near the water below, and eat crabs. The monkey species are separated by their contrasting lifestyles.

When populations are receptive to mating and fertilization in different seasons or at different times, they are in effect isolated by time. For example, female dogs come into estrus, or heat, only once or twice a year; however, cats are continually in estrus until they mate.

Mating is impossible between species with genital organs that are different in shape or size; thus, many species are isolated reproductively by mechanical means. Even in plants and animals that fertilize one another externally, the sperm and eggs of different species may be incompatible and unable to join in successful fertilization (see FERTILIZATION).

However, the most powerful biological isolating factor in animals is probably behavior (see ANIMAL BEHAVIOR). Rituals of courtship and acceptance are essential for breeding and ovulation in a wide range of species (see COURTSHIP). For example, the male bowerbird (family Ptilonorhynchidae) attracts the female by constructing and decorating a bower of twigs, flowers, shells, and stones. If the female does not enter the bower and accept the male, breeding does not take place. In some mammals, the female will not ovulate unless the male of the species engages in certain behavior. Such species-specific behavior, which often includes visual, sound, and olfactory (scent) components, keeps breeding populations isolated and their gene pools distinct.

Each of these prezygotic barriers helps keep populations apart. When they fail, the resulting embryos do not usually develop into normal, viable offspring. These so-called hybrids are common in plant species; hybrid seeds usually fail to germinate. Hybrid sheep and goat embryos usually die before birth.

Hybrids that do develop into adults are usually sterile. The hybrid offspring of a male donkey and a female horse is a mule. The mule is an example of so-called hybrid vigor; it is superior to either parent in strength, endurance, and agility. However, like many hybrids, it is sterile. Sometimes hybrids resulting from the mating of closely related species have partial fertility, but their offspring are typically weak and sterile and develop poorly. This hybrid breakdown is more common in plants than in animals.

## Geographic isolation

In geographic, or allopatric, speciation, a species originates by geographic isolation. A population may be divided into a smaller populations by a volcanic eruption, an earthquake that creates a barrier, a lake drying up, or the covering of an isthmus (a narrow strip of land connecting two land masses) by the ocean. Such geographic events can isolate populations for long periods, during which the populations evolve along separate lines. The populations might be under different selection pressures in their different locations, but there are also chance elements in evolutionary processes, both in natural selection and in genetic drift (see EVOLUTION). Both chance and the differing selection pressures lead the separated populations to diverge (evolve differently). In time, the populations become so different that they speciate. For example, a population of Eurasian brown bears (*Ursus arctos*) was divided by glaciers that formed in the Pleistocene epoch (1.6 million to 10,000 years ago). The western population evolved into the cave bear (*Ursus spelaeus*), now extinct.

If long-separated populations are reunited by further geographic changes, they may be so different that behavioral or mechanical reproductive isolation will maintain the barrier between them.

When species are dispersed over remote areas, such as islands or distant continents, they will adapt over time to the different environments. An example is the different path mammalian evolution took in Australia and its neighboring islands. In the absence of predators or competition for food and space from large placental mammals, pouched mammals, such as wombats (in the family Vombatidae), koalas (*Phascolarctos cinereus*), kangaroos (in the family Macropodidae), and the Tasmanian wolf (*Thylacinus cynocephalus*), proliferated (see MARSUPIALS).

Few placental mammals are native to Australia, but in the rest of the world placental mammals became the largest and the dominant species and drove marsupials in those areas to extinction (see EXTINCTION). Monotremes (the duckbill platypus, *Ornithorhynchus anatinus*, and the spiny anteaters, in the family Tachyglossidae), an order of primitive, egg-laying mammals, are unique to Australia and New Guinea, another Australasian island.

## Adaptive radiation

Multiple geographic isolations, as in the case of an archipelago (group) of islands or valleys separated by impassable mountains, can result in an original

---

### SPECIES EXTINCTION

Extinction has always been as much a part of the evolutionary process as speciation. It has been estimated that 98 percent of all species that have ever existed are extinct. Species become extinct because competitors drive them out or habitats change or as a result of some catastrophe. One theory attributes the extinction of the dinosaurs to habitat changes resulting from the collision of an asteroid with Earth (see DINOSAURS; EXTINCTION).

The main reason for species extinction now is the destruction of habitats brought about by pollution or human exploitation of natural resources. Mass extinctions in the past have wiped out large numbers of species, leaving room for others to develop and proliferate, sometimes through adaptive radiation. The extinction of the dinosaurs, ending their 150-million-year rule over Earth, made possible the present age of the mammals.

### AT RISK

ancestor species very rapidly diversifying into many related species. This diversification is called adaptive radiation. A famous example of rapid speciation from a single ancestor species is that of Darwin's finches. When Darwin visited the Galápagos Islands, he found 14 species of finches that did not live elsewhere. These finches had adapted to the different foods and habitats found on different islands in the Galápagos archipelago. Some species ate insects and others ate plants, the beaks adapting to the needs of the different types of available food. Members of the original finch species arriving on the islands found no competitors. Populations of the finches filled the various ecological niches by adapting in different ways, and in the end, formed different species.

*The Virginia opossum (Didelphis virginiana) is one of many species of opossums that live in the United States. Opossums are the only marsupials that live outside Australia and nearby islands.*

## MUTATION

A mutation is a sudden change in a gene or chromosome. Mutations occur through errors in DNA replication, sometimes as a result of external causes, such as radiation or chemicals. Many mutations are harmful, some are neutral, and some are adaptive. In the case of adaptive mutation, natural selection may favor the mutation, promoting evolutionary change. The average probability of a nucleotide, one of the elements in the DNA of the gene, being changed by mutation in one generation is less than 1 in 100 million. However, the human genome is 3 billion nucleotides long, so most people have some mutations.

In addition to mutations, the genetic makeup of an organism can be changed by human influence, often to produce species with characteristics beneficial to people. The human influence is either indirect, through selective breeding (see SELECTIVE BREEDING) or direct, through genetic engineering (see GENETIC ENGINEERING).

### A CLOSER LOOK

*The banana is an example of a polyploid species, in which there are extra chromosome sets. Polyploid plants tend to be larger and more vigorous than nonpolyploid plants.*

Honeycreepers (birds of the subfamily Thraupinae) provide another example of adaptive radiation. They live only in the Hawaiian Islands. All of Hawaii's 15 honeycreeper species are believed to have evolved from a single immigrant species.

### Sympatric speciation

In some cases, new species are formed in the same location, that is, in sympatry. This sympatric speciation may occur as a result of sudden genetic changes or mutations in part of the breeding population. These changes can occur in one generation and may result in a change in the ecological niche; thus, reproductive isolation may be the result.

An important example of this form of speciation is called polyploidy, in which an extra set or sets of chromosomes are present in the nucleus instead of the usual two. Polyploidy occurs in some amphibians and some hermaphroditic animals, such as snails, earthworms, and planarians (see CHROMOSOMES; HERMAPHRODITES). Many cultivated plants, especially flowering plants, are polyploids, for example, bananas, wheat, and some species of strawberries.

### Endangered species

The creation of new species has always been accompanied by the loss of existing species. Species are now endangered by many factors, but human activity is the most destructive. In the last 400 years, the expansion of humans across the globe has resulted in the disappearance of many species. Hunting, pollution, and the destruction of habitats for building and for agriculture have accounted for most of this loss.

Of the estimated 10 million species on Earth, more than 10,000 are lost each year. Much of this loss is due to habitat destruction, amounting annually to some 125,000 square miles (325,000 km$^2$) of tropical forest, the home of a great many species. The steady increase in the human population is raising the level of carbon dioxide in Earth's atmosphere; as a result global temperature is increasing through the so-called greenhouse effect (see GLOBAL WARMING). These changes are detrimental to species that have adapted to the present atmosphere and the environment it supports.

R. STILLER

**See also:** ANIMAL BEHAVIOR; CHROMOSOMES; COURTSHIP; DINOSAURS; EXTINCTION; FERTILIZATION; FOSSILS; GENETIC ENGINEERING; GLOBAL WARMING; HERMAPHRODITES; MARSUPIALS; MATING; MUTATION; SELECTIVE BREEDING; TAXONOMY.

### Further reading:
Gould, S. J. 2002. *The Structure of Evolutionary Theory.* Cambridge, Mass.: Harvard University Press.
Skelton, P., ed. 1994. *Evolution: A Biological and Paleontological Approach.* New York: Addison Wesley.
Wilson, E. O. 2002. *The Future of Life.* New York: Knopf.

# SPEECH

Humans can communicate vocally by speaking, screaming, crying, or laughing, but speech is humans' main and most versatile form of vocal communication. Speech is a way of expressing thoughts with spoken words, but it is not the only method of expressing thoughts. People can use writing, morse code, or hand signals instead. Speech may seem easy to most people, but a complex sequence of muscle movements is needed to produce it.

## Production of speech

Speech has various components, and the act of speaking involves five distinct processes, namely, respiration, phonation, resolution, articulation, and regulation. Respiration provides a varying flow of air from the lungs to power the production of the voice in the larynx and the formation of words through the nose, mouth, and jaw (see JAWS). When speaking, an individual breathes more quickly than usual, and then exhales over a longer period of time to build up a sufficient amount of air pressure and airflow to produce the varied sounds of speech.

Phonation, the process of producing vocal sound, occurs when air flowing from the lungs causes the vocal cords to vibrate, much as the reed in a clarinet does. Vocal cords are a pair of flexible folds of muscle and ligament in the larynx. The frequency (and hence pitch) of sound produced is varied by adjustments in the tension on the vocal cords.

Resonation amplifies the sounds that come from the vocal cords and fashions them into a human voice by modulating them through the action of the throat (or pharynx), palate, mouth, and nasal cavities. Opening or closing the pharynx affects the softness or harshness of the tone of voice produced.

The palate acts as a valve and directs airflow from the larynx to the mouth and nose. Because the size and thickness of the walls of the nasal cavities differ in every individual, the nasal cavities are most responsible for the unique voice produced by each person.

Articulation involves the production of different speech sounds by the movements of the tongue, lips,

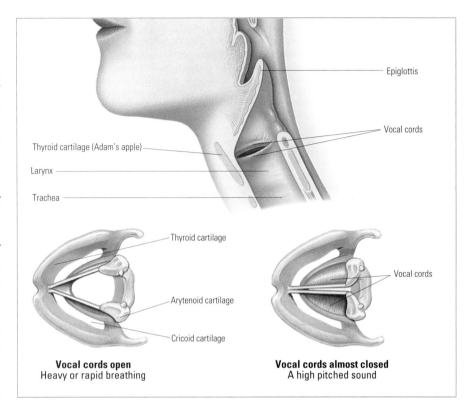

Epiglottis

Vocal cords

Thyroid cartilage (Adam's apple)

Larynx

Trachea

Thyroid cartilage

Arytenoid cartilage

Cricoid cartilage

Vocal cords

**Vocal cords open**
Heavy or rapid breathing

**Vocal cords almost closed**
A high pitched sound

*The vocal cords are located in the larynx and enable humans to make vocal sounds. The sounds are modified by the throat, nose, and mouth to create speech.*

and jaws (see TONGUE). The production of various vowel sounds depends on the placement of the tongue in the mouth, the degree of opening of the mouth, and the position of the jaws and the lips.

For example, the tongue lies flat on the floor of the mouth when creating the vowel sound *uh* (as in "other"). The mouth opens only slightly and the lips are pursed when producing the vowel sound *u* (as in "mute"). The jaws open most widely to form the vowel sound *a* (as in "father").

Consonants require precise placement of the tongue and lips to direct the airstream from the lungs and larynx properly. The lips are responsible primarily for making the sounds for *p*, *b*, and *m*. Sounds for *f* and *v* are formed by placing the upper teeth on the lower lip. Sounds for *n* and *l* are produced by bringing the tip of the tongue in contact with the teeth. Lifting the back of the tongue to the soft palate (the muscular flap at the back of the roof of the mouth) produces the sounds for *g* and *k*.

Regulation is the control process exerted by the brain when it coordinates the operation of the lungs, larynx, pharynx, mouth, tongue, lips, and jaws (see BRAIN). Regulation also directs the formation of meaningful words and sentences and determines whether the words and sentences produced by the voice are conveying the proper message.

The cortex (outer layer) of the brain is the site for storing long-term memory (see MEMORY). Long-term memory is necessary for applying the rules of language to create a specific verbal message. The cortex also stores short-term memory, which processes

## CORE FACTS

- Speech is a system of sounds produced by the vocal cords, which, through the use of language, allows communication with others.
- The components of speech are respiration, phonation (using the voice), resolution, articulation, and regulation.
- Speech sounds are produced using different movements of the tongue, lips, jaw, and vocal cords and include vowel sounds and consonants.
- The cortex of the brain stores long-term memory. Vocabulary and grammatical rules stored in the memory enable an individual to compose words and sentences.

## CONNECTIONS

● Speech requires precise control of the **LUNGS** and the **TONGUE**.

● Individuals who have lost their sense of **HEARING** may communicate using sign language.

● Speech has played a vital role in **HUMAN EVOLUTION**.

## EVOLUTION OF SPEECH

No one knows when prehistoric humans began to speak. Some scientists consider that humans first spoke between 2 and 3 million years ago; others believe speech developed 40,000 years ago during the fourth glacial period.

Human ancestors, like today's apes, undoubtedly communicated through gestures and facial expressions. Later during human evolution, the development of the human brain enabled the long-term storage of the rules of language, as well as the ability to use symbolic reasoning and language as a vehicle for communication. Language was needed by prehistoric humans to support their evolving thinking processes.

Language was also necessary for exchanging information with members of the group or tribe to coordinate the hunting of animals, protect one another from danger, and deal in other more subtle ways with a developing social system. Speech allowed them to convey messages at night or in otherwise poor visibility, shout warnings over long distances, and free their hands for using tools.

## EVOLUTION

messages from others, fashions an appropriate response to individual messages, and tracks the production of words, phrases, and sentences as they are being formed by the voice.

The centers of speech production are in the left hemisphere of the brain in right-handed people and are named after the various people who first described them. Wernicke's area, which is near the temporal lobe (the area at the side of the head at around ear level), is a crucial center for language. An injury to this part of the brain does not affect articulation, but it impairs speech by interfering with the recollection of verbal sounds and with comprehension (understanding). Broca's area, which is located in the frontal lobe (in the forehead area) and is con-

nected to Wernicke's area by neuronal pathways, controls the movement of the muscles of speech. An injury or tumor (swelling) in this area interrupts the coordinated sequence of movements needed for articulation but has no effect on speech comprehension. Individuals who have suffered an injury to Broca's area understand what is being said by others, but they are incapable of making meaningful verbal sounds or speaking using the correct words.

### Development of speech

During the first few weeks of life, babies are usually fairly quiet, making crying sounds only to convey their discomfort. By two to four months, they begin to coo and gurgle to indicate when they are content, and they begin to notice the sounds of speech around them (see CHILD DEVELOPMENT). Babbling, which consists of streams of sounds and syllables repeated over and over again, starts at about four to nine months. Babbling is a critical phase in language development because it indicates that the baby is exploring the use of his or her own voice.

Over time, babies gradually begin to recognize and learn how to form vowel and consonant speech sounds, and they realize that these sounds provide a vehicle for communication (see COMMUNICATION). Between the age of 9 and 18 months, babies start to transform speech sounds into simple words, such as *mama* and *dada*. By the age of two, children can usually utter two-word phrases. By the time they reach the age of four, children have a good knowledge of grammar, a fairly strong vocabulary, and complete mastery of vowel and consonant sounds. By the age of six, most children can use adult syntax (that is, put words together to form meaningful sentences) and grammar.

### Speech therapy

There are approximately 45,000 speech therapists in the United States who treat a wide variety of problems related to the use of speech and language development. Nearly half of all speech therapists work in the public school system, where they educate children about proper speech patterns and correct irregularities and speech impediments.

Speech therapists also work in community speech and hearing centers, helping deaf children learn how to communicate, guiding stroke or head-injury victims through long-term speech and language rehabilitation, and training children and adults in voice modulation so they can prevent damage to their vocal structures from misuse.

In hospital settings, speech therapists usually assess the speaking ability of stroke or head-injury victims so that physicians can plan the most appropriate treatment. Therapists may help patients with comprehension or the production of meaningful words and phrases. They may also teach cancer patients who have had their larynx removed surgically how to produce esophageal speech, a technique that creates vocal sounds by forcing air into and out of the esophagus.

*As part of a speech therapy program, the child pictured below is blowing on a ball to develop his control of intra-oral (within the mouth) air pressure.*

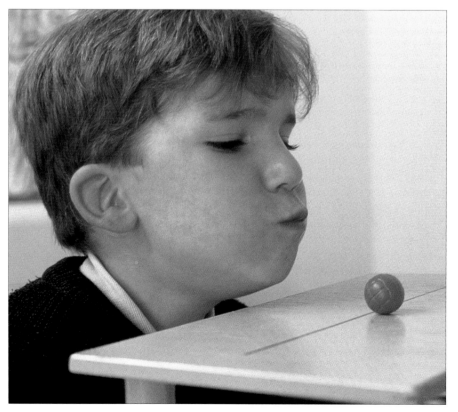

*Sign language is an effective alternative to speech-based language. People who cannot hear or produce speech can use sign language in conjunction with lipreading.*

## Stuttering

When individuals interrupt the flow of certain speech sounds an abnormally high number of times or for an unusually long time, they are said to be stuttering. The interruptions in sound patterns may take the form of repetitions of individual sounds, syllables, or single words, or they may simply prolong the formation of a particular sound.

Approximately 1 percent of all school children worldwide have a stuttering problem, and at least 15 percent of the world's population has stuttered at some point in their lives. However, only 6 percent of those who stutter continue to do so for more than six months. Stuttering tends to run in families; there may be some as yet undiscovered genetic factor that creates a predisposition to stuttering in some people. However, there are also other theories that attempt to explain the development of stuttering.

Speech originates in and is controlled by the left hemisphere of the brain. Some investigators believe that growth of the left hemisphere during fetal development may be delayed in people who stutter. This delay may cause the location of the speech and language centers in the brain to be slightly askew (out of line).

Other researchers believe that when people stutter, the brain hesitates for a split second before initiating the command for forming a particular sound to the muscles that form speech. Still others consider that the brain cells require extra time to process the signals for speech that come from the brain's language and speech centers.

Stuttering typically begins in childhood between the ages of two and five years, and it affects three times more boys than girls. Eighty percent of children with mild forms of stuttering recover without any treatment. Many children with more severe forms recover with speech therapy.

Therapy reduces the fear and embarrassment of stuttering and provides counseling and instruction to modify the speech patterns that occur during stuttering and improve the overall fluency of speech.

K. SANDRICK

**See also:** ANATOMY; BRAIN; CHILD DEVELOPMENT; COMMUNICATION; HEARING; HUMAN EVOLUTION; JAWS; MEMORY; TONGUE.

### Further reading:

Lawrence, J. R., K. S. Harris, and G. J. Borden. 2002. *Speech Science Primer: Physiology, Acoustics, and the Perception of Speech.* Baltimore: Williams and Wilkins.
Zemlin, W. R. 1997. *Speech and Hearing Science.* Paramus, N.J.: Allyn and Bacon.

## USE OF LANGUAGE

There are approximately 6,000 languages spoken in the world, and more than 250 are spoken in North America alone. These languages not only apply different names to various objects and ideas they also depict the many different ways people view the world in which they live.

All languages have five characteristics in common. They (1) use symbols, (2) involve a small number of specific sounds, (3) create a vocabulary by combining meaningful sounds into definite units, (4) link the units of vocabulary together in phrases and sentences to express complex thoughts, and (5) use vocabulary in social interactions.

Speech is therefore not the same as language. Language is the representation of objects and ideas by strings of symbols, which form words. These symbols may be speech sounds, written characters, or hand signals. There are two main facets of language ability: understanding the meaning of words (comprehension) and generating words to express something meaningful. Speech is just one way by which language can be communicated to others.

**SCIENCE AND SOCIETY**

# SPIDERS

**Spiders, arthropods belonging to the class Arachnida, have two main body sections and eight jointed legs**

*Tarantula spiders, such as the red-kneed tarantula (Eurypelma smithi) shown above, are large, hairy, hunting spiders that capture and kill prey using downward-pointing fangs that introduce venom into the victim.*

## CONNECTIONS

● **ARACHNIDS** include spiders, **SCORPIONS**, and mites and ticks.

● Spider **FEEDING** habits involve killing and eating **INSECTS** or even small **MAMMALS** or **BIRDS**.

Long before dinosaurs or even flies existed, spiders roamed Earth. Spider fossils some 300 million years old are evidence of the long history of evolution that has produced more than 30,000 described species. Spiders live worldwide, inhabiting extremes of climate from frozen landscapes to tropical forests and deserts, and have many hunting techniques to capture live prey.

Spiders have eight legs, produce silk, and are strictly carnivorous. Although prey comes in the form of roving insects and other small invertebrates, spiders can ingest only liquid foods. A spider's fangs penetrate its victim's tissues, and venom is injected through them to paralyze the prey. After the spider draws out its fangs, it spits digestive enzymes into the holes created to break down the captive's insides. No wonder the term *arachnophobia* has been given to the human fear of spiders. Indeed, some spiders can kill organisms tens of thousands of times heavier than themselves. However, most spiders are harmless to humans, and their lives revolve around creatures closer to their own size.

### External structure

Like insects, spiders are arthropods, characterized by a hard exoskeleton and jointed appendages. Unlike insects, however, spiders have eight legs rather than six, lack antennae and wings, and have simple rather than compound eyes (see EYES). Insects have three main body sections (head, thorax, and abdomen), but spiders have only two—a fused head and thorax (cephalothorax) and a distinct abdomen.

The Mesothelae are the most primitive group of spiders, characterized by a segmented abdomen and spinnerets (silk spinners) near the middle of the abdomen. The spinnerets are at the end of the abdomen in the two other major groups. The Mygalomorphae, which include tarantulas, have fangs that strike downward and are effective when the prey is pinned against the ground. The Araneomorphae, also called true spiders, have fangs that work from side to side, suitable for piercing prey hanging in a web.

Most spiders measure ⅕ to ⅖ inch (5 to 10 mm). The abdomen is the largest part of the spider, containing its digestive, respiratory, and reproductive systems, as well as glands that produce silk. Some spiders are brightly colored, while others are dull. The main features of the spider's head are its eyes, mouth, jaws, and two leglike appendages (pedipalps) on either side of the mouth. The pedipalps are important for the sense of touch and have been modified in males for use in mating. Spiders do not have true ears and noses. Hairs and slits on the spider's body and legs detect vibrations and chemicals to be tasted or smelled.

### CORE FACTS

■ Spiders belong to the phylum Arthropoda, class Arachnida.

■ Characteristic features include four pairs of jointed legs, two main body sections (cephalothorax and abdomen), pincerlike jaws (chelicerae), and silk and venom glands.

■ Most spiders are harmless, but the black widow produces a neurotoxin capable of causing paralysis and respiratory failure in humans.

■ Spiders live in most environments, with the greatest diversity in tropical rain forests.

■ All spiders make silk, although not all spin webs.

## Anatomy

Spiders' anatomy is specialized for eating animals. They have jaws called chelicerae that grip the prey and hollow fangs connected to poison sacs. The poison sacs lie within the jaws but sometimes extend into the head. In addition to venom, spiders pass into their victims digestive enzymes regurgitated from the intestine. The spider's stomach muscles help suck back down the partially digested liquids.

Spider venom varies in potency and type. The black widow spider (*Latrodectus mactans*) produces a neurotoxin that can cause paralysis and respiratory failure in humans. The brown recluse (*Loxosceles reclusa*) has a potent hemolytic venom that causes the breakdown of red blood cells, which results in the death of tissue in the area around a bite. Generally, the effects of venom are less severe in larger animals. A bite that rapidly paralyzes an insect may cause only a minor swelling in a human. Most spiders are not dangerous to humans. The spiders of the family Uloboridae, which live mainly in tropical and subtropical regions, do not produce venom at all. To catch prey, they rely entirely on their jaws and their tangled, sievelike webs.

Although most spiders have eight eyes, they tend to have poor vision. Different species may have two, four, or six eyes, depending on the spider's hunting method. Web-weaving spiders generally rely on tactile sensation (touch) and less on vision. However, jumping spiders stalk their prey; two main eyes perceive sharp images within a few inches, the remaining six eyes detect motion at a distance. Visual hunters tend to have larger eyes than spiders that do not hunt in this way.

Even without being touched, spiders can sense the presence of predator or prey through bristles (setae) on their legs and body that detect minute vibrations in the air. Some setae can even detect air humidity and temperature. Spiders can also detect pheromones (see PHEROMONES) through holes in the exoskeleton on their tarsi, the end leg segments. Spiders taste with their legs, too, sampling droplets of food or water through hollow hairs.

Coordinating movement can be tricky for a creature with eight legs and poor eyesight, yet a spider can move nimbly and accurately on its web. Slit sense organs connected to membranes near the leg joints help a spider detect vibrations created by nearby prey, predators, and the spider's own body. Sensory receptors, called proprioceptors, relay information about the position of the spider's limbs, its speed, and its direction of travel.

## Respiration

Primitive spiders breathe using respiratory organs called book lungs. Folds ,like pages of a book, are held apart by pillarlike structures within the lung. Air enters the body through a slit in the abdomen. As it circulates between the folds of a book lung, oxygen diffuses into the blood. More advanced spiders rely on organs called tracheae, tubes that lead from openings in the abdomen directly to the tissues. Freshly oxygenated blood flows to the heart and leaves via open-ended arteries, allowing the blood of this open circulatory system to flow freely over the tissues.

## Reproduction

The reproductive opening is on the underside of the abdomen. Male spiders have no reproductive organ for the transfer of sperm directly to the female. Instead, many species deposit sperm on a specially built web. The male than transfers the sperm to the two pedipalps near his mouth. To mate, he inserts his sperm-laden pedipalps into the female genital opening (epigyne). Courtship and mating can be brief or last for hours. When completed, the females can store sperm in sacs called spermathecae until they are ready to release their eggs.

*The body of all spiders consist of two main sections, called the cephalothorax and the abdomen. Spiders also have four pairs of jointed legs, a pair of leglike pedipalps, and multiple silk glands. As in all arthropods, the exoskeleton provides a hard protective body covering, in which the internal organs are contained.*

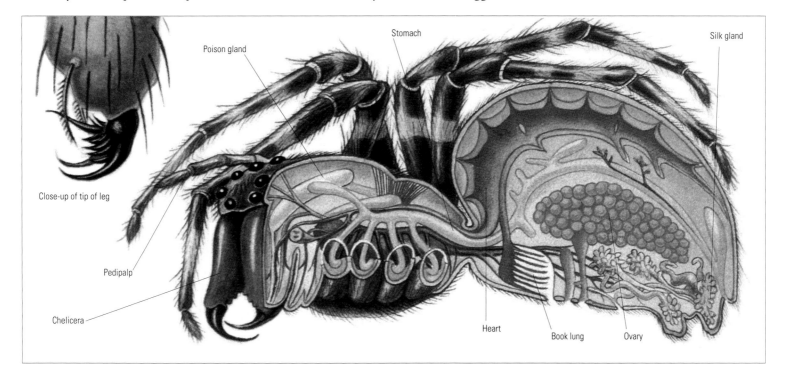

Close-up of tip of leg

Poison gland

Stomach

Silk gland

Pedipalp

Chelicera

Heart

Book lung

Ovary

Female spiders of most species construct a silken sac to protect the eggs after they are laid. The eggs may be left to hatch on their own, although the females of some species guard them while they develop. Some even go so far as to provide the young with flies. The female may care for her young until she dies, when the young will feed on her body.

The smallest spider species may lay only 2 eggs at a time, while larger ones can produce as many as 3,000 eggs at once. A few days after hatching, spiders make the longest journey of their life in a feat called ballooning. The spiderlings (young spiders) crawl to the top of a blade of grass or to the highest point of the web, where they release a strand of silk. Warm rising air catches the silk and carries off the spiders, sometimes as high as 5,000 feet (1,500 m). Some spiders have even landed on ships at sea.

## BIRD-EATING SPIDERS

Bird-eating spiders of the genus *Avicularia* are the largest spiders on record. Their legs span 11 inches (280 cm), outsizing the small birds on which they prey in the Amazon Basin. The spiders live in trees, taking refuge in holes by day and emerging to hunt at nightfall. They feed on insects, small mammals, and birds that are sometimes taken from the nest. When provoked by humans, bird-eating spiders will give a painful bite, although the venom is not particularly potent. Typically, however, bird-eating spiders defend themselves against larger aggressors by scraping the hairs from their back using their hind legs and flinging them at the attacker. The hairs are hooked and thus can urticate, that is, produce rashes on human skin. If flung into the eyes of an aggressor, the hairs may cause temporary blindness. These spiders may also discourage other animals from approaching their nests by lining them with these hairs.

*Despite their formidable appearance, bird-eating spiders, such as* Europelma mesomelas, *shown above, are placid and will attack humans only when provoked.*

## A CLOSER LOOK

## Spider habitats

Spiders live worldwide, from remote mountaintops to kitchen ceilings. One species (*Argyroneta aquatica*) even lives under water. Although spiders can be found in almost any terrestrial region, each species tends to be specialized for a particular habitat. Adaptations may be behavioral, such as waiting underground in the heat of the desert and coming out at night to hunt. Several species show remarkable specialization of body form (morphology). For example, spiders that live among ants have evolved an antlike body shape as disguise, enabling them to enter an ant colony and easily pick their prey.

## Catching prey

Spiders have such a low metabolic rate that they can survive without food for a considerable time— sometimes as long as one and a half years. This ability is critical for creatures that do not pursue prey but wait for prey to come to them.

Crab spiders catch prey by waiting motionless on leaves or flowers. One species blends in with bright yellow petals, and when a nectar-seeking insect arrives, the crab spider quickly grabs it and bites its neck. A Kenyan species of the family Araneidae plays the waiting game by physically resembling fresh bird droppings to attract flies.

Trap-door spiders ambush their prey from below ground, waiting in silk-lined burrows beneath a slightly raised, custom-built trapdoor. When a victim wanders within reach, the spider jumps out and seizes it. Wolf spiders and jumping spiders behave differently by hunting down their prey; wolf spiders stalk their prey and leap on them, acting much as wolves do, hence their name.

The most familiar spiders build webs. Traditionally, scientists believed that web-building spiders waited passively for an insect to blunder into the web by accident. However, research has shown that some spiders use their webs as lures. For example, *Argiope* garden spiders decorate their webs with zigzag patterns of thickened silk. The zigzags reflect ultraviolet light in patterns similar to those reflected by flowers, and so they attract insects.

While most spiders are solitary, a few species live socially on webs large enough to cover trees. When prey hits the web, many spiders attack it and share the prize. Hundreds of individuals may live on a single web in the species *Agelena republicana*.

## Courtship

In many spider species, females are larger than males. About 100 tiny male *Nephila clavipes* spiders equal the weight of one female, for example. Females reach sexual maturity later than males and generally live longer. Tarantulas mature at age 10 years; the male dies within a year of becoming sexually mature, but females may live another 10 years.

One of the most perilous acts of a male spider's life may be to court a female. If he inadvertently triggers her predatory instincts, he may end up as a meal rather than a mate. Male jumping spiders sport

*Web-spinning spiders spend virtually their whole life in contact with the silk webs they manufacture. The structures they create provide an effective method for trapping prey.*

bright colors and perform dances for the females, signaling their sexual intentions. Male web-weaving spiders have a particularly precarious job because their mates have poor vision and attack when the web vibrates. The male *Nephila clavipes* cautiously tiptoes toward the female and climbs onto her; he is the size of prey that she usually ignores. Other spiders may pluck the strands of the web in a rhythm recognized by the female.

The nursery web spider, *Pisaura mirabilis*, brings a silk-wrapped morsel for the female and mates with her while her jaws are busy with the food. During courtship, the male *Xysticus* crab spider binds the female in silk, first grabbing her front legs and circling around her trailing a silken thread. When he decides the female is secure, he crawls head first beneath her abdomen and inserts his sperm-laden pedipalps into her reproductive tract. The entire mating process may take as long as 90 minutes, but only when it is complete does the female unwrap herself from the tangle.

M. CHU

**See also:** ANATOMY; ARTHROPODS; CARNIVORES; COURTSHIP; DEFENSE MECHANISMS; EYES; JAWS; PHEROMONES; PHOBIAS; PREDATION; REPRODUCTIVE SYSTEMS; RESPIRATORY SYSTEMS.

**Further reading:**
Foelix, R. F. 1996. *Biology of Spiders.* 2nd ed. New York: Oxford University Press.
Levi, H. W., and L. R. Levi. 1996. *Spiders and Their Kin.* New York: St. Martin's Press.
Schultz, S. A., and M. J. Schultz. 1998. *The Tarantula Keeper's Guide.* New York: Barron.

## SPIDER SILK

All spiders make silk, although not all spin webs. Spiderlings (young spiders) release a strand of silk that wafts them away on air currents to a new home. Adults of almost all species trail a silk dragline when they walk, enabling them to return home or jump off a web if a predator approaches. The water spider (*Argyroneta*) uses silk to construct an underwater bell-shaped roof that traps the air it breathes. Males produce webs on which to deposit sperm, and females secure their eggs within silken sacs. Perhaps the most conspicuous use of silk is in web construction; about one-third of spider species make round orb webs, but webs can also be shaped like sheets, funnels, tubes, and tents.

Silks used for different purposes differ in properties such as the degree of strength or stickiness. At least seven distinct types of silk glands have been identified, and a single spider may possess several. Silk leaves the body from abdominal openings (usually three pairs), called spinnerets. Each spinneret has hundreds of holes. Silk emerges from the tiny holes as a liquid, and when the spider pulls on it, structural changes cause solidification.

Spider silk can be one millionth of an inch across and stronger than an equivalent (hypothetical) thread of steel. Because of its thinness, it has been used in optical instruments, such as telescopes and microscopes. Its strength and lightness also give it potential to make superior bulletproof vests or parachutes. Future medical applications include the use of spider silk replacements for damaged tendons.

The properties of silk are due largely to the chemical structure of the protein fibroin, which is a key component. Fibroin consists of sheets of polypeptide chains. In silk these chains are almost fully extended, and strong chemical bonds are formed between them. These bonds are hard to break, and thus, silk is very strong.

**A CLOSER LOOK**

# SPLEEN

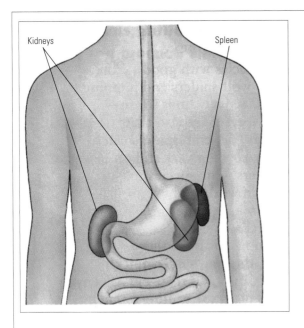

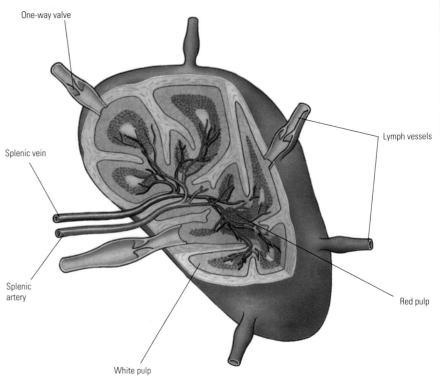

*The spleen (above and right) is a small organ located behind the stomach and above the left kidney. It is an important gland in the body's lymphatic system and also acts as a filter for old red blood cells.*

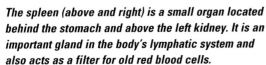

## CONNECTIONS

● The spleen changes its functions before and after birth, and its development is therefore a key part in the study of the **EMBRYO**.

● The spleen has an important role to play in fighting infection and plays an important role in the human body's **IMMUNE SYSTEM**.

Soft, dark red, and bean shaped, the spleen is the largest lymphoid organ in the body (see LYMPHATIC SYSTEMS). Located in the upper left abdomen, it is close to the pancreas, the diaphragm, the left kidney, and the colon. Bands of fibers attached to the membrane lining of the abdominal cavity support the spleen. The adult human spleen is about the size of a fist and weighs about 7 ounces (200 g), although size and weight vary with age and depend on the nutritional status and physical health of the individual. The spleen is approximately 3 inches (8 cm) in length and $\%_{10}$ inch (2.4 cm) thick. However, it may become enlarged because of disease. Ten percent of the population have accessory spleens, which are usually situated near the primary spleen or in the abdomen.

The spleen is surrounded by a dense fibrous capsule, while its interior consists of a fibrous meshwork, red pulp, and white pulp. The red pulp (between 80 and 95 percent of the tissue) is composed of venous sinuses (large blood-filled areas) and cords of tissue called splenic cords. The splenic cords consist of several types of cells, including erythrocytes (red blood cells; see BLOOD), macrophages, lymphocytes, and granulocytes (immune cells; see IMMUNE SYSTEMS). The white pulp consists of lymphatic tissue—mainly lymphocytes arranged around central arteries. The white pulp tissue is thickened in areas, forming splenic nodules (called Malpighian capsules).

## Functions

In the unborn child, the spleen's main function is the creation of red blood cells. After birth, it relinquishes this function to take on a range of other roles, including the disposal of old red blood cells. However, if the bone marrow—the main source of red blood cell manufacture after birth—is diseased, the spleen takes over red cell production.

The red pulp removes worn-out red cells and other waste materials. Blood enters the spleen through the splenic artery and passes along the central arteries in the white pulp. Then the blood enters the red pulp through a series of specialized vessels and drains into the splenic cords. The blood then squeezes into the venous sinuses. Normal red blood vessels are able to change shape easily and can survive being squeezed, but older red blood cells are more rigid and tend to lyse (burst open). The

---

### CORE FACTS

■ The spleen is the largest lymphoid organ in the body.

■ The human spleen is about the size of a fist and weighs about 7 ounces (150 g).

■ Before birth, the spleen manufactures red blood cells; after birth, its main functions are to dispose of old red blood cells, while storing the iron from these cells, and to create white blood cells.

■ Humans can survive when the spleen is removed.

fragments of these red blood cells are destroyed by phagocytic cells. Undamaged red cells then leave the kidney via the splenic vein.

When the spleen removes worn-out red blood cells, it stores the iron from them for later use in the body (see IRON). Its also serves as one of the body's blood reservoirs, storing extra red blood cells. This surplus ensures large enough volumes of red cells to compensate in the event of hemorrhage.

The white pulp is concerned with the production of defensive white blood cells. Antibodies to fight disease originate from B-lymphocytes in the spleen and lymph nodes (see LYMPHATIC SYSTEMS). When the bloodstream becomes infected, the spleen's defensive phagocytes go into action to help fight the disease.

## Disorders of the spleen

There are numerous diseases that can affect the spleen. Splenomegaly, or enlargement of the spleen, is usually an indication of disease elsewhere in the body, including parasitic diseases such as malaria and schistosomiasis, some blood disorders, leukemia, and Hodgkin's disease. In some infectious illnesses the spleen enlarges, just as the lymph nodes do, to fulfill its housekeeping functions more vigorously. When the liver is diseased and blood cannot circulate through it, large volumes of blood collect in the spleen, causing it to become engorged. In hypersplenism, an enlarged spleen removes, or sequesters, too many red blood cells (causing anemia; see ANEMIA) or too many platelets (causing bleeding problems). Tumors originating in the spleen are rare and usually benign, or noncancerous. However, sometimes surgery is necessary to remove such tumors. In a condition called sickle-cell anemia, the spleen is often gradually destroyed by aggregating red cells cutting off the blood supply.

## Removal of the spleen

Although the spleen is important to humans, some people are born without it and are able to survive. Emergency splenectomy—surgical removal of the spleen—has to be performed when the organ is ruptured (for example, in an automobile accident), in some diseases, such as lymphomas, and as part of some major operations, such as the removal of the stomach for cancer. Partial or total removal of the spleen may be recommended in the treatment of some blood diseases, including severe anemia. In such cases, other lymphoid tissues take over the function of the spleen in destroying red blood cells. When only a part of the spleen is removed, the remaining portion rapidly regenerates to roughly its original size and weight.

Because people can live without the spleen, the outlook following a splenectomy is good for most patients and the recovery period does not usually take long. However, because the spleen is an important part of the immune system, patients undergoing splenectomy—and especially children—may have a reduced resistance to infection. A particular

## NONHUMAN SPLEENS

The spleen developed early in the course of vertebrate history and is present in most fish and all tetrapods (four-legged animals). Hagfish, lampreys, and lungfish lack a complete spleen. In hagfish, the splenic tissue lies in the wall of the stomach and intestine; in lampreys it is present in the spiral valve (a fold of mucous membrane projecting into the intestines); and in lungfish the splenic blood-forming tissue is concentrated in the stomach wall. In sharks and rays, the spleen becomes attached to the mesentery (a double-layered extension attaching the stomach and intestines to the body wall).

An elongated spleen is thought to be primitive because it is present in the majority of fish, newts, salamanders, and reptiles. A more compact structure is present in some fish, some amphibians, many birds, and all mammals except monotremes. In the embryos of all present-day vertebrates, red and white blood cells are formed in the spleen; this situation persists in the adult in every group except for mammals. In frogs and toads, the spleen begins to lose its importance as a red-blood-cell forming organ because the hollow bones contain bone marrow. In mammals, bone marrow is the primary site of red-blood-cell formation, and any blood formation in the spleen is usually confined only to white cells.

## A CLOSER LOOK

problem is an infection caused by the bacterium *Streptococcus pneumoniae*. Normally the presence of *S. pneumoniae* excites an immune response that destroys the bacteria; however, in an individual without a spleen, the organism can circulate in the blood and reproduce.

M. RIESKE

**See also:** ANEMIA; BLOOD; CIRCULATORY SYSTEMS; IRON; LYMPHATIC SYSTEMS.

## Further reading:

Bowdler, A. J. 1999. *The Complete Spleen: Structure, Function, and Clinical Disorders.* Totowah, N.J.: Humana Press.

*A light micrograph of a normal human spleen. The red pulp (the main component of the spleen) is seen here as the granular red background. Regions of white pulp (the compact lymphatic tissue) appear center and bottom right.*

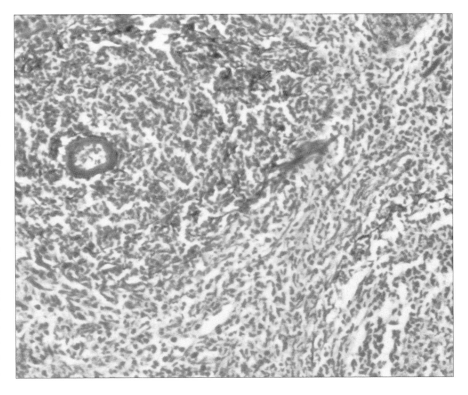

# SPONGES

*The sponge pictured above shows the basic structure of most tubular species, seen here growing on a coral outcrop.*

## CONNECTIONS

● Many sponges live in salt water and are found in **OCEAN HABITATS**.

● Sponges are aquatic **INVERTEBRATES**, just as **CORALS** and **JELLYFISH, SEA ANEMONES, AND HYDRAS** are.

Not so long ago, no bathroom was complete without its sponge, light brown in color, irregular in shape, soft, and squeezable. This accessory was the skeleton of an animal. Now the animal sponge has been almost completely replaced by synthetic plastic versions, although some sponges are still harvested for other specialized uses. Making up the phylum Porifera (meaning "pore bearers"), sponges are the simplest of all multicellular animals, having no specialized tissues or organs. There is also little differentiation in the three layers of cells that make up individuals. There are nearly 10,000 species of sponges, the majority being marine, although about 150 species live in fresh water.

Sponges can range in size from a fraction of an inch high, through branched structures up to 8 feet (2.4 m) tall, to round masses measuring several feet in diameter. In shallow seas, sponges can be brightly colored blue, violet, green, yellow, orange, red, brown, gray, black, or white. These colors appear to be due to the presence of photosynthetic symbiotic micro-

organisms. Deep-sea species are not so brightly colored, being mostly brown, gray, or off-white.

The animal's basic structure is similar to a tube, with a large opening, called an osculum, at one end. The tube contains a number of pores (ostia) through which the sponge draws in water, oxygen, and nutrients; it expels water, carbon dioxide, and waste (mostly ammonia) through the osculum. The exterior body wall is usually composed of a layer of flat cells, called pinacocytes. The inner layer of cells (called choanocytes) have flagella (whiplike protrusions) that circulate the water through a system of channels to a central cavity, called the paragaster. As water passes the cells, small food particles contained in the water are engulfed.

Between the two walls is the mesohyl, a gelatinous material inhabited by ameboid cells (cells that wander in the tissues of fluids of many invertebrates) that help digest nutrients from the water and eliminate waste. The mesohyl also contains the skeleton, a system of interlocking, needlelike fibers called spicules that help the organism maintain its shape. The skeleton may be calcareous (contain calcium carbonate) or siliceous (contain silica), or consist of a fibrous protein called spongin, or a combination of the last two.

The simplest sponges are called asconoid sponges. Because of their simple tubelike structure, they are always small. Larger sponges evolved by folding the body wall to make a larger surface area through which nutrients could be absorbed; they are the syconoid sponges. The most highly evolved sponges, which have extensive systems of chambers and canals, are called leuconoid sponges.

The rate at which sponges can pump water through their body to obtain oxygen and nutrients varies. For example, sponges of the *Leuconia* genus, which are only some 4 inches (10 cm) tall and ½ inch in diameter, can pump more than 5 gallons (22.5 l) of water every day. A large sponge may pump in several hundred gallons of water a day. However, all

### CORE FACTS

■ Sponges are extremely ancient, simple, but very successful multicellular organisms that inhabit both marine and freshwater habitats.

■ The size and appearance of sponges can vary tremendously but the structure is based on a tube that enables them to pump vast quantities of water through their bodies.

■ There are three main types of sponges, which vary according to the simplicity of their body structure: asconoid (simple), syconoid, and leuconoid (which are comparatively complex).

■ Like some other invertebrates, sponges have the ability to regenerate parts of their body when they become damaged or lost.

# CLASSIFICATION

There are four classes of sponges in the phylum Porifera:

● **Calcarea:** Calcareous sponges have spicules made of calcium carbonate with no spongin fibers. Their structure may be asconoid, syconoid, or leuconoid, and these sponges are generally small, seldom exceeding 4 inches (10 cm) in height. They are chiefly shallow-water marine species.
● **Hexactinellida:** The skeleton of these sponges often consists of long siliceous fibers that look like the fiberglass used for insulation, and thus they are called glass sponges. Species such as Venus's-flower basket (*Euplectella*) can be very beautiful. Most hexactinellids are deep-water sponges.

● **Demospongiae:** As many as 95 percent of sponge species may belong to this class. The skeleton may be siliceous or consist of spongin fibers or a combination of both. All of these sponges are leuconoid, and they live from the shallowest coastal waters to the deepest ocean. Among the families in this class are the Clionidae, the boring sponges; Spongillidae, which contains most of the freshwater species; and Spongidae, the marine species harvested as bath sponges.
● **Sclerospongiae:** This small class of sponges, which live in hollows and tunnels of coral reefs, are leuconoid and have a skeleton made up of a combination of both siliceous and spongin fibers on top of a calcareous base.

sponges have the same water canal system. Water enters through perforations called incurrent pores. After being strained of food particles, this water leaves the body cavity through the osculum.

As with most invertebrates, sponges are usually hermaphroditic (producing both eggs and sperm). The ameboid cells of the mesohyl produce the egg cells, or zygotes, and some choanocyte cells develop into sperm. When an egg is fertilized by sperm from another sponge, it develops into a multicellular, ciliated larva. The free-swimming larva is discharged through the parent's water canal system and eventually settles and anchors itself to a substrate. It begins its adult life by turning inside out, bringing its cilia inside to form the flagella of the interior surface. Sponges can also reproduce asexually by budding off new offspring (see REPRODUCTION).

Sponges are sessile (fixed and stationary), living attached to the seabed or other hard structures (see OCEAN FLOOR). They inhabit almost every part of the ocean, from low-tide areas to 26,000 feet (8,500 m) below the ocean surface. Sponges are most profuse around coral reefs and can be either reef builders or destroyers, depending on their habits (see CORAL REEF BIOMES). For example, many species of sponges hold fragments of coral together and thus keep the reef intact. Others, such as the boring sponges (*Cliona*), bore holes in dead corals, weakening the overall limestone structure of the reef.

Many sponges produce toxic substances that help protect them against certain predators. In addition, 9 out of 16 species of Antarctic sponges and 27 out of 36 Caribbean species are poisonous to fish.

P. BARNES-SVARNEY

**See also:** CORAL REEF BIOMES; HERMAPHRODITES; INVERTEBRATES; OCEAN FLOOR; REPRODUCTION.

### Further reading:
Boury-Esnault, N., and K. Rutzler, eds. 1997. *Thesaurus of Sponge Morphology.* Washington D.C.: Smithsonian Institution.
Hooper, J. N. A., and R. W. N. van Soest, eds. 2002. *Systema Porifera: A Guide to the Classification of Sponges.* New York: Plenum Press.

*The bread-crumb sponge (Halichondria panicea), shown above, lives in the lower intertidal zone of the North Atlantic rocky shores, which is exposed at the lowest tides.*

# EVOLUTION OF SPONGES

Sponges are multicellular invertebrates that lack most typical animal features, such as appendages and complex organs. Because they are much less developed than any other group of multicellular animals, one theory is that they developed from single-celled protists containing many nuclei, which were walled off by plasma membranes into separate cells.

Other scientists infer from ribosomal evidence that sponges have an evolutionary origin separate from other animals, departing early on from the main line of animal evolution. In this theory, flagellated protistan cells aggregated to form colonies resembling solid organisms with a ciliated surface. Sponges are believed to have evolved in this way from protozoans called choanoflagellates. These protozoans are made from a single flagellum (a long projection) surrounded by a collar of microvilli. Sponges are the only animals that have collar cells, called choanocytes, that each have a single flagellum, and are very similar to choanoflagellates. In general, sponges represent an evolutionary dead end. They are not believed to have given rise to any other multicellular organisms.

## EVOLUTION

# SQUASH FAMILY

**The squash family is a group of herbaceous plants that typically grow as sprawling, climbing vines**

*Squash plants, such as the melon pictured above, can adapt to difficult growing conditions and provide a valuable source of carbohydrates in some areas.*

## CONNECTIONS

● **POLLINATION** of squashes can be carried out by **BIRDS**, **BATS**, and **BEETLES** or other **INSECTS**.

● Squashes play a valuable role in human **NUTRITION**, although they are less important than **GRAINS** and **LEGUMES**.

Pumpkin and watermelon, spaghetti squash and zucchini, cucumber and loofah—these plants are all members of the family Cucurbitaceae. They are known popularly as squashes, a name that comes from the Algonquin word *askutasquash*, which is said to mean "food eaten raw." This family of climbing, sprawling vines comprises some 120 genera and 830 species, most of which grow in tropical regions. Ninety percent of the species are present in three main areas: Africa and Madagascar, Central and South America, and Southeast Asia. A few species grow in Australia and temperate regions, and several species grow in semidesert habitats.

## Cultivation of squashes

Although they are not as important a food source as grains or legumes (see GRAINS; LEGUMES), squashes play a significant role in the human diet. A large number are cultivated in various parts of the world, and a feature of cultivated species is their ability to adapt to different growing conditions. Many squashes thrive in environments considered marginal for agriculture. Pumpkins, melons, and a variety of other squashes are cultivated for local consumption in many areas and are a valuable source

of carbohydrates. Chayote, or chocho (*Sechium edule*), is, in particular, a staple food for many Latin Americans. This fruit is hard and green or white, usually pear shaped, with a furrowed covering. The watermelon (*Citrullus lanatus*), well known for its delicious fruit, is valued as a commercial crop and is also a useful source of drinkable water in some desert regions.

In the United States, approximately 220,460 tons (200,000 metric tons) of honeydew melons (*Cucumis melo*) are produced each year, worth tens of millions of dollars. Similarly, cucumbers (*Cucumis sativus*) and zucchini (*Cucurbita pepo*) are major food crops widely cultivated for export. Other important food sources are pumpkins and various types of squashes (*C. argyrosperma*, *C. maxima*, *C. moschata*, and *C. pepo*). The dried fruit skeleton of *Luffa cylindrica* is an effective cleaning scourer and is the source of loofah (vegetable) sponges. In earlier times, the dried, hollowed-out fruits of *Lagenieria siceraria* (calabash, or bottle gourd) were used as pots, and this species, in particular, is among the oldest of human-cultivated plants.

## Structure

Most cucurbits are perennial herbs, although some are annual and a few are soft woody lianas, shrubs, or even small trees. They are typically scrambling herbaceous plants with long, trailing stems (up to 50 feet, or 15 m, in certain species of *Cucurbita*), and spiraling tendrils (a characteristic feature of the family; see CLIMBING PLANTS), which are used to cling to any available support. The leaves are arranged alternately; they have long stalks and are usually palmate (similar to a hand with outstretched fingers), and the tendrils grow from the leaf axil (the junction between the leaf stalk and the stem). Most botanists agree that the tendril is a shoot, the lower part being a stem and the upper part a modified leaf.

The flowers, which also grow from the leaf axils, are usually unisexual (separate male and female flowers are borne on either the same plant or different plants) with yellowish petals, and the females have ovaries situated beneath the base of the petals (called inferior ovaries). There are usually five sepals and petals, borne at the top of a cuplike receptacle,

---

### CORE FACTS

■ Most squashes are perennial herbs that grow as sprawling, climbing plants.

■ Squashes (family Cucurbitaceae) grow mainly in tropical regions, such as Africa, Madagascar, Central and South America, and Southeast Asia.

■ The fruit of some squashes provides an important food source in many parts of the world.

and the petals are usually fused into a bell-shaped corolla (see FLOWERS AND FLOWER STRUCTURE).

In some male flowers, the stamens may be fused into a single central column, although more commonly, there are three freestanding stamens; two are double and have four pollen sacs each, and one is single with two pollen sacs. The pollen of Cucurbitaceae varies greatly in size and structure, and the shape of the pollen grains is the basis of classification in the family.

In the New World tropics, hummingbirds are among the principal pollinators, while some species may be pollinated by bats, beetles, or other insects. New World species of *Cucurbita*, including squashes and pumpkins, are pollinated by specialized, solitary bees. Fruits may take the form of berries (some with firm walls, such as the melon, called pepos) or fleshy, dry, or leathery capsules (see FRUITS AND FRUIT PLANTS). Seeds vary in number (see SEEDS AND SEED DISPERSAL) and may be winged and scattered by the wind, eaten and dispersed by animals, or forcibly spurted from fruits that burst open when ripe, such as the squirting cucumber (*Ecballium elaterium*).

The Cucurbitaceae are a well-defined, fairly close-knit family in respect to their growth, flower formation, pollen structure, and biochemistry, but their relationship to other flowering plant families is still being debated. In many ways they resemble the Passifloraceae (passion flowers), which also tend to have long trailing stems, tendrils, and lobed leaves. At one time they were thought to be most closely related to the order Campanulales (bellflowers and lobelias), but present-day botanists now place them nearer to Begoniaceae (begonias) and Datiscaceae (datiscas).

## Classification

Botanists divide the Cucurbitaceae into two subfamilies: the Nhandiroboideae, with 18 genera and about 70 species, and the much larger Cucurbitoideae, with about 100 genera and 750 species.

Plants in the subfamily Nhandiroboideae have two to three styles (the column between the ovary and the pollen-receiving stigma), generally two-branched tendrils, uniform pollen grains with a lined surface ornamentation (striate), and usually winged seeds. Examples include *Xerosicyos*, a shrubby genus from Madagascar, with circular, succulent leaves, sometimes grown as an ornamental plant, and A*lsomitra macrocarpa*, a liana (woody vine) with large fruits and large, winged seeds.

Plants in the subfamily Cucurbitoideae have one style, generally unbranched tendrils, varied pollen structure (not striate), and unwinged seeds. These plants include the edible crop plants cucumber, melon, pumpkin, squash, watermelon, and zucchini.

One of the most bizarre species in the whole family belongs to the subfamily Cucurbitoideae and is called *Dendrosicyos socotranus*. This rare and extremely succulent-stemmed tree grows only on the Indian Ocean island of Socotra.

Certain genera and species in the Cucurbitaceae have not yet been classified completely. Among the least known is the subtribe Cyclantherinae, of which three new species have now been discovered in Central America.

P. STAFFORD

**See also:** AGRICULTURE; ANNUAL PLANTS; CLIMBING PLANTS; FLOWERS AND FLOWER STRUCTURE; FRUITS AND FRUIT PLANTS; GENETIC ENGINEERING; PERENNIAL PLANTS; SEEDS AND SEED DISPERSAL.

**Further reading:**
Capatti, A., G. Vaccarini, D. Garavini, and G. Roveda. 1999. *The Squash: History, Folklore, Ancient Recipes.* London, U.K.: Konemann Publishers.
Damerow, Gail. 1997. *The Perfect Pumpkin.* North Adams, Mass.: Storey Books.
Hazelton, J. W. 2000. *Summer Squash and Squash Blossoms from Seed to Supper.* St. Petersburg, Fla.: Jack's Bookshelf.

*Zucchini (**Cucurbita pepo**), in the subfamily Cucurbitoideae, is characterized by unbranched tendrils and grows, as shown below, on the surface of the soil.*

# STEM CELLS

**Stem cells, unspecialized cells that can divide indefinitely, have the potential to differentiate into specialized cells**

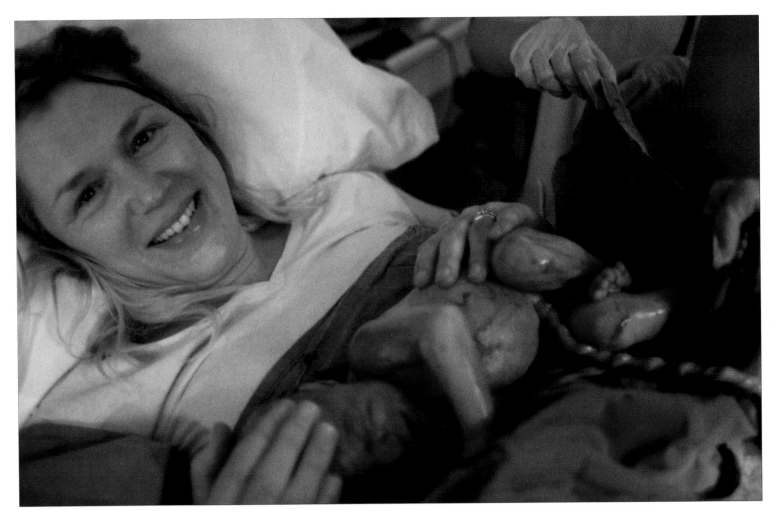

*A woman holds her newborn baby, which is still attached to its umbilicus. Umbilical cord blood cells are a potential source of stem cells.*

## CONNECTIONS

● Research into stem cells often involves **CLONING** embryos.

● Hematopoietic stem cells give rise to all the cells that circulate in the **BLOOD**.

● Stem cells replace dying cells in organs with high rates of cell turnover, such as the **SKIN** and the **INTESTINE**.

Stem cells are the cellular equivalents of a blank canvas. When given the right biochemical instructions, they can replicate (copy themselves), and the resulting daughter cells can turn into the many different types of cells required by the body. This process is called cell differentiation. Stem cells are essential for normal growth and development and to maintain adult tissues. Scientists are interested in stem cells because they may one day provide replacement tissue for diseased organs. Also, stem cells may be important sources of hormones and other biochemicals, and they are an important tool for medical research.

Stem cells differ from other body cells in a fundamental way: unlike most body cells, stem cells can replicate endlessly to produce copies of themselves. Moreover, when a stem cell divides, two things can happen to the daughter cells: they can remain as stem cells, or they can undergo changes that cause them to turn into a specialized type of cell, such as a muscle cell. Once a stem cell has become another type of cell, it is said to be terminally differentiated. It can no longer turn into other types of cells nor can it divide indefinitely. Scientists do not fully understand the exact biochemical changes in a stem cell that lead to terminal differentiation.

Scientists have known for a long time that embryos have stem cells that can change into any type of specialized cell. It is has also become clear that many adult organs contain populations of stem cells, which act as a permanent reservoir to replace (by cell replication and differentiation) other cells that have become damaged or worn out.

### CORE FACTS

■ Stem cells are unspecialized cells that can turn into many other different types of body cells, such as muscle cells or skin cells.

■ Unlike most body cells, stem cells can replicate endlessly to produce copies of themselves.

■ Unipotent stem cells produce only one type of differentiated cell, while pluripotent stem cells give rise to a number of cell types. Zygotes (fertilized eggs) are totipotent because they can produce any cell type.

■ Stem cell research often involves procedures using human embryos.

■ Embryonic stem cells may one day provide a supply of replacement tissue for organs that no longer function properly as a result of sickness or old age. This type of therapy is called therapeutic cloning.

## Embryonic stem cells

When a mammalian egg and a sperm fuse, they form a fertilized egg, a single cell called a zygote. This cell is totipotent; from it all the different cells of an embryo are made. However, as the one-celled zygote replicates again and again by the process of mitosis (see CELL BIOLOGY), the daughter cells form a structure with an outer layer and an inner layer, and by this time the cells have become more specialized. The outer layer forms the placenta, which is the temporary organ that feeds the developing fetus. The inner layer of cells consists of stem cells that are able to replicate and specialize to produce any adult cell type; they are therefore totipotent. This inner layer of cells goes on to form the embryo (see EMBRYO).

## Adult stem cells

In an adult animal, many cells live for only a short time and must be replaced continually by new cells. There are a few exceptions, including cardiac muscle cells and the cells of the eye, which are created in the embryo and persist throughout the lifetime of the animal. The majority of cells, however, carry out simple replication of existing fully specialized (also called differentiated) body cells to produce daughter cells of the same type. Cells that multiply in this way include certain types of skin cells, smooth muscle cells (of the type that make the intestine walls move), the cells that line blood vessels, and the epithelial cells that line the internal passageways of most internal organs, including the liver, pancreas, kidneys, lungs, prostate, and breasts.

Other populations of differentiated cells are generated from stem cells. In adults stem cells replace differentiated cells that cannot replicate because they are so specialized they have lost the ability. Examples include cells in which the nucleus (control center) has been digested, such as red blood cells and keratinocytes in the outermost layers of the skin.

The nucleus contains the DNA that gives the instructions for mitosis; without DNA, mitosis cannot take place. In other cases, the cytoplasm of a cell may contain structures that prevent cell division, such as the fibers inside striated muscle cells, which occur in arms or legs. Alternatively, the biochemistry of a cell may make it resistant to cell division.

Stem cells are never used by the body to perform the functions of the differentiated cells; they exist

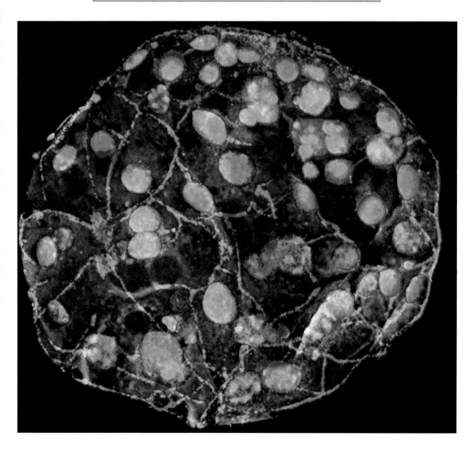

purely to produce new cells when necessary. Those stem cells that produce only one type of differentiated cell are called unipotent, while those cells that give rise to a number of cell types are called pluripotent. Zygotes are totipotent because they can produce any cell type.

There are different types of unipotent stem cells, including muscle satellite cells, a source of skeletal muscle; epidermal stem cells, which give rise to epidermal skin cells; spermatogonia and oogonia, sources of sperms and eggs, respectively; and basal cells of the olfactory epithelium,

*A human embryo at the blastocyst stage. Scientists can remove the embryonic stem cells present within the inner cell mass of the blastocyst. These totipotent stem cells have the potential to develop into any cell type in the body.*

# THERAPEUTIC CLONING

Patients and researchers hope that one day embryonic stem cells might provide a supply of replacement tissue for organs that have become faulty as a result of sickness or have simply worn out from old age. This therapy is called therapeutic cloning. Sufferers of brain diseases such as Parkinson's and Alzheimer's and victims of spinal injury could be among the first patients to benefit (see ALZHEIMER'S DISEASE; BRAIN).

In therapeutic cloning, stem cells genetically identical to the patient's are created and grown into new tissue. In the first step of the therapeutic cloning, the nucleus of a patient's cell is transferred into a donor egg that has had its nucleus removed, a process called nuclear transfer. The resulting stem cell then has all the genetic material and biochemical machinery it needs to become an embryo and has the potential to differentiate into any type of tissue. Reproductive cloning of animals uses the same initial technique as therapeutic cloning, but the resultant embryo is implanted into a female's uterus, rather than used to make new tissues. This technique was used to create Dolly the sheep in 1997 (see CLONING).

To date, such cloning of humans has been banned by all of the world's countries for ethical reasons.

Any tissues grown from stem cells and transplanted back into the patient would avoid the possibility of transplant rejection, which arises when genetically dissimilar tissues are introduced into an organism. Additionally, the risk of viruses being transferred to the patient from foreign cells is also greatly reduced.

From a technical viewpoint, therapeutic cloning still has a long way to go. At present, research, using a number of organisms, including primates, sheep, cows, and pigs, has shown therapeutic cloning to be very inefficient. According to one estimate, it would take around 280 cloned eggs to produce a single colony (called a cell line) of embryonic stem cells. In addition, many of the embryos resulting from nuclear transfer have defects, possibly because gene expression is abnormal in such embryos. Gene expression is the switching on and off of specific genes that enable and control growth, development, and metabolism. The reasons for this abnormality are poorly understood.

**A CLOSER LOOK**

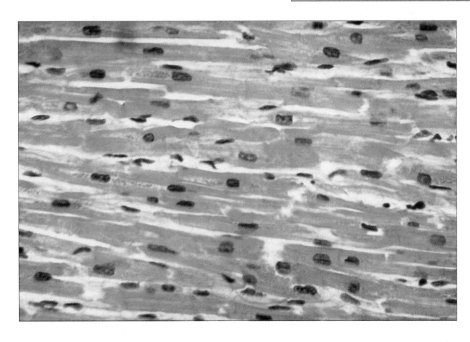

*Just as the cells of the eye do, cardiac (heart) muscle cells, shown above, form in an embryo and last for a lifetime. The majority of other cell types are short-lived and must be replaced continually; some, including red blood cells, are generated from stem cells.*

# EVOLUTION OF STEM CELLS

It appears that stem cells arose very early in evolution because they exist in very primitive organisms; sponges, for example, have pluripotent stem cells called archeocytes. Hydrozoans (simple organisms that include soft corals) have stem cells called I-cells (interstitial cells), which are capable of differentiating into a number of different cell types. I-cells allow the organism to replenish cells, including stinging cells and even neurons throughout an organism's life.

**EVOLUTION**

which generate the olfactory sensory neurons (nerve cells) with which mammals smell.

## Unipotent stem cells: Renewal of skin and muscle cells

The skin is formed during embryonic development, and as with all organs, it grows during childhood. Throughout life, the skin is exposed to damage from a number of sources, including mechanical stress, chemicals, and attack by microorganisms, and its cells must be constantly renewed. This growth and regeneration are carried out by unipotent stem cells, which lie on the basal lamina, the innermost layer of the skin. As the stem cells grow and divide, their daughter cells are displaced toward the skin's surface. As they progress on their outward journey, the cells eventually differentiate into specialized skin cells (keratinocytes), die, and are finally sloughed off after a few weeks. A number of factors control the process of skin renewal, including the production of certain hormones that act to stimulate or inhibit the process.

Unlike the skin, which is in a constant state of renewal, skeletal muscles are regenerated only when necessary, such as when a muscle is injured. Particular stem cells, called satellite cells, are attached to bundles of muscle fibers (cells). Satellite cells remain inactive until muscle damage activates chemical signals that stimulate the satellite cells to replicate and form new muscle cells.

## Pluripotent stem cells: Formation of blood cells

The bloodstream carries a multitude of cell types that have a range of functions. Red blood cells (erythrocytes) transport oxygen to and from body tissues; platelets are essential for blood clotting; granulocytes and macrophages destroy invading microorganisms;

and lymphocytes are responsible for carrying out immune responses, such as the production of antibodies. Each of these cells has a limited life span, ranging from less than a day to a few months. Astonishingly, all of these different cell types are generated continually by the division of a common pluripotent stem cell in the bone marrow called a hematopoietic stem cell. The production and differentiation of blood cells is termed hematopoiesis. A surprisingly small number of rapidly dividing pluripotent stem cells (1 per 10,000 cells in the bone marrow) provide, through their differentiated descendants, all of the blood cells in the human body.

Hematopoiesis begins when a hematopoietic stem cell initially replicates to produce one of the following five combinations: (1) two stem cells, (2) a stem cell and a myeloid cell, (3) a stem cell and a lymphoid cell, (4) two myeloid cells, or (5) two lymphoid cells. The new stem cells continue to replicate to make more pluripotent stem cells, a process called self-renewal. The myeloid and lymphoid cells continue to replicate, becoming more differentiated at each stage. Myeloid cells eventually differentiate into erythrocytes, platelets, macrophages, or granulocytes. Lymphoid cells, on the other hand, differentiate only into lymphocytes.

Once these blood cells have become fully differentiated, they can no longer replicate themselves. The only way to maintain a population of differentiated blood cells is for the hematopoietic stem cells to continue dividing. Several hormones control the activity of the hematopoietic stem cells; these hormones are, in turn, controlled by physiological factors, such as low numbers of red blood cells.

P. DAVIS

**See also:** ALZHEIMER'S DISEASE; BRAIN; CELL BIOLOGY; EMBRYO; LIVER AND GALLBLADDER.

**Further reading:**
Holland, S., K. Lebacqz, and L. Zoloth, eds. 2001. *The Human Embryonic Stem Cell Debate (Basic Bioethics)*, Cambridge: MIT Press.
May, M. 2000. Mother nature's menders: Origins of a stem cell. *Scientific American* (May).
Mooney, D. J., and A. G. Mikos. 1999. Growing new organs. *Scientific American* (April): 60–73.

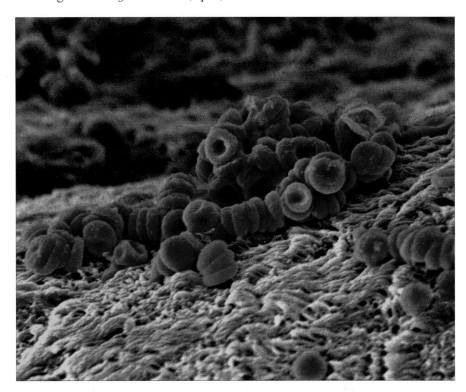

*Red blood cells, shown below on the wall of an artery, do not contain a nucleus and thus cannot replicate to replace worn-out cells. They are renewed instead by the division of pluripotent stem cells in the bone marrow called hematopoietic stem cells.*

## THE ETHICS OF STEM CELL RESEARCH

Stem cell research poses a number of ethical considerations because this research often involves procedures using human embryos. The embryos are created by in vitro fertilization (IVF) and are destroyed after their stem cells have been harvested.

Embryonic stem cells can differentiate into any human cell type. Most adult stem cells are not able to differentiate in this way. Opponents of stem cell research believe that it is morally wrong to destroy embryos, which they regard as human beings, for scientific research. People who are in favor of such research believe that the medical benefits of stem cell research will be of great value to humanity. They claim the benefits outweigh the loss of IVF embryos, which are already being created and destroyed in large numbers daily in fertility clinics all over the world.

The great variation from country to country in policies on human cloning and stem cell research indicates just how contested this issue is. Many governments, such as Germany's, feel that even allowing research into therapeutic cloning, in which stem cells are harvested and used to grow new tissues, is unethical (see CLONING).

The United States has been divided by the argument for and against cloning in research. In 2001 the House of Representatives voted for a bill that would ban all forms of human cloning, including therapeutic cloning. However, some government-funded stem cell research is able to take place on a limited basis, using only so-called established stem cell lines. These cells are human stem cells and their descendants that scientists extracted from embryos before the new legislation was announced. In 2001 researchers in a U.S. laboratory produced the first human embryos using the technique of cloning. For unknown reasons, only one of the embryos progressed to the six-cell stage, at which point it stopped dividing. The researchers hope to use these cloned cells for stem cell research.

The British government, in contrast, allows research with human stem cells on the condition that the cloned embryo is destroyed in the laboratory within 14 days of creation.

Many of the ethical problems of stem cell research could be bypassed if researchers could reprogram adult cells directly without cloning a human embryo. To do so, researchers would need to uncover the steps that stimulate the nucleus of an adult human cell to grow into an embryo transplanted into a denucleated egg cell. Initial research into this field is yielding some positive results.

For example, some researchers have managed to program neural stem cells (cells that normally differentiate into nerve cells) to differentiate into blood cells when injected into the bone marrow.

### SCIENCE AND SOCIETY

# STEMS AND STEM SYSTEMS

**Stems and stem systems provide the structural support, bearing the leaves, flowers, and fruits, in vascular plants**

*The stems of bamboo plants often grow in dense stands, developing from subterranean stems called rhizomes.*

Plant stems are like the skeleton and circulatory systems of animals. Their main purposes are to support the leaves and flowers and to carry water, food, and nutrients between the different parts of the plant. The stems and leaves of a plant may both be involved in photosynthesis (food production; see PHOTOSYNTHESIS), and some stems are able to store surplus food and water until they are needed. In many plants, the stems are also important in vegetative reproduction; see REPRODUCTION).

## Development of stems

Plant cell division and the creation of new tissue are restricted to several localized areas called meristems, or growing points, unlike animal cell division. The main areas of growth in a plant occur at the tips of the shoots and roots and are called apical meristems. In the root tips, the delicate meristem tissue is protected by a thin layer of cells called the root cap (see ROOTS AND ROOT SYSTEMS); in the shoot, the meristem tissue is protected by newly formed leaves and in some cases by bud scales.

Initially, the cells produced by the meristem are all similar, and they are as long as they are broad. As the meristem continues to form new cells, the recently formed cells lying behind the meristem begin to elongate (grow longer) and differentiate into various types of cells. Growth in plants occurs mainly by the elongation of existing cells rather than by the addition of new cells.

The cells first differentiate into one of three types, the protoderm on the outside, the ground meristem in the middle, and the procambium, which lies within the ground meristem. Cells in the protoderm become the epidermis, a single layer of cells that form the outside skin of the stem. The outer walls of the epidermis become thicker and covered with a waxy substance, called cutin, to form the cuticle, which is impermeable to water and gases and protects the stem cells from damage and drying out. On young stems there are usually small openings in the epidermis called stomata, which allow the exchange of water and gases and enable the stem cells to manufacture food by photosynthesis.

The ground meristem cells become the pith, located in the center of the stem, and the cortex, which forms a layer below the epidermis and surrounds the vascular tissue. The cortex contains several different types of cells, including parenchyma, collenchyma, and sclerenchyma. The most common type of cell is parenchyma, unspecialized thin-walled cells that are about as broad as they are long. Their main function is to act as packing tissue, but they can also manufacture and store food. Collenchyma cells are elongated and have irregularly thickened walls; they strengthen the stem but can also manufacture food. Sclerenchyma are also strengthening cells, but they have lignified (woody) walls. They may be short (called sclereids) or elongated (called fibers). The pith consists largely of parenchyma cells that have a similar function to those of the cortex. Usually, the pith and the cortex are connected by structures called pith rays.

The procambium develops into the vascular tissue (see VASCULAR SYSTEMS), which occurs as strands or as a complete cylinder between the pith

## CORE FACTS

■ Plant stems support the various plant organs, such as the leaves, flowers, and fruits, and can also manufacture and store food.

■ Food and water are transported between the different parts of the plant by the phloem and xylem tissues, respectively, which run along the length of the stem.

■ The main growing region of the stem, the apical meristem, is located at the tip of the shoot, from which all the visible plant organs are formed.

and the cortex. The vascular tissue consists largely of xylem and phloem, vessels that transport water and food, respectively, in the plant. The main function of phloem is to transport dissolved organic and inorganic materials created by photosynthesis in the leaves to other parts of the plant by a process called translocation. The main function of xylem in the stem is to transport water and nutrients absorbed by the roots to the leaves by a process called transpiration (see TRANSPIRATION AND TRANSLOCATION).

## Buds

Buds are highly condensed undeveloped shoots. They consist of a short stem with leaf primordia (tiny folded-up leaves) and have meristem tissue at their tips. They are surrounded and protected by bud scales, which are specialized leaves. Flower buds are similar to bud scales, but the buds contain the immature flower parts, which are themselves highly evolved and specialized leaves.

Leaf buds are resting structures that protect the shoot tip during the periods of dormancy that occur in many trees and shrubs during the cold or dry season. Terminal buds are produced at the tip of the stem, and lateral buds in the leaf axils (the junctions between the leaf and the stem). Usually once the dormancy period is over, only the terminal bud develops. The lateral buds can remain dormant for many years but become active if the stem is damaged, such as by pruning. The terminal bud normally produces hormones called auxins that inhibit the growth of the lateral buds. When the leading bud is removed, growth of the lateral buds is no longer inhibited, and they are allowed to develop, creating side shoots. In some species, buds can also develop in places away from the leaf axils. These buds are called adventitious buds.

## Secondary growth

In most annual and biennial plants, no further growth occurs after the initial formation, elongation, and differentiation of cells. However, in many longer-lived plants, particularly trees and shrubs, secondary growth occurs along the length of the stems. This growth takes place in the vascular cambium, which is situated between the xylem and phloem cells. Initially, the cambium consists of groups of cells, which eventually link up to form a complete cylinder. The cells of the cambium then divide to form the vascular tissue—xylem on the inside and phloem on the outside.

The layers outside the vascular cylinder must also increase in size to compensate for the expansion of the inner layers. This growth occurs in a layer of cells called the cork cambium, just below the epidermis layer. The cork cambium produces new cortex cells on the inside and corky cells on the outside. These cells become impregnated with suberin (a waxy material) and form the outer layers of the bark, which are impermeable to water and gases. In places, however, the cells are more loosely packed to allow gases to reach the phloem beneath. These

*The diagram below shows the development of a woody stem as a result of secondary growth, which is characteristic of trees and shrubs.*

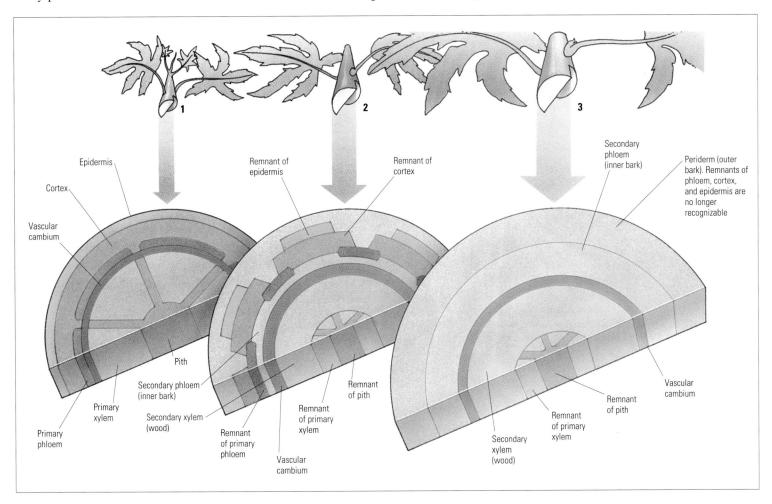

## DIFFERENT TYPES OF WOOD

The stems of different woody plants produce different types of wood. Hardwood, for example, is the wood of angiosperms, while softwood is the wood of gymnosperms. The difference is that gymnosperm wood, such as pine, is anatomically simpler than angiosperm wood and generally has no vessel elements.

The pattern and grain present in wood relates to different structures in the stem. The main structures involved are the annual rings, concentric rings that result from differences in cell size and cell wall thickness in the cells of the secondary xylem. Large cells with relatively thin walls represent the period of maximal growth in the early part of the growing season. Smaller cells with thicker walls represent the period of minimal growth later in the season.

Wood may also contain knotholes. As a woody stem increases in width over the years, the branches it bears also grow with it as long as they are alive. When a branch dies, it no longer continues to grow with the base of the stem. The basal portion of an embedded dead branch is called a knot, and the mark it leaves on the stem when the branch falls off is called a knothole.

### A CLOSER LOOK

*Whistling thorns (Acacia spp.) have evolved specially enlarged hollow thorns; these popular nesting sites for ants help defend against other insects attacking the plant.*

## VEGETATIVE REPRODUCTION

Asexual reproduction in flowering plants does not usually involve the formation of flowers, seeds, and fruits. Instead, the vegetative structures of plants, particularly modified stems, such as tubers, bulbs, and rhizomes, form offspring. In asexual reproduction, part of an existing plant becomes separated from the rest of the plant (by the death of the connecting tissues). This part then grows into a separate, genetically identical plant (a clone). Humans have taken advantage of this ability; for example, a potato plant (*Solanum tuberosum*) produces several swollen underground stems, called tubers. Each tuber can be replanted and will grow into a new plant. Vegetative propagation can also be induced in the laboratory by isolating meristem tissue. This procedure is called tissue culture.

### A CLOSER LOOK

areas, called lenticels, are often visible as raised bumps on the bark of the tree. With increasing age, there is a buildup of oils, resins, and tannins in the xylem that prevents the cells from conducting water. This wood becomes darker in color and is extremely resistant to decay.

### Variation and adaptation

The stems of different plant species may differ greatly in size and shape, but each is adapted to best fit its environment. Rather than wasting energy to produce a robust stem, some species use other plants and objects as support. Some plants twine around their support, while others cling to it; often these plant species have hooked prickles on the leaves and stems, as do blackberries (*Rubus* spp.) and greenbriers (*Smilax* spp.), or wiry, twining tendrils, as do grape vines (*Vitis* spp.; see CLIMBING PLANTS).

Insects, nematodes, fungi, bacteria, viruses, and chemical and mechanical injuries can result in abnormal growth of the stem or an abnormal outgrowth (called excrescence) on the stem. This growth is called plant gall, and many species have evolved various defense mechanisms to guard against it.

Many species have also evolved ways of helping to protect their stems from being eaten by animals. Plants such as roses (*Rosa* spp.) and acacias (*Acacia* spp.) produce sharp thorns. Other plant species produce a variety of chemicals to make them less palatable. These include tannins, present in tea (*Camellia sinensis*) and oaks (*Quercus* spp.); latex, present in spurges (*Euphorbia* spp.) and rubber trees (*Hevea brasiliensis*); and resins, present in many conifers (division Coniferophyta or Pinophyta).

Although most stems can store food and water to some extent, in some species stems inflate to increase their storage capacity. This inflation is common in species that grow in arid situations, where the plants may have fleshy (succulent) stems and leaves that contain cortical or mesophyll cells that store large amounts of water. In cacti (family Cactaceae), the leaves are reduced to spines to protect the inflated stems, which carry out photosynthesis as well as storing water.

Several types of modified stems are produced underground for food storage and overwintering, including rhizomes, stem tubers, bulbs, and corms (see BULBS AND CORMS; TUBERS AND RHIZOMES).

N. STEWART

**See also:** BULBS AND CORMS; CLIMBING PLANTS; PHOTOSYNTHESIS; REPRODUCTION; ROOTS AND ROOT SYSTEMS; TRANSPIRATION AND TRANSLOCATION; TUBERS AND RHIZOMES; VASCULAR SYSTEMS.

### Further reading:
Evert, R. F. 1998. *Topics in Botany Lab Separates; Woody Stems.* New York: W. H. Freeman.
Raven, P. H., R. F. Evert, and S. E. Eichhorn. 1999. *Biology of Plants.* 6th ed. New York: W. H. Freeman/Worth Publishers.

# STOMACH

The stomach is a specialized organ
that holds food and helps in
the process of digestion

Heartburn is not a malady of the heart but a common burning sensation in the chest caused by the malfunction of another important organ, the stomach. This organ engages in a complex combination of muscle contractions and acid and enzyme activity to help break down food. When the delicate balance within the stomach is upset, many problems, from heartburn (reflux of the stomach's acid contents into the eosophagus) to vomiting, can occur.

The human stomach holds a meal until its physical churning and chemical actions have made the food ready for the rest of the digestive system (see DIGESTIVE SYSTEMS). The stomach wall can stretch to accommodate a meal of up to ⅓ gallon (1.2 l). The stomach then intermittantly releases small portions of food to the rest of the digestive system. Without the stomach's storage ability, small amounts of food would have to be eaten every 20 minutes to regulate the flow to the intestines.

## A specialized organ

All animals subject food to mechanical and chemical processes that break it down into molecules that can be absorbed by the body. In simple animals such as protozoans, cnidarians (see JELLYFISH, SEA ANEMONES, AND HYDRAS), and sponges (see SPONGES), this breakdown takes place inside the cells. More complex animals, with and without an internal skeleton (see INVERTEBRATES; VERTEBRATES), have specialized organs to break down food. One of these organs, present in complex organisms from leeches to humans, is the stomach.

The size and structure of the stomach vary with the diet and eating habits of animals. Carnivores (meat eaters; see CARNIVORES) have an expandable, single-chambered stomach, probably because they eat large meals with periods of fasting in between. Herbivorous organisms eat frequent meals of plant material, which is hard to digest, and may have extra chambers in their stomach to allow them to digest the cellulose (see CELLULOSE).

Organisms that change their body form as they mature, such as some insects and amphibians, also

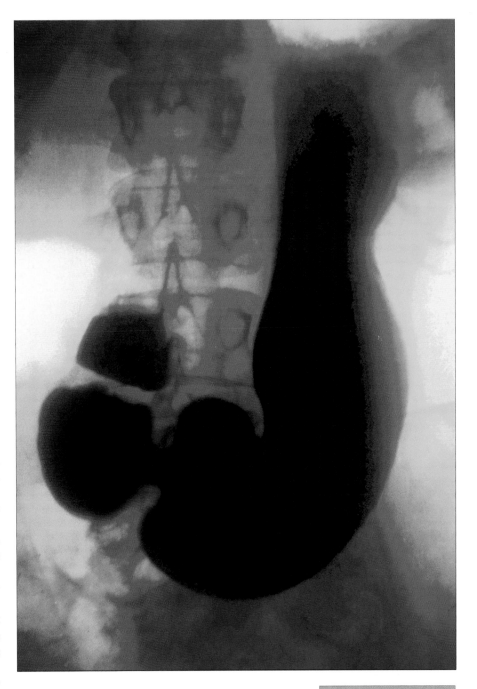

This X ray reveals the human stomach to be a curved, saclike organ (black, at center). It receives food from the esophagus (top right).

modify their stomach. The butterfly caterpillar, for example, has a stomach adapted for digesting large amounts of leaves with low nutritional value, while the adult butterfly has a stomach adapted for digesting nectar.

Chewing gives digestion a head start; food is chopped up and mixed with the digestive enzymes present in saliva. Animals that swallow their food without chewing must rely exclusively on internal digestion to break down the food. In reptiles, for example, breaking down a rodent swallowed whole

---

### CORE FACTS

- The stomach stores food temporarily and begins the breakdown of nutrients.
- In the stomach, strong muscular contractions called peristaltic waves and strong gastric juices convert chewed food to liquid chyme.
- Only water, salts, alcohol, and small amounts of glucose (sugar) are absorbed directly from the stomach.
- The stomach is not essential to life. Many people survive gastrectomy, the surgical removal of all or part of the stomach.

---

### CONNECTIONS

- **EMOTIONS**, such as anger and fear, can affect the secretions and contractions of the stomach.

- Food has to pass through the stomach of **RODENTS** twice before digestion is complete.

into a usable form may take several weeks. In many birds, the stomach includes a section for extra storage, a compartment that adds digestive juices, and a muscular gizzard that grinds food with the help of small stones swallowed by the bird.

Ruminant (or cud-chewing) animals, such as cows (see RUMINANTS), have a specialized stomach to digest coarse, fibrous plant materials into usable nutrients. The stomach of ruminants is large relative to the animal's size and has four major compartments. The first, the rumen, serves as a temporary storage area while the animal continues feeding. Between periods of eating, material from the rumen is brought up to the mouth so that it can be finely ground and mixed with more saliva. The food is then returned to the rumen, where colonies of bacteria and protozoans help digest cellulose, and passes through the other compartments of the stomach, where further digestion takes place. The digested food then enters the small and large intestines, where further digestion and absorption take place.

Rodents, lagomorphs (rabbits and hares; see RABBITS AND HARES), and caveomorphs (such as guinea pigs) also process food twice to complete digestion. On the first trip through the rodent's stomach and digestive system, the food is coated with enzymes to help break it down (see ENZYMES). Some of the food is only partially digested when it is excreted; the droppings are then eaten along with new food. This behavior is called coprophagy.

## The human stomach

In humans the digestive system includes the mouth, esophagus, stomach, small intestine, large intestine, and rectum. The upper end of the human stomach connects to the esophagus, and the lower end opens into the duodenum (the first part of the small intestine). The stomach is a J-shaped muscular organ that can expand and contract depending on the amount of food it contains. When the stomach is nearly empty, it looks like a tube. When it is filled with food, it becomes much larger and more rounded.

Chewed food from the esophagus enters the stomach through a muscular one-way valve, the cardiac sphincter. Muscles encircling the stomach walls then squeeze food back and forth with powerful rhythmic contractions called peristaltic waves. The stomach muscles, contracting about every 20 seconds, crush food to a pulp and move it toward the pyloric (intestinal) end of the stomach. The processed food, a creamy substance called chyme, flows out of the stomach into the duodenum and through another valve called the pyloric sphincter.

In addition to muscle contractions, the action of acids and enzymes produced by the stomach lining break down food for further digestion in the small intestine. Gastric juice, secreted by stomach glands, contains water, salts, hydrochloric acid, and the enzymes pepsin and rennin. Pepsin speeds up protein digestion, while rennin causes milk to clot, coagulating the protein in milk into an insoluble protein that takes longer to leave the stomach. As well as its digestive functions, hydrochloric acid kills most harmful microorganisms. Another digestive juice, salivary amylase, is formed from saliva and enters the stomach with the food. In the stomach, ptyalin converts 75 percent of the cooked starch in a meal to malt sugar (maltose) before being destroyed by hydrochloric acid in the gastric juice. Sugar digestion is completed in the small intestine.

Vertebrate stomachs are lined by a mucous membrane with folds called rugae (see MUCOUS MEMBRANES). These folds allow the stomach to expand and contract as food passes in and out. Most of the surface is covered with mucus-secreting epithelial cells. Scattered throughout the lining are many small glandular pits lined with cells that produce gastric juice. Below the mucous membrane, the submucosa forms a thin layer of loose connective tissue between the inside of the stomach and the encircling layers of muscle.

*The diagram below shows the muscular stomach, the stomach lining, and the gastric glands, which release secretions containing enzymes that speed up the digestion of food.*

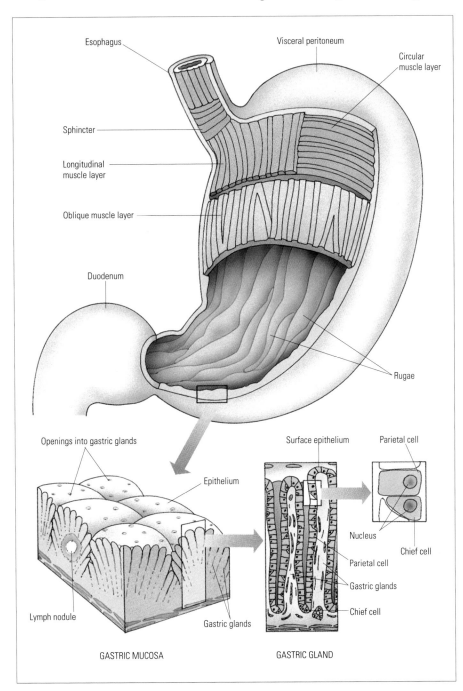

GASTRIC MUCOSA

GASTRIC GLAND

# DISORDERS OF THE STOMACH

Nausea is a disagreeable sensation in the stomach that is felt when the muscles of the stomach wall slow down or stop their movement and digestion is reduced. Nausea can help prevent the body from absorbing a poisonous substance that has been swallowed. Some poisonous substances cause nausea by stimulating nerve endings in the lining of the stomach or intestine. Nausea can also arise when the blood carries poison to cells in the brain stem.

Expelling the contents of the stomach—vomiting—often follows the feeling of nausea and further protects the body from absorbing toxic substances present in the stomach. The stomach contents are expelled by movements of the abdominal muscles and the diaphragm, a large muscle at the bottom of the ribs. In this muscular activity, called retching, the diaphragm moves downward and the abdominal muscles contract, squeezing the stomach contents upward. An individual vomits when his or her retching becomes intense enough to force the stomach contents through the esophagus. Some animals, including horses, are unable to vomit. These animals are more vulnerable to the effects of any poisonous plants they may ingest. Induced vomiting is associated with some eating disorders (bulimia and anorexia; see EATING DISORDERS). Where there is repeated vomiting, gastric juice can dissolve tooth enamel and damage the esophagus and mouth.

A stomach (gastric) ulcer is a raw area that develops in the lining of the stomach. It arises when gastric juices begin to digest the stomach lining. People with gastric ulcers experience a burning, gnawing pain in the upper part of the abdomen or the lower chest. Although the exact cause of such ulcers is not known, there is evidence that the stomach lining is irritated by bile juices regurgitated into the stomach from the duodenum. People who smoke, drink alcohol, consume large amounts of painkillers that contain aspirin, or eat irregular, hurried meals run a greater risk of developing gastric ulcers. Probably 1 in 5 men and 1 in 10 women in western nations get either a stomach ulcer or a duodenal ulcer at some time in their life. Doctors have discovered that a bacterium, *Helicobacter pylori*, is responsible for many stomach ulcers. The bacterium survives in the stomach's acidic environment by using urea to make ammonia, an alkaline substance that neutralizes the stomach's acid.

Indigestion, which occurs when too much acid is produced in the stomach, causes a wide range of symptoms, including abdominal

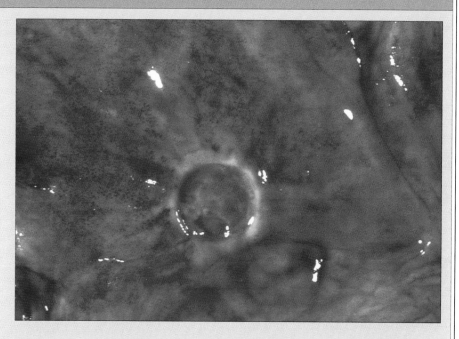

*A stomach ulcer is a raw area that develops in the stomach lining. Those who drink alcohol and smoke are more likely to develop one.*

pain, nausea, and vomiting. Heartburn arises when the acid is pushed back up toward the esophagus in a process called esophageal reflux. Heartburn causes a burning pain in the chest and occasionally, an acid taste in the mouth. Both disorders are aggravated by spicy and rich foods, stress, and alcohol.

To diagnose stomach disorders, physicians may order a barium X ray; the patient swallows a liquid containing the metallic chemical barium, which is visible on X rays. The liquid's progress down the digestive tract is recorded on a series of X-ray pictures.

Treatment of stomach disorders often involves changes in eating habits or emotional states to reduce or neutralize the stomach acid in digestive juice. Taking antacids and drugs that reduce acid secretion, avoiding irritating foods, and practicing relaxation techniques have proved effective. The human stomach is a simple organ that helps digestion, but it is not essential to life. It has been wholly removed from people who have cancer of the stomach, and large parts of it have been removed from patients who have gastric ulcers. These people must modify their diets so that they eat many small meals, but their prognosis (outlook) is generally good.

## A CLOSER LOOK

The time taken to empty the stomach depends on the individual and the type of food eaten. Water passes almost immediately through the pyloric sphincter into the small intestine. In most people, the stomach empties in three to five hours. When it is empty, peristaltic waves (involuntary contractions) create feelings of hunger and churn up gases that make a growling sound. The sight, smell, and taste of food stimulate the production of saliva and digestive juices. Emotions also affect the stomach's action; fear, anxiety, and anger strongly affect stomach secretions and contractions, and unpleasant sights, disgusting odors, and severe pain can cause stomach upset.

P. WEIS TAYLOR

**See also:** CARNIVORES; CELLULOSE; DIGESTIVE SYSTEMS; DIGESTIVE TRACT; EATING DISORDERS; ENZYMES; INVERTEBRATES; JELLYFISH, SEA ANEMONES, AND HYDRAS; MUCOUS MEMBRANES; RABBITS AND HARES; RUMINANTS; SPONGES; VERTEBRATES.

**Further reading:**
Chivers, D. J., and P. Langer, eds. 1994.
*The Digestive System in Mammals: Food, Form, and Function.* New York: Cambridge University Press.
Vander, A., J. Sherman, and D. Luciano. 2001.
*Human Physiology.* New York: McGraw-Hill.

# STRESS

*Conflict between teenagers and their parents commonly cause extremely stressful situations.*

## CONNECTIONS

● Stress stimulates the **LIVER** to increase the rate at which it converts **AMINO ACIDS** and fatty acids to glucose.

● **HORMONES** in the bloodstream trigger the movement of **BLOOD** from the internal organs to the muscles when the body is under stress.

Stress arises from many causes. Some causes are physical, such as an infection; others are environmental, for example, exposure to extreme heat. Many causes of stress are psychological. For a student, the prospect of a major examination can trigger stress; for an athlete, an upcoming competition can have the same effect. Emotions such as fear and anger are also powerful sources of stress in individuals. The death of a near relative or loved one, financial worries, and the demands of school or the workplace can also cause stress.

## Effects of stress

The body's first response after experiencing stress is often called the fight or flight phenomenon; the body reacts in a way that prepares it either to flee a stressful situation or to fight and defend itself. This response to stress is controlled by the hypothalamus, a small region of the brain (see BRAIN). The hypothalamus is connected to most of the body's sensory systems, as well as to other parts of the brain. These systems can send a signal to the hypothalamus when a stressful situation is perceived. Once the individual perceives a stressor, the hypothalmus sends messages to the sympathetic nervous system (see NERVOUS SYSTEMS). These messages stimulate the adrenal medulla (the interior of the adrenal gland, one of

which sits above each kidney) to secrete epinephrine (often called adrenalin) and norepinephrine (often called noradrenalin; see ENDOCRINE SYSTEMS; EPINEPHRINE AND NOREPINEPHRINE). These hormones, once released into the bloodstream, trigger a number of changes: the heart beats faster, the breathing rate increases, and blood moves from the internal organs to the muscles. The body interrupts other nonessential processes, such as digestion.

After this initial, very rapid response, the hypothalamus stimulates the glands' production of the hormone cortisol. The release of cortisol occurs when the brain, interpreting an event as stressful, sends a message to the hypothalamus. The hypothalamus then sends its own message to the anterior (front) part of the pituitary gland, located at the base of the brain. This gland secretes a hormone into the bloodstream that specifically causes the adrenal cortex (the outer tissue of the adrenal gland) to secrete cortisol into the bloodstream.

Cortisol produces a wide range of effects in the body that help a person either cope with the stress itself or react to whatever is causing it. For example, it provides the body with a ready supply of energy. Specifically, cortisol promotes the chemical breakdown of stored proteins into amino acids and stimulates the liver to produce glucose more rapidly (see METABOLISM). This action results in an energy supply for use in stressful situations, as well as amino acids that can be used to make new proteins (such as those needed to repair injured tissue). Cortisol also counteracts the relaxation of the circulatory system, ensuring that the body functions at peak efficiency.

Stress is not reserved for humans. All living organisms undergo stress in some form or another and react to it in different ways. In wild animals psychological stress can be a result of threats from predators or conflict arising from social relationships. These stresses can give rise to displacement activities; for example, the feeding animal may direct

## CORE FACTS

■ Stress has physical and psychological causes. The body reacts to stress in a way that prepares it to fight the situation or flee from it.

■ Hormones are released when the body is under stress. Some hormones trigger increased heartbeat and breathing rate and the movement of blood from the internal organs to the muscles. Other chemicals provide for a ready supply of energy to improve endurance.

■ Physiological responses to prolonged or repeated stress may have a negative impact on those suffering psychological stress. Increased cholesterol levels, hypertension, and stomach ulcers are thought to be the health effects of excessive stress.

its attention to inedible particles on the ground because the animal cannot decide on the appropriate response to the stressful situation. Severe stress can lead to abnormal behavior and the development of gastric ulcers (in humans).

Penning animals together in close quarters leads to elevated levels of stress-related hormones. This hormonal increase causes the type of behavior most commonly seen in zoos—animals pacing back and forth or rocking from one foot to the other.

## Health impacts

The body's response to physical stress is beneficial, provided it is not prolonged. For example, cardiovascular exercise, such as swimming, running, or aerobics, places a mild stress on the heart and helps it grow stronger.

However, bodily changes usually do not help people cope with psychologically induced stress. It is seldom possible to react to modern causes of psychological stress by fight or flight. For example, a student may be upset about receiving a disappointing grade on an assignment, but fighting or fleeing will not solve the problem or improve performance next time. Because the hormones and other substances involved are not decomposed by vigorous physical action, they may feed back into the body, the result being anxiety and other reactions.

Some people suffer prolonged, repeated stress, for example, those who work in a demanding job. All the processes that are helpful in dealing with momentary stress can be harmful if they continue for long periods. High cortisol levels appear to impair the immune system and thus make a person more susceptible to disease. Chronic stress produces higher levels of gastric acids in the stomach, which may promote the development of ulcers. The cardiovascular effects of stress, such as increased pulse rate, may lead to hypertension. Moreover, stress contributes to an increased cholesterol level. These two effects explain why physicians often advise people with heart disease to reduce the amount of stress in their lives.

## Delayed effects

People who experience a profoundly stressful event, such as active combat during war, are often affected by that stress for years or decades, a condition called post-traumatic stress disorder (PTSD). To the military, the phenomenon is as old as warfare itself, although it has been known by different names in the past: shell shock during World War I and battle fatigue during World War II.

Whatever term is used, the symptoms of PTSD remain unchanged. They include depression, nightmares and insomnia, flashbacks to the original traumatic event, violent behavior, and jumpiness. Researchers think that suffering a severely traumatic event may make one's body more sensitive to future changes in the body's epinephrine levels. In that case, a sufferer might be severely affected by an epinephrine increase that would have little effect on healthy people. Post-traumatic stress disorder is not

## STRESS IN PLANTS

Plants are said to be stressed in any situation in which they are prevented from growing and metabolizing normally. Stresses usually impose a complex range of physical and biochemical effects on plants. Water stress provides a good example.

The principal effect of water stress is reduced cell growth. With less water present, the pressure inside plant cells falls, and thus, cell expansion is reduced. As the stress increases, a wide range of metabolic processes become disrupted, the level of certain enzymes drops, and cell membrane and protein synthesis become impaired. In response to stress, certain plant hormones accumulate, causing closure of the stomata, the pores in the plant epidermis. This closure reduces further water loss but also decreases gaseous exchange and thus reduces photosynthesis and respiration.

Other limiting factors, such as temperature, light, and soil nutrients, may cause stress when present in extremes. Lack of nutrients leads to deficiency syndromes, yet high concentrations can be toxic.

Periods of stress of one form or another are universal among plants, which have consequently evolved strategies to minimize their impact. These strategies are essential because, to be competitive, it is as important to capitalize during optimal conditions as it is to survive episodes of stress with minimal disruption.

### A CLOSER LOOK

limited to combat veterans. Anyone who has experienced a major calamity can be at risk. For example, survivors of plane crashes have also been diagnosed as suffering from the disorder.

V. KIERNAN

**See also:** BRAIN; ENDOCRINE SYSTEMS; EPINEPHRINE AND NOREPINEPHRINE; HORMONES; MENTAL DISORDERS; METABOLISM; NERVOUS SYSTEMS.

**Further reading:**
Rothschild. B. 2000. *The Body Remembers: The Psychophysiology of Trauma and Trauma Treatment.* New York: W. W. Norton.
Sapolsky, R. M. 1998. *Why Zebras Don't Get Ulcers: An Updated Guide to Stress, Stress-Related Diseases, and Coping.* New York: Freeman.

*Piglets forced to live close together in small rearing pens, below, can experience high levels of stress-related hormones.*

# SUBURBAN HABITATS

## Suburban habitats are residential areas between a city center and the surrounding countryside

*The raccoon (Procyon lotor) has adapted well to the environment of suburban areas. These animals often feed on human garbage, which is usually quite accessible in residential districts.*

## CONNECTIONS

● **GRASSES** are the most common plants in suburban areas.

● Inadequate human **WASTE DISPOSAL** often attracts many animal **SPECIES** to suburban areas, where **FEEDING** may be easier than it is in the species' natural habitat.

A suburb is a residential area on the outskirts of a central city. Its environment provides a transition between that of the undeveloped, more natural landscape and that of the paved-over downtown area (see URBAN HABITATS).

Suburbs are definitely not a new phenomenon. Historians think that even the earliest cities in the Middle East (established thousands of years ago) had suburbs where city workers lived. One resident of a suburb of the ancient city of Babylon wrote to the king of Persia in 539 BCE, "It is so close to Babylon that we enjoy all the advantages of the city, and yet when we come home we are away from all the noise and dust." Many occupants of modern suburbs would describe their homes in much the same way.

Some of the first U.S. cities, such as Boston (founded in 1630) and Philadelphia (founded in 1681), quickly developed suburbs, but they were quite close to the central city—usually within walking distance—because of the lack of mass transportation. However, from the early 1800s, successive development of transportation systems, such as the building of an extensive network of good-quality roads and, later, railroads allowed people to live at greater distances from the central city and yet commute back and forth from their jobs. The establishment of these transportation systems triggered an exodus from the central city, with more and more people living at greater distances away from the city. This was accelerated by the development and increasing availability of the automobile, particularly after World War II (1939–1945).

Approximately 46 percent of Americans now live in the suburbs, while 31 percent live in cities. This population pattern causes traffic headaches: the workers' daily convergence on the city overwhelms the mass transportation systems and causes large traffic jams on freeways and highways.

### Plants in suburbia

By definition, suburbia's setting is midway between that of the inner city and that of the surrounding agriculture on natural lands. Thus, suburban habitats have more open space and greenery than urban areas but less than the countryside. Moreover, suburbia tends to have a narrower range of plants than the country and more imported or exotic plants.

Perhaps the most ubiquitous plant in suburbia is grass, in the form of carefully tended lawns on which residents may expend large amounts of water to keep them green. Usually the homeowner mows the lawn regularly, sometimes throwing the clippings in the trash. At other times, the clippings are mulched so that the photosynthetic productivity of the lawn grass can be used to enrich the soil and thus benefit other suburban plants and animals.

Weeds, such as dandelions (*Taraxacum* spp.), are particularly common in the surburbs. The wind-borne pollen of the ragweeds *Ambrosia artemisiifolia* and *A. trifida* is a common cause of hay fever in North America.

### Animals in suburbia

Many of the animals seen in the surburbs are visitors from the more rural areas. Some of the best-known residents of suburbia are raccoons (*Procyon* spp.). These animals have shown an uncanny ability to adapt their patterns of life in the wild to the different circumstances of suburbia. Being nocturnal, raccoons are able to avoid much direct contact with

---

**CORE FACTS**

■ The environment of suburban habitats is usually dominated by residential areas.

■ The suburban environment provides a transition between the built-up area of a city center and the open countryside.

■ Most of the plant life in the suburbs is restricted to trees, grasses, and other plant species found growing in lawns.

■ Animal species found in the suburbs are often migrants from the surrounding rural areas.

humans, although they make dens for themselves in human structures, such as chimneys, and they root through trash cans in search of food. Raccoons are often regarded as pests that must be exterminated or trapped and relocated. The common raccoon (*Procyon lotor*) is the major rabies vector (an organism housing disease and transmitting it to other organisms) in the southeastern United States.

The suburban environment can have an impact on animal populations. Lizards, for example, grow larger and lizard populations are denser than in the wild, probably because food and water are more accessible and often there are fewer predators. However, suburban development eliminates much of the native plant cover and so may also eliminate the many reptiles and amphibians that depend on these plants.

Owls (families Strigidae and Tytonidae) are common suburban birds that often nest in human-made structures such as church steeples and barns. Owls are raptors (birds of prey; see BIRDS OF PREY); human development may lead to larger populations of the owls' prey, such as mice, lizards, and insects. However, a suburban environment also poses new threats to owls. For example, little owls are attracted to roadways after rainstorms because they can find earthworms there, a place where the owls are also at risk of being hit by automobiles.

In the suburbs, the trees are usually too sparse to support many native bird populations, such as fly-catchers (subfamily Muscicapinae), that are dependent on a specific food source. Bird populations therefore tend to be composed of generalist feeders.

The pigeon (family Columbidae) is an excellent example of a generalist feeder. It is not native to North America, where it was introduced in the 1700s. Pigeons find shelter for their nests in a variety of artificial structures, such as buildings, and generally depend on humans for food. The American robin (*Turdus migratorius*) also eats a variety of plant and invertebrate food, such as slugs, beetles, and berries, and nests in branches, awnings, and porch trellises.

Other birds have also found suburban life to their liking, and many nest inside buildings. The chimney swift (*Chaetura pelagica*) has been attracted to suburbs by the combination of appropriate nesting areas (tall chimneys) and gardens or parks that serve as a source of insects. The American kestrel (*Falco sparverius*) nests in hollow trees and in a variety of buildings. Other common suburban birds include crows, sparrows, blackbirds, and house finches.

## Living off humans

Many of the animals that live in suburban habitats do so because they can live off the waste that humans produce around them. One obvious example is the house mouse (*Mus musculus*), which has followed humans wherever they have moved around the globe; the mouse is probably the most widely distributed mammal beside humans. Another example of great historical importance is the black rat (*Rattus rattus*), which is responsible for the epidemics of

## PET PROBLEMS

Many city dwellers keep cats and dogs as pets. These pets are more common in the surburbs, where there are parks and gardens in which they can roam, than in urban areas. However, in the surburbs there are many abandoned cats and dogs that have lost their domestic habits. These wild (feral) animals often prey on smaller animals and have been known to attack humans. Many of them cannot survive on their own because they do not know how to hunt and cannot find shelter. They may also contract rabies. In 1994 hundreds of people in Maryland had to receive rabies vaccinations after contact with an infected feral kitten.

bubonic plague that swept through Europe in the 1300s. The disease was transmitted to humans from rats infected by fleas that carried plague.

Less threatening examples of animals abound. Raccoons, for example, eat dog and cat food that have been left out by humans for their pets. Opossums (family Didelphidae) and coyotes (*Canis latrans*) root through human trash in search of food. Thus, human garbage provides a new energy source for animals, allowing new food chains to be built. For example, the waste may sustain a mouse population, which, in turn, is preyed on by small predators, such as cats. However, the limited food resources in a suburban environment cannot generally support the larger predators that, in turn, would hunt the smaller ones. As a result, large populations of the smaller predators may develop.

V. KIERNAN

**See also:** BIRDS OF PREY; URBAN HABITATS.

## Further reading:

Hadidan, J., ed. 1997. *Wild Neighbours: The Humane Approach to Living with Wildlife*. Golden, Color.: Fulcrum Publishers.
Wheater, C. P. 1999. *Urban Habitats (Habitat Guides)*. New York: Routledge.

*Some birds of prey, such as the common kestrel (*Falco tinnunculus*) shown below, may nest in a variety of buildings in the suburbs. These birds are often attracted to suburban habitats by the presence of large numbers of their prey species.*

# SURGERY

**Surgery is the treatment of disease or injury by invasive operative procedures**

relief; see ANESTHESIA) at their disposal. Until the mid-19th century, the memorable feature of most operations was speed rather than surgical finesse. The mortality (death rate) from surgery—especially from infection and shock—was enormous. It was only with the arrival of effective anesthesia that surgery began to come into its own.

## Pioneering anesthesia

The introduction of ether anesthesia, pioneered at Massachusetts General Hospital in 1846, was followed by the development of a number of surgical specialties, including neurologic (brain and nervous system) and thoracic (chest) surgery. Innovators began devising all manner of complex operations, including nephrectomy (kidney removal) and various bowel procedures, which had not been possible before. Splenectomy (spleen removal), first attempted as far back as 1549, was revived as a treatment for trauma and for certain blood diseases.

## Landmark advances

From the mid-19th century to the early years of the 20th century, a number of landmark advances contributed fundamentally to the success of surgical treatments. These advances included the acceptance of the germ theory of disease, which in turn prompted measures to limit infection; the discovery of blood groups, which was essential for safe transfusions; and the development of surgical anastomosis techniques—the rejoining of the severed ends of blood vessels or other tubular structures, such as the intestine.

By the early 20th century, access had been gained to all three of the major body cavities—the chest, the abdomen, and the interior of the skull, although not all the new procedures would stand the test of time. Some, such as thoracoplasty (the contriving

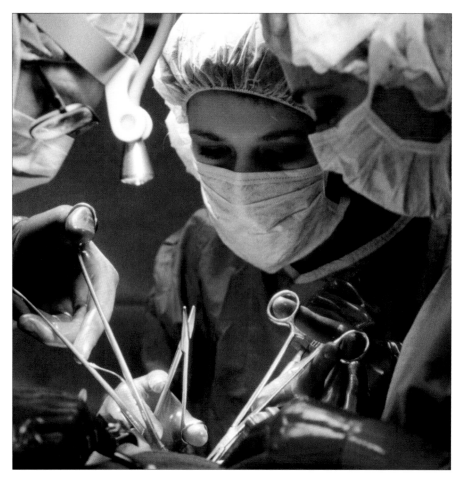

*Surgery is carried out in the carefully controlled environment of the operating theater, in which the surgeon is supported by other medical staff.*

Imagine someone having his or her arm cut off by a surgeon—a terrible enough procedure in itself—but imagine the operation without anesthesia. This situation was exactly the fate of many patients needing surgery before the 1850s. Pain, infection, and shock were three formidable problems for patients, and surgeons had few tools for lessening them.

The practice of surgery, that is, using some form of instrument on the body for curative means, can be traced back to earliest times. It is known from archeological finds, for example, that prehistoric people undertook trephining—the procedure of cutting a circular hole in the bone of the skull—as long as 10,000 years ago. The reason for this practice is unknown; most likely it was carried out by witch doctors to release evil spirits.

For centuries in Europe, surgery was carried out not by medical doctors but by barbers and hangmen. In the mid-16th century, the Frenchman Ambroise Paré (1510–1590) elevated surgery to a respectable profession and, as a military surgeon, greatly reduced the death rate among the wounded.

Throughout recorded history, many procedures, such as limb amputation, removal of cataracts, and lithotomy ("cutting for stone," that is, removal of stones from the urinary bladder), were carried out. However, early surgeons did not have anesthesia (pain

## CONNECTIONS

● The need for exploratory surgery has been greatly reduced by the development of noninvasive imaging techiques such as **ULTRASOUND** and **MAGNETIC RESONANCE IMAGING**.

### CORE FACTS

■ Acceptance of the germ theory of disease (which helped limit infection), the discovery of blood groupings (essential for safe transfusions), and the development of surgical anastomosis (rejoining, for example, the severed ends of blood vessels) contributed to the advance of surgery from 1850 to the early 20th century.

■ Ether anesthesia for surgical patients was not available until the mid-19th century; surgeons now have highly sophisticated techniques , such as microsurgery and keyhole surgery, and laser scalpels at their disposal.

■ Modern surgery is either elective (there is a choice) or nonelective (it must be performed if the patient is to live).

■ The most frequently performed open heart procedure is coronary artery bypass grafting; dangerously narrowed coronary arteries are replaced by lengths of vein taken from the patient's leg.

of partial collapse of a lung to treat pulmonary tuberculosis), were replaced in due course by more effective treatments. Nevertheless, surgery in general was increasingly seen as a viable form of therapy for many categories of disease and injury.

As the century progressed, all the major elements of modern surgery were gradually brought together. These elements included specialized instrumentation and equipment and trained operating room personnel who, by now masked, gloved, and gowned, carried out operations in accordance with the aseptic principle of excluding infection as much as possible.

In 1935 came the breakthrough that went a long way toward minimizing the effects of life-threatening shock. This innovation was the invention of an efficient delivery system for transfused blood. Although blood had been transfused in the past, it could not be supplied to the patient in large quantity—a serious drawback because traumatic or surgical blood loss often required considerable replacement. The answer, invented in London, England, was the continuous drip, an intravenous infusion system for feeding donated blood at a controlled rate directly into one of the patient's veins. This important advance led to the establishment of the first blood banks.

The anesthesiologist was a relative latecomer to the operating suite; until World War II (1939–1945), surgeons tended to administer anesthesia. By then it was widely recognized that operating safety depended to a great extent on the presence of a highly trained physician-anesthesiologist with the ability not only to put the patient to sleep but also to maintain him or her in a stable condition during surgery.

## Major developments

Meanwhile, there had been two further developments that would have important implications for surgery. The first, during the early years of World War II, was the introduction into clinical use of penicillin, the first antibiotic (see ANTIBIOTICS). Scottish microbiologist Alexander Fleming (1881–1955; see FLEMING, ALEXANDER) had discovered penicillin more than 10 years earlier following accidental contamination of a culture plate by the *Penicillium notatum* mold. However, it was not until 1940 that penicillin was isolated from the mold, enabling commercial production. This new so-called wonder drug was closely followed by the discovery of other antibiotics to combat a wide range of life-threatening infections. Antibiotics are now used perioperatively (before, during, or after surgery) to prevent or treat infection.

The second development was especially welcomed by general surgeons who perform mostly abdominal operations. For years they had wanted to use ever-deeper levels of anesthesia to relax the muscles of the abdomen and diaphragm, but deep anesthesia carries a significant risk of sudden death. However, in 1942 Montreal surgeons injected patients with a purified preparation of curare, the poisonous compound used by South American Indians on their arrowheads to paralyze muscles.

A black, resinous substance obtained from the bark of certain South American trees, curare inhibits nerve stimulation of voluntary muscle—an effect called neuromuscular blockade—and effectively relaxes the skeletal muscles. The drug was used at one time to control severe muscle spasm in conditions such as tetanus, but the purified curare allowed operations to be performed with much lighter anesthesia and thus reduced the risk of patient death.

So World War II produced many positive changes in medical and surgical procedures. The immediate postwar years brought refinements, particularly in the areas of resuscitation (an emergency life-support technique), wound treatment, and the transport and care of very sick patients. The early postwar years also saw the introduction of teamwork into surgery. This new sense of professionalism in the operating room and improved technical expertise paved the way for the development of so-called high-profile surgery—procedures such as organ transplants (see TRANSPLANTS) and coronary artery bypass grafting (CABG).

## Entry to the heart

The last recesses of the body to be explored surgically were the chambers of the heart. The limited amount of surgery involving the heart or its great vessels (closed-heart procedures) had been performed with the heart still beating. Surgeons had to operate quickly on the parts they could actually see. Anything more had to await the development of the heart-lung machine, which takes over the functions of both the heart and the lungs so that the patient's heart can be stopped.

The heart-lung machine provides the patient with an extracorporeal circulation—a system that draws blood away from the body, removes the carbon dioxide, and returns it, freshly oxygenated, into the circulation. The equipment also cools

*From the early 20th century, physicians recognized that to reduce the possibility of infection being introduced in the operating theater, operating room personnel must be masked, gloved, and gowned.*

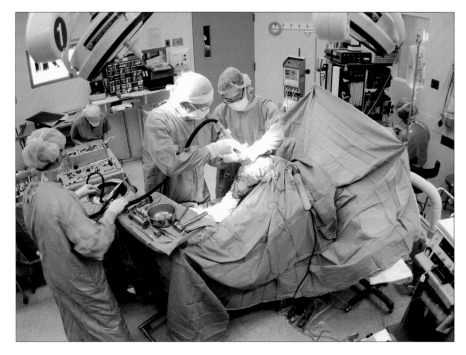

## INTRICATE WORK

Microsurgery is a term used to describe procedures undertaken using an operating microscope and tiny precision instruments. It is used for intricate tasks, such as suturing minute nerves or blood vessels or treating a lesion that lies close to some vital structure in, for example, the brain or spinal cord. Microsurgery is also invaluable in ophthalmology (the study of the eye structure, function, and disease), in otorhinolaryngology (ENT; the study of the ears, nose, and throat), and in surgery to replace severed body parts. The scope of plastic surgery—any operation carried out to repair or reconstruct skin or other body parts—has been broadened over the last 30 years by the development of microsurgery techniques to join blood vessels; thus, the transfer of blocks of skin and muscles from one body part to another, the reattachment of severed limbs, and the transplantation of a wide variety of organs are now possible.

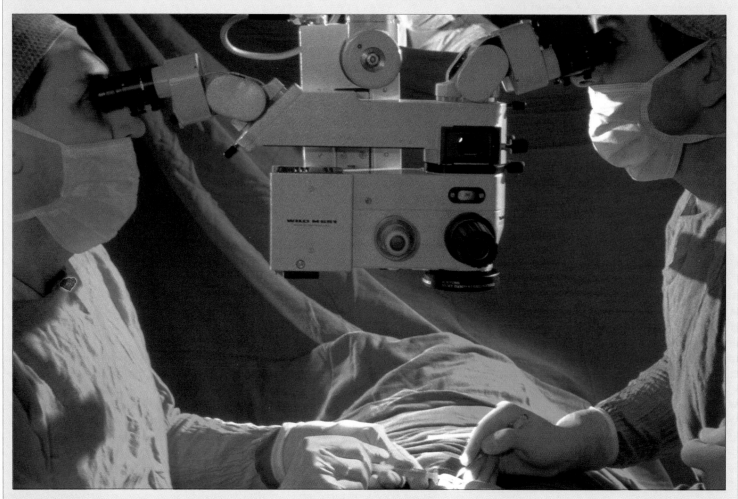

*The twin optic binocular microscope allows two surgeons to see the same detailed view of an operation while carrying out a delicate microsurgical procedure. A video camera can also be mounted on the microscope, and via a live feed to the internet, another physician at a different hospital can consult during the operation. The resulting video may be used in training.*

### A CLOSER LOOK

the blood during prolonged surgery and rewarms it as the operation is completed before returning it.

The prototype was invented by Dr. John Gibbon of Philadelphia, who first demonstrated its use in surgery in 1953. However, another 20 years passed before what is now the most frequently performed open-heart procedure, coronary artery bypass grafting, was developed. This operation replaces diseased sections of the coronary arteries, which carry the heart's blood supply. Dangerously narrowed vessels (owing to accumulation of plaque, a fatty deposit), which cause ischemic heart disease (deficient blood supply), are replaced by lengths of vein taken from the patient's own leg. Bypass surgery relieves the intense pain of angina and restores an adequate blood supply to the patient's heart muscle.

### Elective or nonelective surgery

Modern surgery is either elective, that is, the patient has a choice, or nonelective, in which case the patient has no choice. Nonelective surgery includes life-saving operations that must often be performed on an emergency basis. One of the most common nonelective procedures performed is appendectomy, the removal of an acutely inflamed appendix before it ruptures (usually causing a potentially lethal infection called peritonitis). A large proportion of trauma surgery (treatment of patients with acute physical injury) is also nonelective.

With elective surgery, the element of choice includes which of several techniques to opt for, whether to schedule surgery or to forego surgery in favor of some other form of treatment. One of the most successful and widely performed elective procedures is hip replacement—removing a diseased joint and inserting an artificial one.

The elective choices vary to some extent, owing to changing trends or advances in medical technology. For example, the introduction over the last 25 years of noninvasive imaging techniques such as ultrasound (see ULTRASOUND), computerized axial tomography (CT) scanning (see CT SCANNING), and magnetic resonance imaging (MRI; see MAGNETIC RESONANCE IMAGING) has greatly reduced the need for exploratory surgery. Laparotomy (opening up the abdomen) was and still is the most common exploratory procedure but is now performed less often.

Among the specialties that have been revolutionized by these noninvasive techniques is neurologic surgery, where the CT scanner has now become the principal diagnostic tool.

## Undergoing surgery

For a major operation performed under general anesthesia, the patient is usually brought into the hospital at least 24 hours in advance. This procedure gives doctors time to complete the various preoperative preparations, such as having the person fast for some hours so that the stomach empties before anesthesia is administered. The preoperative medication, given an hour or two before surgery, usually consists of a sedative and an anticholinergic drug, such as atropine, to dry up the bronchial secretions and assist smooth muscle relaxation.

Once the patient is brought to the operating suite, another hour's preparation may be necessary before surgery. First, anesthesia is given by injecting a fast-acting sedative, such as thiopentone, which depresses brain activity. Once unconscious, the patient is intubated: a breathing tube, called an endotracheal tube, is passed down the throat so that the patient can be kept anesthetized with an inhaled anesthetic, such as halothane; oxygen is also delivered through this tube. Heart and other electronic monitors are connected up to warn the surgical team of any change in the patient's condition.

Hemostasis (control of bleeding) is essential during surgery to prevent excessive blood loss. Any major vessels that have to be severed are compressed with clamps (called hemostats) and then either tied off or sutured (stitched); tiny blood vessels are cauterized (heat sealed). Suction equipment and gauze sponges clear away blood from the site of the operation.

Surgical wounds are closed in layers, with the edges of each layer of tissue being brought together and sutured. There are two types of sutures: absorbable catgut (now made from sheep's intestines), used for rapidly healing, internal tissues, such as the gut; and nonabsorbable sutures (made of silk, cotton, linen, or synthetics) for slower-healing, external tissues, such as the skin. Metal clips, skin-closure strips, or cyanoacrylate glues may also be used to close incisions.

After surgery, the patient is nursed in the recovery room until the anesthetic has worn off and his or her body has returned to normal functioning. Most patients make a prompt recovery, although complications can sometimes occur after an operation. One of the most worrying problems is deep vein thrombosis (DVT), or clot formation, usually in the legs. If a blood clot breaks away, it can be carried in the bloodstream to lodge in some distant site, such as the pulmonary artery supplying the lungs, a potentially fatal development called pulmonary embolism. Postoperative infections are also a major complication and can be fatal.

Not all surgery is performed while the patient is unconscious. In many cases, an epidural (spinal block) or local anesthetic may be administered instead, which numbs the nerves in the chest and the lower half of the body. In this method of pain relief, the anesthetic is injected via a hollow needle and a catheter (a thin, flexible tube). The catheter is inserted into the epidural space (the space around the membranes surrounding the spinal cord, within the spinal canal) in the middle and lower back and remains in place to allow further doses of local anesthetic to be given if necessary. An epidural can be used to relieve pain during and after surgery. A spinal tap (or lumbar puncture) can also be used to achieve extensive anesthesia without loss of consciousness. Here a hollow needle is inserted in the lower part of the spinal canal to inject local anesthetic. The needle is then removed, and the puncture site covered with sterile tape.

*An anesthetist administers drugs to a patient prior to surgery. Anesthetists are responsible both for putting the patient to sleep and for maintaining and monitoring the patient's stability throughout surgery.*

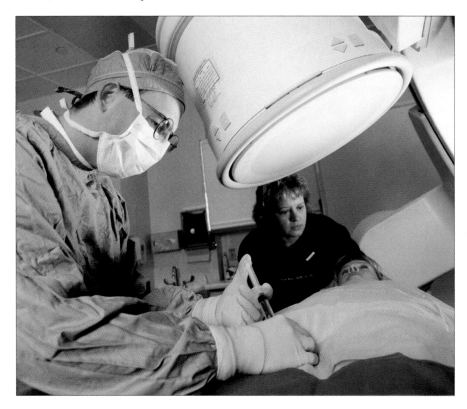

Wound infection is now far less common than it was in the past, but chest infection is not uncommon, particularly in patients who smoke. Urinary retention (an inability to pass urine) can occur after abdominal or pelvic operations; it may be prevented or relieved by bladder catheterization (passing a tube into the patient's bladder to drain off urine). After abdominal surgery, there is also a risk of paralytic ileus—absence of movement in the intestine—in which case the patient is restricted to intravenous fluids (fluid administered directly into the veins) until gut motility is restored.

With the high success rate of many operations, some may now even be carried out unnecessarily, a classic example being the Cesarean section. This operation is used to deliver a baby through a vertical or horizontal incision in the abdomen and uterus and is supposed to be performed when it is impossible or dangerous to deliver the baby normally. In the past 25 years, the number of Cesarean sections performed in the United States has increased dramatically to around 25 percent of all births. It has also become the single most commonly performed invasive procedure in many other countries. There is now some debate as to whether these operations are all strictly necessary. A major concern is that physicians may be performing unnecessary operations to lessen their liability to malpractice lawsuits when babies are born with problems owing to a lengthy natural delivery.

*Laparoscopic techniques enable surgeons to operate through a small hole in the patient's body wall and to perform operations using a television monitor screen to view the instruments inside the body.*

## A quiet revolution

Operating suites and conventional surgery have gradually been overtaken by minimal-access procedures that do not involve cutting into the body. Keyhole, or minimal access surgery (MAS), is performed either using an endoscope (a device for viewing the body's interior) or by passing fine instruments through a catheter (tube) inserted into the body via a large blood vessel. The growing list of minimal-access procedures, many of which require only local anesthesia, have enabled the expansion of outpatient surgery, where patients are admitted to the hospital, operated on, and return home in one day.

One of the best-known examples of minimal-access surgery is percutaneous transluminal coronary angioplasty (PTCA), an alternative procedure to coronary artery bypass grafting, performed on selected patients with ischemic heart disease. In coronary angioplasty, a balloon-tipped catheter is passed into a large artery in the groin and advanced until the tip comes to rest in a coronary vessel narrowed owing to plaque buildup. The balloon is inflated to compress the plaque against the artery wall and thus reopens the vessel for blood flow. Nearly half a million angioplasties are performed in the United States each year.

Although some endoscopic surgery had been practiced over many years, it was the introduction of the computer chip TV camera in 1986, enabling video-guided surgery, that accelerated the shift toward minimal-access surgery. In the same year, the first cholecystectomy (gallbladder removal) carried out using a laparoscope, a type of endoscope, was reported. Endoscopic surgeons have applied the technology to other procedures, such as appendectomy (removal of the appendix), nephrectomy (removal of one or both of the kidneys), and hysterectomy (removal of the uterus). The laser—the so-called bloodless scalpel (see the box on page 1575)—features in many of these procedures.

In skilled hands and for selected procedures, minimal-access surgery is safer and less traumatic than conventional surgery; it involves either out-

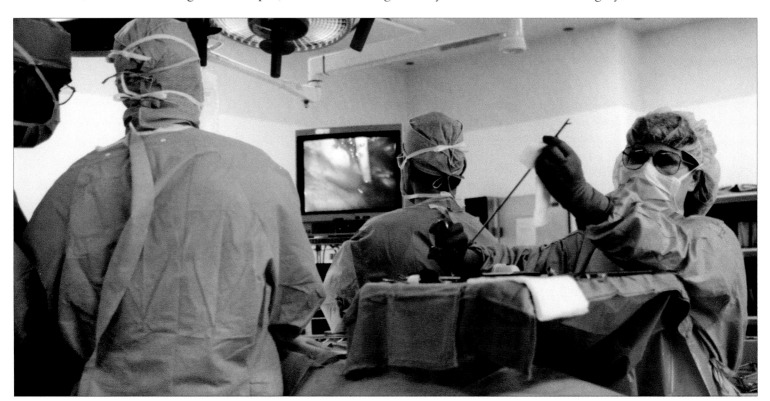

patient attendance or a shorter stay in the hospital. It is hard to know whether or not individual procedures are as effective because experience with the new technology is too recent. However, minimal-access surgery seems set to take over to a very great extent.

P. PRATT

**See also:** ANESTHESIA; ANTIBIOTICS AND ANTI-MICROBIALS; CT SCANNING; FLEMING, ALEXANDER; MEDICINE, HISTORY OF; TRANSPLANTS.

**Further reading:**
Griffith, H. W. *Complete Guide to Symptoms, Illness, and Surgery*. 4th ed. New York: The Body Press/Perigee.
Muth, A., and K. Bellenir, eds. 2002. *Surgery Sourcebook: Basic Consumer Health Information about Major Surgery and Outpatient Surgeries*. Detroit: Omnigraphics.
Youngson, R. M. 1993. *The Surgery Book: An Illustrated Guide to 73 of the Most Common Operations*. New York: St. Martin's Press.

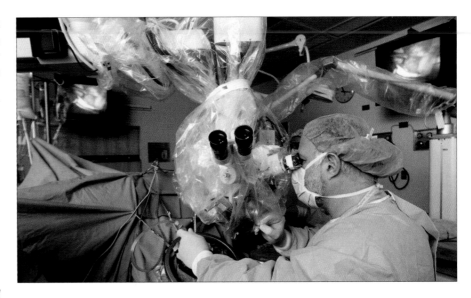

*A surgeon uses a microscope and a laser scalpel to remove a brain tumor. The brain can be seen on monitors on the wall of the operating theater.*

## THE "BLOODLESS SCALPEL"

A uniquely useful tool in surgery is the so-called bloodless scalpel—the laser. With precision control, it can be used to cut, coagulate, or vaporize body tissues with little or no bleeding. The cost of buying laser equipment is quickly offset by a reduction in operating time, faster patient recovery, and therefore, shorter hospitalization.

Named after the lasing medium (usually a gas), the instruments most often used in surgery are: the precision carbon dioxide ($CO_2$) laser, whose shallow depth of penetration avoids damage to delicate underlying structures; the argon-ion laser, widely used in eye surgery; and the deeply penetrating neodymium-YAG (Nd-YAG) laser.

The laser's effects on tissue depends on its wavelength (measured in nanometers), the power of its beam, and the nature of the tissue being treated. The infrared light from a $CO_2$ laser is almost entirely absorbed within the first 0.1 mm of tissue it encounters, and so this instrument can be used much as a scalpel is. The blue-green light of the argon laser, which has proved so successful in eye surgery, passes through the cornea and lens but is absorbed by the retina and can be used to prevent and treat detachment of the retina and to destroy small tumors of the retina.

The laser was first developed for medical use in 1960 and entered service in ophthalmology (the study of the anatomy, functions, and diseases of the eye), a specialty still at the forefront in laser usage. However, this immensely valuable tool has also been introduced into a number of other specialties, including the treatment of disorders of the male and female reproductive systems; the urinary tract in males and females; the nervous system; the bones and joints and their associated muscles, tendons, and ligaments; and the ears, nose, and throat and in general thoracic surgery (concerned with operations on organs within the chest, excluding the heart). In general surgery, one of the most successful applications is laparoscopic laser cholecystectomy (removal of the gallbladder), pioneered in 1989. This procedure entails at most a 48-hour stay in the hospital and full recovery within 10 days, compared with 10 days' hospitalization and up to 3 months' recovery time for the conventional operation.

A laser may be introduced using a gastroscope (a light, flexible, tubular instrument passed through the mouth for examination of the esophagus, stomach, and duodenum) to coagulate bleeding ulcers in the stomach. In advanced lung cancer, thoracic surgeons may use laser treatment to remove a tumor blocking a patient's airway. In the treatment of the male reproductive system, lasers are inserted into the urethra (the tube that runs through the penis to the bladder) and used to treat enlargement of the prostate gland and the consequent difficulty with urination, a condition estimated to affect up to 70 percent of men over the age of 50.

Minimal-access techniques using lasers have been developed for a number of operations on the female reproductive system, including an alternative treatment to hysterectomy (removal of the uterus) for heavy menstrual periods. In this procedure, light from an Nd-YAG laser is passed down an optical fiber inserted into a hysteroscope, an instrument used to view the interior of the uterus. The surgeon then uses the laser tip to remove unwanted tissue.

Unlike the Nd-YAG, the carbon dioxide laser cannot be used in association with the fiber optics of a flexible endoscope. Instead, it is used with a rigid endoscope fitted with a series of mirrors to direct and focus the beam. Neurological surgeons use the precision-cutting capability of this laser scalpel to remove otherwise inoperable tumors of the brain and spinal cord, which would cause fatal bleeding if simply cut with a scalpel.

Laser-assisted operations on the brain are some of the most modern applications, sometimes replacing the procedure of gaining access to the brain by means of a bone flap raised in the skull. These operations are often undertaken to relieve a buildup of fluid in the brain and are performed through a small hole drilled in the cranium.

In eye surgery, the argon-ion laser remains a potent weapon against damage to the retina that can occur as a complication of diabetes. It also has a role in the treatment of glaucoma (abnormally high pressure within the eye), the surgeon minimizing harmful fluid buildup by improving drainage within the eye. The Nd-YAG laser is also used to remove fragments of lens remaining after surgery to remove cataracts (clouded lenses).

A new treatment for some localized cancers, called photo-radiation therapy, makes use of the light sensitivity of certain biological pigments. Injected into a vein, a solution containing one of these photosensitive pigments concentrates in a tumor. Stimulated by laser light, the pigment converts oxygen into a toxic form, killing the cancer cells without destroying the surrounding tissues.

Many laser procedures are now performed on an outpatient basis, enabling the delivery of precise and highly specific treatments without the need for hospitalization. Portable lasers are being introduced to bring this mode of treatment to rural hospitals and medical centers.

# SWIMMING

**Swimming is the ability to move in water using limbs, fins, tail, or any other specialized features**

*Butterfly fish (Chaetodon larvatus) are laterally flattened. This adaptation enables them to swim quickly and slip into narrow crevices on the coral reefs where they live to escape from predators.*

A person trying to run through water moves as if in slow motion, even though his or her arms are pumping furiously. Water is denser than air and creates much more resistance against the body as someone tries to move through it. Aquatic animals have evolved bodies and ways of moving that minimize water resistance. When a human swims, the body position adopted and the limb movements used also reduce water resistance so that movement through the water is much easier.

### Swimming like a fish

Fish have inhabited oceans, rivers, and lakes for hundreds of millions of years and have evolved very efficient body designs for movement through water. Adaptations include streamlining, a spindle (fusiform) shape—rounded and tapering from the middle toward each end—flattening of the lateral parts, compression of the upper and lower abdominal parts (dorsoventral parts) of the body, or thinning (attenuation). Many fish combine these adaptations. Tuna and soldierfish are both fusiform and laterally flattened, for example, while trumpetfish are attenuated and cylindrical.

The more body surface there is pushing against water, the less efficient locomotion is. Fish have evolved a streamlined shape that presents a very small amount of body surface to the water in the direction of movement. To minimize the drag of water on the moving body, the head and tail are tapered and the side fins can be tucked flat against the body. The water moves easily around the head, flows over the thickest part of the body, and converges behind the tail.

In fusiform fish, the body is thickest about one-third of the way behind the head. This body shape enables water to flow easily over the body and converge at the tapered tail. Examples include sea bass, cod, billfish, and some species of marlin.

Seen head-on, laterally flattened fish, such as butterfly fish, appear squashed with flattened sides. Fish flattened from top to bottom (as opposed to side to side) are said to be dorsoventrally compressed (*dorso* means "back," and *ventral*, "belly"). Examples include stingrays and skates.

Many eels have an attentuated body shape. Moray eels are long and thin, and thus, it is easy for them to squeeze into rock crevices and find food.

## CONNECTIONS

● Many aquatic organisms, including some **INSECTS**, **SEABIRDS**, and **WATERBIRDS AND WADERS**, are also specially adapted for **FLIGHT**.

● **WHALES, DOLPHINS, AND PORPOISES** have streamlined bodies and fins and are often mistaken for **FISH**.

## CORE FACTS

■ Aquatic animals have evolved specialized body forms and features for efficient locomotion in water.

■ Water is a dense medium; thus, a streamlined, fishlike body is the most efficient way to minimize the amount of body surface in contact with water and reduce resistance during locomotion.

■ Some insects, squid, salamanders, and aquatic birds have developed a variety of body shapes and features that enable them to swim.

■ Whales and dolphins have evolved a blowhole on the top of their head. This development allows these animals to take in air easily before diving.

■ Many single-celled aquatic organisms swim using flagella (whiplike extensions) or cilia (tiny hairs).

## Fish locomotion

Fish usually swim by undulating, creating a traveling wave. The front of the body curves, and this curve passes along the body to the tail. In most fish, this curve passes along the body in a side-to-side motion; in flatfish, this curving wave appears to pass along the body in an up-and-down motion, but since these types of fish lie on their sides, the motion is really side to side.

Fish fins have many functions, among them propulsion, steering, braking, and maintaining stability. The main propulsion in most fish comes from the caudal (tail) fin, while other fins help keep the fish stable. To prevent pitching (the head being moved up and down), fish stabilize themselves using pectoral fins on the lower front of the body. Some fish can also swim slowly by sculling their pectoral fins. To counteract rolling from side to side, fish extend their fins outward. To resist yawing (spinning on the vertical axis), fish erect their dorsal (back) fin(s). To slow down fish extend and curve all their fins to increase drag, a maneuver that enables them to stop.

Most fish maintain buoyancy (the ability to float or maintain a specific depth) using an organ called a swimbladder. Swimbladders hold gases delivered by the bloodstream. The more gas in a swimbladder, the more buoyant the fish and the nearer the surface it can hover or swim. If the fish wants to descend, the gas is removed from the swimbladder.

## Like a fish in water?

A number of other animals can swim or are aquatic. Although many species have evolved unique ways to move through water, most adaptations for swimming are based on the fish model. Humans swim best when the body is elongated and flattened as much as possible and the arms are moving in a line with the body. Arms and legs take the place of fins, providing propulsion and controlling direction and stability.

The same principles apply to many nonaquatic swimming mammals, such as bears and muskrats. The body is held as horizontal as possible, and the limbs are used for propulsion and stability. In both humans and other land animals, the lungs take the place of the swimbladder and provide much of the buoyancy. By taking deep breaths and keeping the lungs filled with air, the animal does not have to work too hard to stay afloat and move. Sharks do not have swimbladders and must move constantly so that their fins can create lift to prevent them from sinking. Their bouyancy is increased to nearly neutral by a large, oil-filled liver, which results in a slow sink rate.

## Invertebrate adaptations

Invertebrates are among the most abundant aquatic animals. Although some animals, such as lobsters, walk on the sea bottom, many others swim. Some sea-dwelling worms swim by undulating much as fish do. Other creatures, including squid and octopuses, swim using hydraulics. They have a funnel-shaped siphon on the ventral (lower) surface, and when surrounding muscles contract, water shoots like a jet through the narrow siphon. The force produced propels the animal in the direction opposite to the ejected water.

Some insects swim under water using specially adapted legs or wings. For example, the backswimmers, or water boatmen, use their hind legs as underwater oars. Because insects are primarily terrestrial organisms, they do not have gills or other organs for underwater breathing. Gnat and mosquito larvae have developed "snorkels" that protrude from their bodies. When they need air, they rise toward the surface and

*An octopus (**Eledone cirrhosa***) swims by jet propulsion, rapidly expelling water from its mantle cavity. The force the water jet creates enables the octopus to swim fast in pursuit of prey for limited distances.*

## SWIMMING CELLS

Many flagellate microorganisms swim by using one or two whips called flagella attached to their body, which behave like oars or undulate (move in waves) to provide locomotion. Some microorganisms may have many flagella arranged in clusters around their body. Others (mainly protozoans) have cilia (tiny hairs) on their body surface that move in a coordinated, oarlike fashion, beating or pushing water in a single direction (usually backward to propel the organism forward).

How do microorganisms without appendages get around? Amoebas and similar organisms move by creating their own temporary appendages, called pseudopods (false feet; *pseudo* means "false," *pod* means "foot"), in a type of locomotion sometimes called streaming. The amoeba extends a cytoplasm-filled part of its body outward as a type of false limb. Once the pseudopod is extended, the rest of the amoeba's body flows into it. The limb extends in the desired direction, the rest of the amoeba's body empties into it, and the limb then becomes the main body. Streaming is a very effective form of locomotion, but all organisms that use it, even aquatic species, must adhere to a solid surface to move.

## A CLOSER LOOK

inhale through the snorkel, the insect remaining submerged. Diving beetles have adapted the "aqualung" method of breathing under water. They collect a bubble of air at the surface and submerge, keeping the bubble in contact with the spiracles, through which the insect breathes (see GILLS AND SPIRACLES). As the oxygen is used up, the air pressure in the bubble decreases and more oxygen (dissolved in the water) enters the bubble to equalize the pressure. Some water beetles can remain submerged for 36 hours.

### Vertebrate adaptations

Crocodiles, salamanders, and tadpoles are among the many reptiles and amphibians that swim with an undulating motion. A swimming crocodile presses its legs against its body and propels itself forward with side-to-side undulations of its tail. Adult frogs use their strongly webbed hind feet to propel themselves through water by making jumping movements. The body of these highly aquatic animals is generally streamlined and moves with little resis-tance through water.

*Otters have several adaptations for life in the water. They have tightly packed underfur and long, water-repellent guard hairs. Their body is streamlined, and most species have webbed paws.*

Most aquatic birds are also adapted for swimming. The loon is one of the best adapted, having a highly streamlined head, neck, and body. Like most aquatic birds, loons use their compressed, blade-shaped, and strongly webbed hind feet for propulsion. Their hind feet and legs are so well adapted to swimming that loon locomotion on land is extremely awkward.

Most birds have webbed feet with which they swim under water and paddle on the surface, but some, such as grebes and coots, have lobed toes, and others just have a broadened base to their toes, which provides a surface area for swimming. Sea turtles (see TORTOISES AND TURTLES), auks, and penguins have webbed hind feet that are used primarily as rudders, wings shaped like flippers for forward propulsion, and short feathers that give them a more streamlined body.

As most birds have a lightweight body that is less dense than water, they are able to fly, land on water, and float. Diving birds decrease buoyancy by squeezing much of the air out of their feathers. Wildfowl can float and swim for long periods of time because, as they preen their plumage, they spread oil into it from glands under their tail; preening sheds water from the feathers and thus prevents them from becoming waterlogged. Cormorants have especially wettable feathers that make it easier to lose air, and they have to spend a long time drying their wings after diving. The body of diving birds has a high density so that they can sink more easily. Grebes are said to increase their weight by swallowing small stones.

Marine mammals, particularly cetaceans, such as whales and dolphins, are the most popular and well-known aquatic mammals. They are so well adapted to their watery habitat that some people mistake them for fish. They have streamlined, fusiform, fishlike bodies, front limbs shaped like paddles, and fins. Unlike those of fish, however, marine mammal tail fins are horizontal and propel them forward by moving up and down (a fish's vertical tail fin moves from side to side). Cetaceans use their flippers and their dorsal fin to maintain stability and to steer in water.

Other mammals, although not fully aquatic, may spend a good deal of time in water. Expert swimmers, such as otters, seals, and rodents (such as beavers), use their hind legs and tails for propulsion and usually have webbed, paddlelike feet. Fur seals and polar bears swim primarily using their front legs.

Many mammals have a dense underlayer of fur with long guard hairs on top that make their coat water-repellant. A seal's skin also contains many oil glands that give the fur an oily coating.

N. GOLDSTEIN

**See also:** ADAPTATION; ANATOMY; FEET; GILLS AND SPIRACLES; HANDS; OCEAN FLOOR; OCEAN HABITATS; SALAMANDERS AND NEWTS; TORTOISES AND TURTLES.

### Further reading:
Counsilman, J. E. 1994. *The New Science of Swimming.* Englewood Cliffs, N.J.: Prentice-Hall.
Vogel, S., and S. T. Betty. 1996. *Life in Moving Fluids.* Princeton, N.J.: Princeton University Press.

# SYMBIOSIS

**Symbiosis is an intimate association between two organisms of different species**

An offer that benefits both individuals might be "I'll scratch your back if you'll scratch mine." It is a pleasant enough association but hardly a matter of life or death. Yet in nature organisms that live and have evolved together may form various types of beneficial, intimate associations on which their lives sometimes do depend.

The term *symbiosis* literally means "living together" and is used to describe several different relationships between two organisms. Symbiotic associations can be classified by the type of mutual helpfulness they exhibit, but sometimes no hard-and-fast line can be drawn between them. The terms used to describe these different types of associations seem to imply a value judgment, for example, that the most altruistic associations are morally preferable and better than more one-sided relationships. However, such associations are simply adaptations that have evolved to help one or more species survive.

If two organisms interact in such a way that one of the partners benefits while the other neither benefits nor comes to any harm, the relationship is called commensalism. This term generally refers to the associations between larger, nonparasitic organisms, such as multicellular plants and animals. For example, small pilot fish are almost always seen swimming with large barracudas or sharks for protection.

If two organisms interact so that both receive a necessary benefit or the survival of both depends on their intimate association, the relationship is called mutualism. For example, wrasse are small fish that feed on the external parasites of large fish; even the most voracious predatory fish appear to enjoy a good cleaning, and both species benefit. There are two types of mutualism: obligatory mutualism, in which the association is vital to both species, and facultative mutualism, in which the association benefits both species, although both could survive independently of it. If one of the organisms benefits at the expense of the other, their relationship is called parasitism (see PARASITES).

*This black rhinoceros* (Diceros bicornis) *has a symbiotic or mutualistic relationship with the oxpecker birds* (Buphagus *spp.*) *that perch on its body.*

## Parasitism

Parasites live inside (endoparasites) or outside (ectoparasites) their host and benefit at the latter's expense. Although the parasite may harm or weaken its host in some way, it does not usually kill it; it is in the parasite's interest to keep its host alive (see ANIMAL DISEASES; INFECTIOUS DISEASES).

Endoparasites include flukes, which can damage internal tissues and organs; the malaria parasite (*Plasmodium* spp.), which is carried in the blood, having been introduced by a mosquito's bite; and tapeworms, which live in a vertebrate host's

## CORE FACTS

- Symbiosis describes the relationship between two organisms of different species. There are three main types of symbiosis: commensalism, mutualism, and parasitism.
- In a commensal relationship, one partner benefits and the other may or may not benefit but is not harmed.
- Mutualism, in which both partners benefit, may be obligatory (neither organism can live without the other) or facultative (both organisms could survive independently).
- In a parasitic relationship, one organism benefits by living in or on another organism, while harming the host.

## CONNECTIONS

- Some **FUNGI** have a symbiotic relationship with the roots of plants.

- The **BACTERIA** living in the stomachs of cows and other **RUMINANTS** enable them to digest the **CELLULOSE** present in plants.

intestines. Ectoparasites include fleas, lampreys (jawless fish), and vampire bats, all of which attach to their host and feed on flesh or blood. As it can be disadvantageous for parasites to debilitate their hosts and thereby make them more liable to predation, scientists believe there may be an evolutionary relationship between parasitism and commensalism; commensalism may have arisen from parasitism.

## Commensalism

A commensal species may gain a number of benefits from its partner. Some species gain nutritional benefits, either by utilizing pieces of food not consumed by their hosts or by obtaining food independently as a result of the actions of their partner. In northern Europe, ptarmigan (grouselike birds) follow caribou foraging on plants growing in the slightly frozen tundra. The birds eat the insects exposed in the ground as the caribou graze. They do not hurt the caribou or compete for their food and yet benefit by using the caribou to provide an otherwise inaccessible food supply. Similarly, two types of birds, lapwings and plovers, often follow a farmer's plow and gorge on

*Bromeliads (air plants) grow perched on the branches of rain forest trees. The relationship is commensal because the plants benefit by being closer to sunlight but generally do not harm the trees.*

insects turned up with the soil. Two types of insects, silverfish and army ants, also share a commensal relationship. Certain species of silverfish live with the ants and share the food caught by the ants. While the silverfish gain nutrients, the ants derive no apparent benefit and are not harmed by the relationship.

Transportation is another benefit of a commensal relationship. For example, humpback whales often have barnacle encrustations on their body. These tiny mollusks do not harm or benefit the whales, but the mollusks benefit by being carried through the water, filtering microscopic food particles from passing ocean currents.

Many commensal species obtain protection from their host species. For example, sea anemone tentacles contain stinging cells that deter predators, and yet clown fish live safely among them, immune to the poison they carry. The anemone protects the fish (at no expense to itself) and provides food leftovers. Anemone fish (*Amphiprion akallopisus*) also take refuge among the stinging tentacles in a somewhat mutualistic relationship; the anemone protects the fish, which removes the anemone's waste.

The deadly Portugese man-of-war jellyfish has numerous long, curly tentacles wafting beneath its body, each of which is covered with stingers containing lethal toxins. Scientists have shown that the man-of-war fish, which dart deftly around the tentacles, are not immune to the poison but use the tentacles for protection, by expertly swimming among them without touching them.

A small aquatic fern called *Azolla* floats on the surface of freshwater ponds and wetlands. Inside sealed cavities within its floating leaves live blue-green algae called *Anabena*. The algae do not harm or benefit the plant, but they are protected by the fern in an ideal oxygen-free habitat (the algae are nitrogen fixers, which function only in oxygen-free environments; see NITROGEN CYCLE).

Sometimes commensal associations can prove to be indirectly detrimental to one of the species. For example, bromeliads (air plants) grow perched high on the branches or wrapped around the trunks of rain forest trees (see EPIPHYTES). They benefit by being high in the canopy and closer to sunlight and generally do not harm the trees. However, heavy rains often fill the cup-shaped bromeliads, and if many plants are growing on the same branch, the weight may cause the host branch to break off.

## Mutualism

In the endless, often deadly competition for resources, many species have evolved associations with others sharing their habitat. Most of these associations are mutualistic in that both partners benefit.

Tropical acacia trees are highly sought-after food for many species of insects, caterpillars, and herbivores. As a defense, many acacias grow large thorns from their leaf bases, which, in some trees, have become an integral part of a highly efficient mutualistic relationship with some ant species. The thorns are hollow and become the permanent residence of fierce stinging ants. The acacias have also evolved nectaries containing sugars for the ants to feed on. The acacias benefit, too, because the resident ants vigorously defend their home tree against any animal that tries to eat its leaves. Any intruder is immediately met by hordes of stinging ants that chase it away or sting it to death. Acacias with this mutualistic relationship look leafy and untouched compared with other antless tropical trees.

Ants of the genus *Azteca* have a similar mutualistic relationship with tropical *Cecropia* trees. The trees provide nutritious sugary nectar for resident ants, which in turn benefit the trees by eating any bromeliads that may grow on a branch and thus prevent the loss of branches unable to support water-filled bromeliads.

Some ant species have evolved mutualistic associations in which they engage in insect husbandry, tending to sap-sucking aphids and feeding on a type of honeydew, a sweet sugary substance secreted by the aphids as they feed on plants. The ants gently stroke the aphids with their antennae, inducing them to secrete drops of their sugary milk. This association is mutualistic, however. The aphids benefit because the ants transport them periodically to plants with the tenderest, tastiest, and most nutritious leaves.

Another example of a mutualistic relationship is that between sea anemones and hermit crabs. Sea anemones often attach themselves to shells inhabited by hermit crabs; they provide camouflage for crab and in return take uneaten food left by the crab.

## Obligatory mutualism

Some corals and algae exhibit obligatory mutualism, in which both partners are completely dependent on one another. A coral is a polyp that lives within the hard shell it secretes (see CORALS). Minute marine algae live inside the coral and are protected by it. These algae are photosynthetic; they produce food (sugars) using the Sun's energy and provide essential nutrients for the coral. Neither organism can live without the other. Scientists have noted with alarm the bleaching of coral worldwide. Coral is bleached when its resident algae die; without the algae, the coral also dies. Scientists think pollution, global warming, and disease may cause the bleaching.

A lichen is a plantlike organism that illustrates obligatory mutualism between a fungus and an alga (see LICHENS). Lichens grow in regions inhospitable to other plants, on bare rocks and in places too exposed to extremes of drought and cold for either the alga or the fungus to survive independently. Fungi produce hyphae (threads) that help anchor the lichen to the surface on which it grows, and their tissues also take in water needed by the algae. The algae photosynthesize to make sugars that nourish the lichen and also supply other essential nutrients.

Cows and other ruminants illustrate another example of obligatory mutualism. They eat plants with indigestible cellulose cell walls, but the rumen compartment of their four-chambered stomach contains countless bacteria specializing in cellulose

breakdown. Both organisms benefit, the bacteria obtaining their energy through fermentation of glucose and the ruminants obtaining nutrients released or synthesized by the microorganisms.

## Facultative mutualism

Facultative mutualism occurs when two species benefit from their association, but both could survive independently. For example, the tuatara, a lizard native to New Zealand, shares a burrow with the

*Some ants live in a mutualistic partnership with sap-sucking aphids. The ants gently stroke the aphids with their antennae and induce them to secrete drops of their sugary milk, on which the ants later feed.*

## THE EVOLUTION OF MUTUALISM

According to many scientists, prokaryotes, the earliest and simplest single-celled organisms, developed a degree of cooperation and eventually formed a new revolutionary type of cell. The eukaryotic cell probably originated from a mutualistic association of prokaryotic cells that came together to improve their efficiency in carrying out necessary life functions. Over millenia, small prokaryotic cells evolved ever more intimate associations with each other and were eventually incorporated into the new eukaryotic cells. These prokaryotic cells became internal organs in the eukaryotes: mitochondria, chloroplasts, and perhaps other organelles vital to cell functioning. The evolution of eukaryotic cells led to the evolution of multicellular life; without this ancient mutualism, no multicellular life would exist on Earth.

Mutualism also played a vital role in the colonization of the land by plants. The soil was relatively barren before plants invaded the land, and without an input of organic material, there were few nutrients to form the humus that nourishes plants. The first plants to colonize land probably were able to do so because of the mutualistic relationship they had with fungi. Fungi were (and still are) often intimately associated with plant roots and helped them obtain nutrients from a poor soil. In return, the roots provided the fungi with essential nutrients. Without such an association, vegetation might never have succeeded in growing on land.

Numerous scientific studies have shown that the evolution of mutualism tends to improve the environment shared by species. For example, if species A has a wholly antagonistic relationship with species B, dominant individuals in both species will eventually have genes that maximize the destruction of the other. What follows then is a deterioration of both species and environment. However, if in the course of competing for resources, species A and B find it is better to cooperate in a mutualistic way, both will eventually produce dominant individuals adapted to improve the mutualistic association. Evolution will produce increasingly mutualistic tendencies in both species, because such an association helps both to survive and use resources.

### EVOLUTION

## FOR THE LOVE OF HONEY

In the West, humans get their honey in convenient glass jars; elsewhere, other animals have evolved extraordinarily complex mutualistic associations for satisfying their desire for sweet food. For example, the honeyguide, a small, brown African bird, has evolved a remarkable behavior. First, it finds an active honeybee nest and then flits about looking for an animal to help it use the nest. It attracts a honey badger, a carnivore that prefers to feed on honey and bee larvae, by fanning its tail and emitting a special call. It then leads the badger toward the bees' nest (hence its name, honeyguide). The honey badger goes to work, ripping the nest apart and gorging on the honey, immune to the bee stings because of its thick skin.

The honey badger certainly benefits from this association because it gets some honey; the honeyguide also gets food—not honey but beeswax. The bird waits patiently until the honey badger has plundered the bees' nest and then flies in for its reward. Honeyguides are one of the few animals known that can digest beeswax because they have a mutualistic association with a microorganism living in their digestive tract that can break down the substance.

Curiously, honeyguides can enter active bees' nests and steal beeswax by themselves. They also feed on bees, often catching them in midflight. The birds have thick skins and are not susceptible to or afraid of bee stings. Why, then, have they evolved this complex mutualistic behavior with honey badgers? No one knows for sure.

Honey badgers are not the only beneficiaries of the honeyguide's behavior. The birds will readily attract human helpers as well. In Africa, some parents teach their children how to listen for and follow the honeyguide. After removing honey from the bees' nest, the human helper usually breaks off a sizable chunk of the nest and leaves it for the honeyguide.

## A CLOSER LOOK

sooty shearwater (a bird). The association is convenient: the tuatara sleeps in the burrow during the day and leaves to hunt insects at night, while the shearwater hunts by day and sleeps at night. The lizard helps the bird by devouring insects and vermin that might infect the bird; the bird helps the lizard by loosening the earth to enable the lizards to burrow; by defecation and shuffling movements, the bird also encourages more insects to settle, providing the lizard with more food. Although both species benefit from the association, the tuatara is capable of digging its own burrow, and both could survive alone.

Some fungi live among the roots of many plant species. The association between the roots and fungi is called a mycorrhiza, which means "fungus root." Plant species with mycorrhizae grow more successfully in poor soils than do plants without the fungi. It is thought that the fungus supplies the plant with nutrients, especially phosphorus. The plant supplies the fungus with photosynthetic products, the raw materials for cell metabolism.

N. GOLDSTEIN

**See also:** ANIMAL DISEASES; CORALS; EPIPHYTES; INFECTIOUS DISEASES; LICHENS; NITROGEN CYCLE; PARASITES.

### Further reading:
Douglas, A. E. 1997. *Symbiotic Interactions.* 2nd ed. New York: Oxford University Press.
Skelton, P. 1994. *Evolution: A Biological and Paleontological Approach to Biology.* New York: Addison-Wesley.
Silverstein, A. 1998. *Symbiosis (Science Concepts).* Brookfield, Conn.: Millbrook Press.

*Cleaner wrasse are small fish that feed on the external parasites of large fish. Both species benefit from the intimate association and have a mutualistic relationship.*

# INDEX